SUPPORTING BEHAVIOR FOR SCHOOL SUCCESS

Also Available

Developing Schoolwide Programs to Prevent and Manage Problem Behaviors:
A Step-by-Step Approach
*Kathleen Lynne Lane, Jemma Robertson Kalberg,
and Holly Mariah Menzies*

Managing Challenging Behaviors in Schools:
Research-Based Strategies That Work
*Kathleen Lynne Lane, Holly Mariah Menzies,
Allison L. Bruhn, and Mary Crnobori*

Systematic Screenings of Behavior to Support Instruction:
From Preschool to High School
*Kathleen Lynne Lane, Holly Mariah Menzies,
Wendy Peia Oakes, and Jemma Robertson Kalberg*

Supporting Behavior for School Success

A Step-by-Step Guide to Key Strategies

Kathleen Lynne Lane
Holly Mariah Menzies
Robin Parks Ennis
Wendy Peia Oakes

THE GUILFORD PRESS
New York   London

© 2015 The Guilford Press
A Division of Guilford Publications, Inc.
370 Seventh Avenue, Suite 1200, New York, NY 10001
www.guilford.com

All rights reserved

Except as indicated, no part of this book may be reproduced, translated, stored in a retrieval
system, or transmitted, in any form or by any means, electronic, mechanical, photocopying,
microfilming, recording, or otherwise, without written permission from the publisher.

Printed in the United States of America

This book is printed on acid-free paper.

Last digit is print number: 9 8 7 6 5 4 3 2 1

LIMITED PHOTOCOPY LICENSE

These materials are intended for use only by qualified professionals.

The publisher grants to individual purchasers of this book nonassignable permission
to reproduce all materials for which photocopying permission is specifically granted in
a footnote. This license is limited to you, the individual purchaser, for personal use or
use with individual students. This license does not grant the right to reproduce these
materials for resale, redistribution, electronic display, or any other purposes (including
but not limited to books, pamphlets, articles, video- or audiotapes, blogs, file-sharing
sites, Internet or intranet sites, and handouts or slides for lectures, workshops, or
webinars, whether or not a fee is charged). Permission to reproduce these materials
for these and any other purposes must be obtained in writing from the Permissions
Department of Guilford Publications.

Library of Congress Cataloging-in-Publication Data

Lane, Kathleen L.
    Supporting behavior for school success : a step-by-step guide to key strategies /
Kathleen Lynne Lane, Holly Mariah Menzies, Robin Parks Ennis, and Wendy Peia Oakes.
        pages cm
    Includes bibliographical references and index.
    ISBN 978-1-4625-2139-5 (pbk. : alk. paper) — ISBN 978-1-4625-2140-1 (hardcover : alk.
paper)
    1. Classroom management.   2. Behavior disorders in children—Prevention.   I. Title.
    LB3013.L287 2015
    371.102′4—dc23
                                                                          2015011765

GARY PUBLIC LIBRARY

To my husband, Craig: Thank you for being so supportive and loving—
you are my "matchie" and I would not want to imagine this world
without you in it.

To my son, Nathan, and my daughter, Katie:
being your mom is such a gift.

Nathan: It continues to be a gift to watch you become such a confident,
intelligent, and compassionate man. Thank you for understanding me.

Katie: It continues to be a gift to watch you become a confident,
intelligent, and civic-minded young woman.
Thank you for stretching me.

What do I love about each of you? Everything . . . 100%.
Because of the three of you, my life is better than I ever expected.
—K. L. L.

To my coauthors, Kathleen, Robin, and Wendy,
who were unfailingly generous throughout this endeavor.
—H. M. M.

To my husband, John:
Thank you for the love, support, and laughter you give me daily.
—R. P. E.

In memory of my stepmother, Pamela Bounds Peia. I feel blessed
to have such compassionate, strong, and talented women in my life.
—W. P. O.

About the Authors

Kathleen Lynne Lane, PhD, BCBA-D, is Professor in the Department of Special Education at the University of Kansas. Prior to entering academia, Dr. Lane served as a classroom teacher of general and special education students for 5 years and provided consultation, intervention, and staff development services to five school districts in Southern California for 2 years as a Program Specialist. Her research interests focus on school-based interventions (academic, behavioral, and social) with students at risk for emotional and behavioral disorders (EBD), with an emphasis on systematic screenings to detect students with behavioral challenges at the earliest possible juncture. She has designed, implemented, and evaluated comprehensive, integrated, three-tiered (CI3T) models of prevention in elementary, middle, and high school settings. Dr. Lane is coeditor of the journals *Remedial and Special Education* and *Journal of Positive Behavior Interventions*. She also serves on several editorial boards, including *Exceptional Children*, the *Journal of Special Education*, and the *Journal of Emotional and Behavioral Disorders*. Dr. Lane is the coauthor of books including *Managing Challenging Behaviors in Schools*, *Developing Schoolwide Programs to Prevent and Manage Problem Behaviors*, and *Systematic Screenings of Behavior to Support Instruction*.

Holly Mariah Menzies, PhD, is Professor in the Charter College of Education at California State University, Los Angeles, and the program coordinator in mild–moderate disabilities in the Division of Special Education and Counseling. Her scholarly interests focus on inclusive education and school-based interventions. She serves as an associate editor for *Remedial and Special Education*.

Robin Parks Ennis, PhD, BCBA-D, is Assistant Professor in the Eugene T. Moore School of Education at Clemson University. Dr. Ennis worked as a special education high school teacher in both resource and inclusive settings for several years. Her research interests and numerous publications are in the areas of positive behavior interventions and supports, instructional strategies, and students with EBD. Dr. Ennis serves on the editorial boards of *Behavioral Disorders, Beyond Behavior, Intervention in School and Clinic,* and *Remedial and Special Education.*

Wendy Peia Oakes, PhD, is Assistant Professor in the Mary Lou Fulton Teachers College at Arizona State University. Her scholarly interests include practices that improve the educational outcomes for young children with EBD, including CI3T; the implementation of evidence-based academic and behavioral interventions; and professional learning for preservice and inservice educators in implementing evidence-based practices with fidelity. Dr. Oakes is an associate editor for *Remedial and Special Education* and the *Journal of Positive Behavior Interventions.* She serves on the executive boards for the Council for Exceptional Children—Division for Research and the Council for Children with Behavioral Disorders.

Acknowledgments

We begin by thanking . . .

- The university professors committed to high-quality research to inform educational practices for all learners.
- The university professors committed to high-quality teacher preparation experiences for future educators.
- The expansive network of individuals of the PBIS OSEP Technical Assistance Center committed to high-quality work on the national priority of school climate transformation.
- The individuals committed to the high-quality technical assistance providers who support the professional learning of the educators.
- The district leaders committed to high-quality professional learning opportunities for all faculty and staff.
- The educators committed to high-quality learning experiences for *all* students.
- The families committed to supporting their children's learning experiences.
- The students—may you know how much we *all* want to support you in having a learning experience that gives you all the academic, behavioral, and social skills you need not only to love learning but also to have a joyful life.

We respect each of you more than words can express. We are thankful to those who have taught us and to The Guilford Press for the opportunity to share this resource with you.

Contents

Chapter 8   A Look at Instructional Choice   173

Chapter 9   Tips for Success: A Few Closing Thoughts   200

References   219

Index   235

Purchasers can download and print larger versions of select
materials from *www.guilford.com/lane4-forms*.

CHAPTER 1

Teacher-Level Strategies to Manage Behavior and Support Instruction

An Overview

The shift to a knowledge-based economy and the use of digital and electronic technologies has resulted in significant changes in education since the 1990s; in addition, schools have looked to new models that address much more than academic competence. Being an educator is an increasingly complex task, often conducted in less than optimal conditions (Lane, Oakes, & Menzies, 2014). Teachers' responsibilities have become broader in scope with a very high level of accountability (Ravitch, 2010; Richards, 2012), while at the same time school districts have experienced decreased financial support (Lambert & McCarthy, 2006).

Historically, educators were responsible for teaching core content areas, with very little attention to developing social skills, providing instruction in social and emotional learning, or taking an instructional approach to behavior. Furthermore, formative assessment and the concept of benchmarking student performance to inform instructional programs did not yet exist. The focus was predominately on input—the type of training teachers received or that districts provided—rather than student outcomes. Techniques for managing challenging behaviors were largely reactive and punitive in nature: waiting for students to have a problem and then responding with negative consequences (Walker, Ramsey, & Gresham, 2004). And not until the passage of Public Law 94-142 in 1974 (what we now know as the Individuals with Disabilities Education Improvement Act [IDEA], 2004) were all students with disabilities assured of the right to a free and appropriate education in the least restrictive environment.

More than 40 years later, the breadth of instructional responsibilities has expanded dramatically. In fact, in a recent keynote address at the 2014 National

Positive Behavior Intervention and Support (PBIS) Leadership Forum: PBIS Building Capacity and Partnerships to Enhance Educational Reform, held in Rosemont, Illinois, Michael Yudin, Assistant Secretary for the Office of Special Education and Rehabilitation of the U.S. Department of Education, issued a call for educators and educational systems to "pay as much attention to students' social and behavioral needs as we do academics." He indicated it is imperative for students to get the academic, behavioral, and social supports they need, as the students with greatest need are often missing the most instruction.

Fortunately, contemporary society has a better understanding of the importance of social and emotional development for academic skills, and schools are now addressing these issues. Educators teach social skills and character development programs that emphasize nonviolence, antibullying, and cooperation. They also work in conjunction with other professionals (e.g., behavior specialists, school psychologists, social workers, and counselors) to be responsive to students' mental health needs. Another important area of change is the view that students with special needs are the responsibility of both the general and special education communities (Lane, Menzies, Ennis, & Bezdek, 2013). The role of collaboration between general and special education teachers has taken center stage, as the larger educational communities (including school personnel such as psychologists, social workers, reading specialists, instructional coaches, and behavior specialists) work together at a systems level to detect and support students at the first sign of concerns. Rather than taking a wait-to-fail stance, many schools use reliable, valid academic and behavior screening tools to determine which students may need support beyond what is typically offered to all students (Gresham & Elliott, 2008a).

Since the passage of IDEA (2004) and the No Child Left Behind Act (2002), an empirical approach to figuring out "What Works?" to meet students' academic, behavioral, and social needs in a reliable, effective manner (Institute of Education Sciences and What Works Clearinghouse) drives educational practice. The focus on "evidence-based practices" has moved to the forefront of teaching as a guiding principle for determining whether or not a given practice, strategy, or program should be introduced or maintained (Cook & Tankersley, 2013; Gast & Ledford, 2014). Time is at a premium, and other resources (financial and otherwise) are too scarce to use strategies, practices, and programs that lack sufficient evidence. As such, it is important that we carefully consider how to leverage our current resources to make certain all students get what they need (Yudin, 2014). Schools and districts are also more attentive to issues regarding treatment integrity (Cook & Tankersley, 2013), meaning they implement evidence-based practices in the manner the research indicates will yield the desired changes in student performance.

This is especially true given the wide range of students who attend public schools today, many of whom experience a vast range of risk factors that contribute to behavioral challenges such as noncompliance, off-task behavior, and aggression (referred to as *externalizing behaviors*), as well as anxiety, depression, social withdrawal, and even self-injurious behaviors (referred to as *internalizing behaviors;* Walker & Gresham, 2013). Although teachers are less likely to notice internalizing behaviors, as they usually do not interfere with instructional activities in the way externalizing behaviors do, internalizing issues are no less serious, as both types of disorders contribute to negative outcomes within and beyond the school setting (Bradshaw, Buckley, & Ialongo, 2008; Crick, Grotpeter, & Bigbee, 2002).

In the past, many educators often assumed students with these emotional and behavioral disorders (EBD) would be supported by special education teachers. Yet the problem extends far beyond the 1% of school-age children and youth who receive special education services under the category of emotional disturbance. In fact, recent point prevalence estimates indicate that 12% of school-age students have moderate to severe and 20% have mild to severe EBD (Forness, Freeman, Paparella, Kauffman, & Walker, 2012). This finding suggests the vast majority of students with behavioral challenges will be served by the general education community in general education classrooms.

The good news is that many states, districts, and schools across the country are embracing a systems-level approach to serving *all* students, including those with special needs, English language learners, and other at-risk populations. A wonderful partnership is developing between the general and special education communities as they share ownership of all students' education. This is a great step forward, helping many teachers combat the isolation and stress educators have experienced historically. Teaching has traditionally been a job in which educators enjoyed very little time with their colleagues and were seen as the sole individuals responsible for student learning in a given school year (Brunsting, Sreckovic, & Lane, 2014; Drago-Severson & Pinto, 2006). The move toward systematic and collaborative responsibility for meeting students' academic, behavioral, and social needs holds benefit for students and teachers alike.

Working Collaboratively to Support Learning for All Students

Across the country, teaching and research communities are focused on developing multi-tiered systems of supports designed to offer students a continuum of assistance according to their individual needs. This model originated in the mental health field and was adapted for application in the field of education. When these models were initially introduced, you might recall seeing a graphic with a right triangle to describe the continuum of positive behavior interventions and supports (PBIS) available to meet students' behavioral needs and another right triangle (facing the opposite direction) that described the continuum of response to intervention (RTI) to address students' academic needs—particularly in the area of reading. Then, as time passed, you might have seen these two triangles appear on the same graphic but with a space in between the sets of continua. Although perhaps unintended, the message that occurred during the early years of innovation suggested that students' academic, behavioral, and social needs should be addressed separately. Many schools developed multiple decision-making teams to support students, such as (1) grade-level teams committed to examining data from academic screenings to determine students' academic needs, (2) behavior-support teams that reviewed office discipline referral (ODR) data and behavior screening data to determine students' behavioral needs, and (3) still another team that considered students' social and emotional needs. The challenge here: ensuring that students who have more than one risk factor are supported in all areas of need and in an integrated fashion. This is especially important as these problems are inter-related. For example, challenging behavior is sometimes a result of low academic skills, so these issues should be addressed together. Some multi-tiered systems, such as RTI in reading, would have provided academic support but may not have had the capacity to identify the need for behavioral support.

In the last several years, the use of comprehensive, integrated, three-tiered (CI3T) models of prevention to meet students' academic, behavioral, and social needs is moving to the forefront of multi-tiered systems (Lane, Carter, Jenkins, Magill, & Germer, 2014; Sugai, 2013). George Sugai (2013) gave a compelling keynote address at the Northeast PBIS Network Leadership Forum in which he traced the history of PBIS. As he painted a picture of the future of PBIS, he emphasized the importance of integrating academic and behavioral domains at each level of prevention: Tier 1 (for all, primary prevention), Tier 2 (for some, secondary prevention), and Tier 3 (for a few, tertiary prevention).

Sugai (2013) offered a vision that a well-designed, integrated model would include (among other things) explicit instruction in social skills or character education, with the use of validated curricula, strategies, and practices selected by district leadership teams according to district- and site-level needs. Sugai described a model in which social skills would be explicitly taught as part of Tier 1 practices to level the playing field for all students—providing a common language and expectations, as well as specific skills for success. For example, all teachers would provide instruction on the skill of active listening, with some of the lessons cotaught by school counselors as part of regularly scheduled schoolwide lessons. During social skills time, this specific skill might be taught using a *tell, show, do* structure (Elliott & Gresham, 2007). Then, later in the day, one teacher might remind students about the skill as they move into a cooperative learning activity during social studies: "Before you start working in your learning groups, I want to remind you to use your active learning skills. Who can tell me what that might look like?" In essence, the skills are taught and revisited across the instructional day, demonstrating for students how they can be applied to support instructional activities.

Intentional teaching of self-determined behaviors, social skills, or conflict resolution skills in a blended model offers students multiple opportunities to practice and receive reinforcement for demonstrating these skills. As students acquire and build fluency in social and behavioral skill sets, they will become more successful in negotiating relationships with their teachers, other adults, and peers in the school. This Tier 1 effort also supports positive learning experiences for students who require additional instruction to master these skills. By ensuring that all students have exposure to key skills such as listening to and following instructions, making their needs known in a respectful way, and resolving conflicts in a peaceful manner, students requiring additional instruction will have multiple peer models and multiple methods of accessing reinforcement as they continue to master these skills. In addition, they acquire skills that support positive interpersonal relationships in employment, in their daily lives, and in the community overall (Lane, Oakes, & Menzies, 2014; Sugai, 2013; Walker et al., 2004).

These models are grounded in data-informed decision making, relying on multiple sources of information (e.g., academic and behavior screening data, attendance data) made accessible and efficient using technology-based systems. Sugai (2013) discussed the importance of analyzing multiple sources of data in conjunction rather than in isolation, with careful attention to treatment integrity data at each level of prevention (Bruhn, Lane, & Hirsch, 2014). For example, to accurately connect students to relevant research-based strategies at Tiers 2 and 3, it is important to ensure that the students had access to the Tier 1 efforts. Moreover, if a student was in a class in which the Tier 1 reading intervention was not being implemented as planned (with integrity) or the weekly social skills were not taught regularly or in which the PBIS tickets were not being distributed paired with behavior-specific praise (BSP; see Chapter 3), then it is not possible to conclude that the student requires Tier 2 or 3 supports (Codding & Lane, 2014). Instead, the teacher needs support in fully implementing all Tier 1 components with integrity. However, if Tier 1 practices were in place, if attendance data indicated the student was at school regularly, and if systematic screening data suggested additional supports were needed, then supplemental assistance would need to be delivered in an effective, efficient manner (Lane, Oakes, & Menzies, 2014).

It is encouraging to us that there are many talented researchers, technical assistance providers, and district leaders, such as Steve Goodman, Kevin Harrell, Amy Henry, Rob Horner, Terry McEwen, Kent McIntosh, James Palmiero, Lisa Powers, George Sugai, and Leah Wisdom, all working on various approaches to designing, implementing, and evaluating integrated, multi-tiered system of supports. This integration of academic, behavioral, and social domains makes sense. In a recent special issue of *Preventing School Failure* (Lane, Oakes, & Menzies, 2014), we offered a series of articles describing a step-by-step approach for how to design, implement, and evaluate a blended, multi-tiered model that our research team refers to as a CI3T model of prevention. It explains the features deemed essential for success by Sugai (2013), including a systematic approach to designing CI3T models.

In this book, we extend the focus of multi-tiered models to include low-intensity, teacher-delivered supports that can be easily integrated into routine instructional practice—ideally as part of Tier 1 but also in instances in which screening data suggest that students may not be responding to Tier 1 efforts but before connecting them to Tier 2 and 3 supports. The low-intensity strategies explained in detail in each chapter can be used in a CI3T model, as well as independently. In fact, teachers will pick and choose among the strategies depending on the needs of their particular students and the school context. However, a multi-tiered approach is exponentially more powerful and, with that in mind, the next part of the chapter provides a description of the CI3T model. This background information will help demonstrate how the strategies can be used as Tier 2 supports. In addition to explaining how each strategy is used, the chapters provide illustrations of how they can be integrated into a multi-tiered approach. This chapter concludes with a brief introduction to each of the strategies.

A Systems-Based Approach: CI3T Models of Prevention

As we have discussed, CI3T models of prevention include a data-informed continuum of supports developed to meet students' academic, behavioral, and social needs (see Figure 1.1). In essence, the model addresses these three domains (or building blocks) to create a structure for supporting all students in inclusive

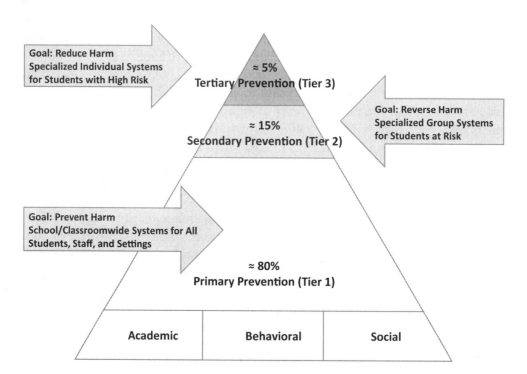

FIGURE 1.1. The comprehensive, integrated, three-tiered (CI3T) model of prevention (Lane, Kalberg, & Menzies, 2009). From Lane, Oakes, and Menzies (2014). Reprinted by permission of Taylor & Francis (*www.tandfonline.com*).

environments by capitalizing on the talent and expertise of school personnel who collaborate together and in conjunction with parents and community members (Lane, Kalberg, & Menzies, 2009).

In a CI3T model, school-site leadership teams examine multiple sources of data to inform the decision-making process, including data from attendance records (absenteeism and tardiness), ODRs, academic screening tools (e.g., AIMS-web; *www.aimsweb.com*), and behavior screening tools (e.g., the Student Risk Screening Scale [SRSS]; Drummond, 1994). Student performance measures are analyzed in conjunction with treatment integrity data (to determine how well the plan is being implemented) and social validity data (to determine stakeholders' views about the goals, procedures, and outcomes). During the analysis process, school-site teams focus on accurately examining (1) the overall level of risk evident in a school (often used as part of school improvement plans), (2) the extent to which Tier 1 efforts were able to meet students' needs, (3) which students may require more intensive supports, (4) the appropriate Tier 2 and 3 supports that may hold benefit for each student, and (5) circumstances in which low-intensity supports implemented by teachers for an entire class may be warranted (Lane & Walker, in press).

CI3T models include regularly scheduled planning time for school-site leadership teams, grade-level teams, and department-level teams to examine these data, assess implementation, solicit stakeholders' opinions, and review student performance (academically, behaviorally, and socially).

Tier 1: Primary Prevention

All students access Tier 1 efforts just by virtue of attending school (Lane, Robertson, & Graham-Bailey, 2006). Tier 1 includes: (1) academic instruction as defined by local or state standards and, for some states, addressing Common Core State Standards (National Governors Association Center for Best Practices & Council of Chief State School Officers, 2010); (2) social skills instruction using a validated curriculum to address the school's (or district's) focal area (e.g., developing character, teaching social skills, preventing bullying); and (3) participation in a school-wide PBIS framework to teach expectations for success in all key settings (Lane, Menzies, et al., 2013).

In the academic domain, the CI3T team defines the roles and responsibilities for all stakeholders (students, teachers, parents, and administrators) to increase the likelihood that the core curricula are implemented with integrity. This is critical, as part of closing existing achievement gaps among students is closing the gap in access; some students do not succeed because the school is unable to provide an adequate learning environment. To illustrate, teachers have the responsibility of teaching the core reading and math programs with integrity, including allocating the appropriate time or dosage (e.g., 4 days a week, 90-minute session). In addition, they might be asked to incorporate starting and closing activities for each instructional segment and to differentiate instruction (process, content, and products; Tomlinson, 2005) to support student engagement. Teachers might also be asked to communicate daily with parents using a Web-based system to post work requirements and provide information on grades. Students may be asked to bring required materials, arrive on time and stay all day, and give their best effort. Parents may be asked to support students in being present for the full school day, to provide a space at home to facilitate homework completion, and to check the Web-based communication system.

In the social domain, the school-site team selects an evidence-based social skills curriculum to address the school's or district's identified area for growth. For example, if analysis of ODR data indicate students need social skills to improve interactions with teachers and peers, the team may select to implement the Social Skills Improvement System—Classwide Intervention Program (Elliott & Gresham, 2007), which involves directly teaching all students 10 critical social skills (often referred to as academic enabler social skills; Kettler, Elliott, Davies, & Griffin, 2009). To support implementation, the team would again define roles and responsibilities for all stakeholders to assist with efforts in this domain.

The behavioral domain involves establishing a PBIS framework (which is not a curriculum). Faculty and staff determine schoolwide expectations (e.g., respect, responsibility, and best effort) for all students in each key setting in the building (e.g., classrooms, hallways, and cafeteria). Teachers (often in collaboration with school counselors) provide instruction to all students, giving them opportunities to practice and to receive reinforcement for meeting defined expectations.

Treatment integrity data for each component are monitored to make certain the plan is implemented as designed. Social validity data are also monitored to obtain stakeholder perspectives on the goals, procedures, and outcomes. Student progress is examined using the data sources to determine whether additional assistance may be required (Lane, Oakes, Menzies, & Harris, 2013).

Tier 2: Secondary Prevention

Secondary supports include low-intensity strategies, some of which include small-group interventions. This level of prevention includes a range of research-based strategies, practices, and programs, such as the Check-In/Check-Out program (Crone, Hawken, & Horner, 2010), self-management strategies (Mooney, Ryan, Uhing, Reid, & Epstein, 2005), and small-group instruction focusing on common areas of concern (e.g., conflict resolution groups). Again, the goal is to address students' academic, social, and behavioral needs in an integrated fashion, with an expectation that 10–15% of the student body will need this level of prevention. Tier 2 supports are additive in nature, meaning they are used to supplement (not replace) Tier 1 efforts.

For example, if a fourth-grade student scores below benchmark on AIMS-web (*www.aimsweb.com)* winter reading assessments while also being rated as moderate risk on the Student Risk Screening Scale, this student may join a Tier 2 reading intervention to increase fluency (e.g., Six-Minute Solution; Adams & Brown, 2007). This group may be led by a reading specialist in a general education classroom during the school's intervention block, offering an additional 30 minutes of instruction to supplement Tier 1 efforts (a recommended 90-minute instructional block). To increase the likelihood of the student participating in the support, she may also have a self-monitoring checklist with the reinforcement system tied back to the schoolwide plan (e.g., a PBIS ticket).

Tier 3: Tertiary Prevention

Tertiary supports are even more intensive, reserved for the 3–5% of students needing more than Tier 2 support or those with multiple risk factors. Examples include functional assessment-based interventions (Kern & Manz, 2004; Lane, Oakes, & Cox, 2011), wraparound services (Eber et al., 2009), and intensive reading supports (Denton, Fletcher, Anthony, & Francis, 2006).

For example, a seventh-grade student scoring in the extremely-elevated-risk category on the BASC-2 Behavioral and Emotional Screening Scales (BASC-2 BESS; Kamphaus & Reynolds, 2008) who also fails two courses during the first quarter may be supported with a functional assessment-based intervention to increase participation in class and reduce disruption.

In brief, each school offers a comprehensive, integrated, coordinated system of support. These models hold several benefits, two of which are transparency and access.

Benefits of CI3T Models: Transparency and Access

In an effort to ensure that all stakeholders are aware of the continuum of supports and how to access them, we recommend that school-site leadership teams create a blueprint of the full CI3T model. Particular attention should be given to describing the available secondary and tertiary supports. We suggest including all of the following: a description of the support, schoolwide data (and the specific scores) that could be analyzed to determine which students might benefit from this support (also referred to as inclusion criteria), progress monitoring data (which includes student performance data, as well as treatment integrity and social validity data) to see how the students are responding, and exit criteria that indicate when the support should be faded. These are referred to as secondary and tertiary intervention grids.

By developing these grids, teachers, support staff, parents, and students can be fully aware of all existing supports for students—both enrichment and remediation. Having a detailed written plan facilitates transparency and clarity. In essence, these grids take the guesswork out of determining supports available for those students for whom primary prevention efforts are insufficient.

In addition, CI3T models of prevention offer other benefits. For example, they provide a coordinated approach for addressing students' multiple needs, address instructional barriers of time and collaboration, offer increased opportunity for equal access to supports, and provide an equitable method and formal structure for the legal mandate of "search and serve" processes.

A Focus on Teacher-Level Strategies

Before connecting students to Tier 2 and 3 supports, we advocate an intermediate step: a look at what can be done at the teacher level to introduce low-intensity, easy-to-implement, highly effective strategies to support desired behaviors and facilitate the instructional process. Intensive assistance in the form of Tier 2 and 3 supports should primarily be used when less intensive efforts are unsuccessful. Usually, these low-intensity strategies are conceptualized as Tier 1. However, teachers can examine their classroom management and instructional techniques as an additional consideration when considering students' performance. Teachers' actions profoundly influence their students, and sometimes alterations in classroom practice can dramatically change student behavioral and academic performance. In addition to revisiting classroom procedures and basic instructional practices, teachers can adopt low-intensity strategies. Examples of these include increasing the rates of BSP (Thompson, Marchant, Anderson, Prater, & Gibb, 2012), introducing instructional choice (Kern & State, 2009), and increasing students' opportunities to respond (Partin, Robertson, Maggin, Oliver, & Wehby, 2010; see also Chapter 2, this volume). Each strategy can be incorporated into instructional time to decrease disruption, increase students' level of engagement, and ultimately increase *all* students' access to the curriculum.

To be very clear, we are not suggesting behavior screening data be used to evaluate teachers. Instead, we recommend behavior screening data be expanded in use to inform teacher-driven supports and to help focus professional development to support teachers in becoming knowledgeable and confident in using these strategies as part of their instructional repertoire (Lane, Oakes, & Magill, 2014).

Purpose

As you may have gathered, this book is designed for the busy teacher, paraprofessional, behavior specialist, school psychologist, social worker, mental health provider, administrator, technical assistance provider, and/or teacher preparation professor who may already have knowledge of specific behavioral strategies but needs a quick and easy guide for implementing them. It is also appropriate for those who are new to positive behavior supports.

As we have worked with schools and districts across the country over the past 15 years to design, implement, and evaluate CI3T models of prevention, a number of professionals have asked for a book that provides detailed (but user friendly!) instructions on how to implement specific strategies for managing behavior. We respectfully offer this book to address this charge.

In Chapters 2 through 8 we introduce specific teacher-level strategies as follows: opportunities to respond (OTR; Chapter 2), behavior-specific praise (BSP; Chapter 3), active supervision (Chapter 4), instructional feedback (Chapter 5), high-probability requests (Chapter 6), precorrection (Chapter 7), and instructional choice (Chapter 8). Each chapter follows the same easy-to-use format. We begin with an overview of the strategy, define it, and then explain why it is effective.

Then we offer a look at some of the supporting research for the strategy. We feature a few key studies and provide enough detail about them so you can see what the strategy looks like in various settings and with different types of students (e.g., students receiving special education services). For the interested reader, we also include a table (Table 1, "Supporting Research") of representative studies for other applications of the strategy. These are not exhaustive reviews of the literature, but they provide a sample of the research conducted to date for each strategy introduced.

Next, we provide a brief discussion of the benefits and potential challenges of implementing the strategy discussed. This information is intended to inform the decision-making process when choosing which low-intensity support to employ in the classroom.

Then we focus on the details of how to implement the strategy in the classroom, providing a checklist for success. In this section, we provide a step-by-step approach for implementing the strategy featured in each chapter. To help guide the reader, there is a table containing an implementation checklist (Table 2), as well as a hypothetical illustration of how these steps can be used in in a CI3T model (Box 1). These illustrations span the preschool through high school continuum. For example, in Chapter 8 you will read an illustration of instructional choice at the elementary level, and in Chapter 4 you will read an illustration of active supervision at the middle school level. In each illustration, you will see a graph of student performance across the intervention process (Figure 1), a sample treatment integrity form (Figure 2) to determine the degree to which the intervention is being implemented as planned, and an example of a social validity form (Figure 3) to see what people think about the goals, procedures, and outcomes.

Because it is critical to determine how well a strategy is working, we include a section on how to examine the effects. This section is written to help answer the question, How well is it working? This section offers practical design considerations to show how to assess the strategy in a classroom (and explains why this is important!), how to make sure the strategy is in place (how to measure treatment integrity), and how to determine what stakeholders think about the strategy before getting started and after the strategy is under way (how to measure social validity). We wrap up each chapter with a brief summary.

In the final chapter of the book we offer tips for success. Here we focus on understanding how the seven strategies noted in this text can be used within and beyond the context of multi-tiered models. We included a table summarizing the teacher-driven, PBIS strategies discussed in this book, as well as some considerations for professional learning to help you move forward. Because these strategies are grounded in applied behavior analysis (ABA) principles, we offer a very brief primer on ABA principles (Baer, Wolf, & Risley, 1968; Cooper, Heron, & Heward, 2007). In particular, we focus on issues of reinforcement central to supporting desired behaviors that facilitate the instructional process. Here you will read about the differences between positive and negative reinforcement and the differences between reinforcement versus punishment. In addition, we discuss how using PBIS can lead to an improved school climate. We close by introducing additional resources for you to explore as you look for efficient, effective methods for meeting students' multiple needs in an integrated fashion.

As always, we admire and respect your commitment to assisting students in meeting their academic, behavioral, and social needs in an integrated way. We hope you will find these strategies to be effective and feasible, with sufficient detail provided to assist you in introducing these strategies at your school or district in the days ahead. For now, grab a nonfat decaf pumpkin-spice latte and read on! (And feel free to treat yourself to the whipped cream!) We look forward to receiving your feedback and wish you every success as you move ahead!

CHAPTER 2

A Look at Increasing Opportunities to Respond

Increasing opportunities to respond (OTR) is a strategy that helps students review material, acquire skill fluency, and commit information to memory while simultaneously increasing on-task behavior and reducing misbehavior. As with the other strategies in this book, it is a powerful tool for improving academic success and also contributes to a classroom climate in which students feel successful (Trussell, 2008). This is a critical aspect of promoting student success. Classroom environment can seem like an intangible and amorphous concept—hard to define and even harder to operationalize—but deliberate and frequent use of techniques such as OTR is part of orchestrating an optimal learning environment. OTR has the added benefit of being easy to implement and can be used from preschool through high school. Once the technique is learned, it is simple to prepare an OTR lesson, as it requires no special materials.

OTR has its origins in the premise that when instructional pacing is optimized, then students are maximally engaged and less likely to misbehave or be off task (Sutherland & Wright, 2013). Keeping 25 or more students simultaneously engaged in a lesson is no easy accomplishment, and (not surprisingly!) teachers can have difficulty keeping engagement high. Instructional pacing should be rapid enough to sustain interest, but not so rapid that students are lost—goals that almost seem in contradiction (Kounin, 1970). OTR is a technique for improving instructional pacing that enhances engagement during whole-group, small-group, and individualized instruction.

The first empirical studies on OTR (Carnine, 1976; Darch & Gersten, 1985) were part of a body of research looking for instructional methods that increased achievement for students with learning disabilities. These particular studies examined whether a rapid rate of presentation resulted in lower off-task behaviors than a slow rate of presentation. Researchers found that a faster rate did, in fact, decrease off-task behaviors, as well as increase participation and accuracy in responding. Pairing the strategy with feedback (Cavanaugh, 2013; Darch & Gersten, 1985) was even more effective. This research was novel because it was the earliest to use instructional strategies related to academic content to improve behavior. Today there is a greater focus on addressing classroom and instructional variables to improve behavioral performance, and OTR is a practice that promotes good behavior, as well as academic achievement (Sutherland & Wright, 2013).

What Is OTR?

Just as the term implies, the OTR strategy is designed to offer students frequent opportunities, within a set time period, to respond to teacher questions or prompts about targeted academic material. This is best done with material or concepts students have a basic understanding of, as the goal is to help students respond to teacher inquiries rapidly and accurately, which promotes their engagement as they practice the information or skill. During the designated instructional period, the teacher initiates a high number of questions or cues to which students respond. Students are expected to reply very quickly, and the teacher immediately provides feedback on whether or not the response is accurate.

OTR can be conducted so that students respond individually or in unison. A variety of response formats is available, including the use of small whiteboards, electronic devices such as iPads, showing thumbs up or down, or using electronic response systems (Sutherland & Wright, 2013). Regardless of the system used, the teacher scans all the answers, quickly evaluates students' responses, and comments on their answers verbally, visually, or with a cue. For example, an OTR sequence might sound like this when used in a whole-class format with students responding in unison with small whiteboards:

> "Students, please solve for the product of 28 × 4."
> After 10 seconds: "Hold up your whiteboards."
> "I see almost all of you found the correct answer is 112. Nice work!"
> "Now, solve for the product of 32 × 3."

The teacher would continue with the routine until she had offered an adequate number of questions/prompts to practice the concepts. The technique can also be used in small groups or individually, allowing the teacher to provide more personalized feedback to specific students, although the goal is still to initiate many opportunities for students to respond, so feedback will be necessarily brief.

OTR is composed of three main elements. The first is identifying the content or skills to be targeted. Then an extensive set of questions or prompts is developed that will offer practice with the material. Finally, the session itself is conducted with a high rate of questioning, rapid student responding, and immediate teacher feedback (Sutherland & Wehby, 2001; Sutherland & Wright, 2013).

Why Is OTR Effective?

Teachers use a variety of instructional arrangements (e.g., small groups, direct instruction, cooperative learning) to promote students' engagement with their academic work. Each format is chosen with the targeted instructional goals and academic content in mind. OTR can be used with an individual or in small-group or whole-group formats, and it can greatly improve whole-group instruction. Undifferentiated whole-class instruction is often a less effective teaching practice than other instructional models; however, there are instances in which it is appropriate and certainly efficient. For example, practice is especially important when learning skills such as memorizing multiplication facts, identifying letter names, developing phonemic awareness, and identifying sight words. In upper-grade and secondary classrooms, each content area has a body of information that must be committed to memory. Fluency and automaticity in the basics of any content or skill frees students to tackle complex and nuanced concepts. Basic information is easily practiced in a whole-group format. It has the advantage of allowing the teacher to quickly determine students' proficiency with the material and to decide whether more practice is needed and which students may require more intensive assistance. (Of course, there are other, quite powerful whole-class formats, such as direct instruction or Socratic questioning.)

Teachers must always balance efficiency against available time. Time is a scarce commodity in schools because of class size, the wide range in student abilities, and the scope of the curricula teachers are expected to cover. Under these constraints, whole-group delivery is a reasonable instructional choice, but it is especially important to promote every student's participation and engagement in order to ensure its effectiveness. Too often the typical pattern of interaction is one in which the teacher intersperses instruction with a question, a student is chosen for a response, and the teacher indicates whether or not the response is correct (Cazden, 2001). Then the entire sequence is repeated, and another student is asked to respond. The pacing in such a format tends to be at a less optimal rate than in other instructional modes. It is often a passive rather than an active learning situation (Van Bramer, 2003). Unfortunately, this may provide an easy opportunity *not* to participate, as students could be daydreaming or engaged in off-task behavior difficult to detect.

OTR can greatly increase active participation. Students have several chances to offer an answer compared with typical instruction. Also, feedback is rapid and matter-of-fact, which reduces the pressure of answering incorrectly. Students are sometimes reluctant to participate because they are worried about having the wrong answer. Participating becomes even easier when the responding is conducted with whiteboards or another mode (e.g., response cards, communication cups [green, yellow, and red], and electronic response systems) that allows the entire class to reply at the same time. When students feel less stress about incorrect answers, they are more likely to take a chance and answer them. Creating safe opportunities to participate frequently contributes to a positive classroom environment (Delisle, 2012). Students will feel more comfortable in a climate in which participation is valued and incorrect responses do not carry such high stakes. OTR is an efficient, high-success instructional technique used to review or practice academic material in a way that maximally engages the highest number of students.

Supporting Research for Increasing OTR

A multitude of studies beginning in the 1970s document the positive effect the OTR strategy has on increasing engaged time, improving academic outcomes, and preventing misbehavior for a wide variety of students (Burns, 2007; Conroy, Sutherland, Snyder, & Marsh, 2008; Sutherland & Wehby, 2001). They also demonstrate how OTR can be used to intervene in the negative cycle that students with challenging behaviors tend to experience (Sutherland, Wehby, & Yoder, 2002). Students with significant behavior issues tend to have frequent, negative interactions with their teachers. Compared with their peers, they also experience less positive feedback. This creates a situation in which the student and teacher are locked into a negative interaction loop. OTR is a strategy that can help break this intractable pattern, because it allows students to interact successfully over academic material (Conroy et al., 2008). Significantly, studies demonstrate that OTR is effective in both general and special education settings for a variety of students. Studies that examine some of these issues are discussed next and appear in Table 2.1.

Decreasing Disruptive Behavior in an Elementary Self-Contained Classroom

Haydon, Mancil, and Van Loan (2009) examined whether the use of OTR would improve the behavior of a fifth-grade girl, Bree. Bree presented significant problems for her general education science teacher, Mr. Smith, including "fighting with her peers, being off-task during instruction, and calling out in class" (p. 269). In addition to her chronic disruptive behavior, Bree scored at risk for externalizing behavior patterns on the Systematic Screening for Behavior Disorders (Walker & Severson, 1992). Bree was the type of student who could achieve at grade level but whose behavior was extremely challenging in a general education setting.

The researcher met with Mr. Smith, who was a first-year teacher, for a 30-minute training on how to use OTR. They reviewed the definition and purpose

TABLE 2.1. Supporting Research: Opportunities to Respond (OTR)

Authors and journal	Students	Intervention setting	Intervention	Measures	Design
Carnine (1976) Effects of two teacher-presentation rates on off-task behavior, answering correctly, and participation (JABA)*	N = 2 first-grade students, 1 teacher, and 1 student teacher	A first-grade classroom during small-group reading instruction.	Teacher and student teacher used a scripted reading curriculum (DISTAR) and presented items in a fast-rate presentation (the delay was 1 second or less) and in a slow-rate presentation (the delay was 5 seconds or more).	*Dependent variables:* 1. Teacher presentation rate. 2. Student responding. 3. Off-task behavior. *Social validity:* Not measured	ABABAB design across conditions
Sutherland, Wehby, & Yoder (2002) Examination of the relationship between teacher praise and opportunities for students with EBD to respond to academic requests (JEBD)	N = 20 teachers and 216 students, southeastern urban school district	20 K–8 self-contained classrooms for students with EBD	The researchers did not implement an intervention but were looking at the transactional nature of teacher praise and rate of OTR in order to describe the conditions under which teachers were likely to have higher rates of OTR.	*Dependent variables:* 1. Correct student response 2. A variety of teacher behaviors including: OTR, praise, reprimands, academic talk, and other talk *Social validity:* Not measured.	Correlation as well as a sequential analysis using time windows
Godfrey, Grisham-Brown, Schuster, & Hemmeter (2003) The effects of three techniques on student participation with preschool children with attending problems (ETC)	N = 5 students, 1 teacher; public preschool	Preschool classroom first thing in the morning	During the morning calendar activity, OTR techniques using response card and choral responding were implemented.	*Dependent variables:* 1. Active responding 2. On-task behavior 3. Inappropriate behavior *Social validity:* Students and teacher were asked which condition they preferred. All preferred the response card format.	Alternating treatments

(continued)

17

TABLE 2.1. (continued)

Authors and journal	Students	Intervention setting	Intervention	Measures	Design
Sutherland, Alder, & Gunter (2003) The effect of varying rates of opportunities to respond to academic requests on the classroom behavior of students with EBD (JEBD)*	N = 9 students with emotional disorders, 1 teacher; 70% free and reduced-price lunches; urban elementary school	A self-contained classroom for students with EBD during mathematics instruction.	1. The teacher was asked to make a prediction about his rate of OTR per minute, and then the observed rate was shared. 2. The benefits of increased rates of OTR were discussed and examples were provided. 3. A goal of three OTR per minute was set. After each session, the teacher's rate of OTR per minute was told to him. 4. The teacher was taught to self-graph his rate of OTR per minute.	*Dependent variables:* 1. OTR 2. Teacher praise 3. Correct response 4. Disruptive behavior 5. On-task behavior *Social validity:* Not measured.	ABAB withdrawal
Haydon, Mancil, & Van Loan (2009) Using opportunities to respond in a general education classroom: A case study (ETC)	N = 1 student, 1 teacher; >90% free and reduced-price lunches; elementary (K–5 grades)	A general fifth-grade education classroom in science.	Changed instructional format so that the rate of OTR was increased to at least three per minute, and students responded chorally.	*Dependent variables:* 1. Disruptive behavior 2. Correct responses 3. On-task behavior 4. Rate of OTR *Social validity:* Not measured.	ABA single subject

18

Study	Participants/Setting	Description	Dependent variables	Design
Haydon et al. (2010) A comparison of three types of opportunities to respond on student academic and social behaviors (JEBD)*	N = 6 students, 6 teachers; elementary school	Six different second-grade general education classrooms during whole-class instruction of content vocabulary and syllable practice.	On a randomized schedule, teachers implemented either individual responding, choral responding, or a mixed mode responding (choral and individual) at a rate of approximately five OTR per minute.	*Dependent variables:* 1. Disruption 2. Off-task behavior 3. Active student responding *Social validity:* Teachers were asked their perceptions about the ease of implementation, its effectiveness, and likelihood of future use.	Alternating treatments
Haydon & Hunter (2011) The effects of two types of teacher questioning on teacher behavior and student performance: A case study (ETC)	N = 2 students, 1 teacher; 90% free and reduced-price lunches; middle school (grades 6–7)	A general education 7th-grade health science class.	1. Instructional delivery was changed to increase OTR (at least three per minute) and praise statements. 2. Two response conditions were compared: single student and unison.	*Dependent variables:* 1. Teacher redirection and praise statements 2. On-task behavior 3. Correct responses 4. Correct responses on test *Social validity:* Teacher and students completed a survey about the acceptability and usefulness of each intervention.	ABCBC

Note. In terms of treatment integrity, many authors reported the strategy (OTR) as a dependent variable, reporting interobserver agreement. ETC, *Education and Treatment of Children;* JABA, *Journal of Applied Behavior Analysis;* JEBD, *Journal of Emotional and Behavioral Disorders;* *indicates full text is available through Google Scholar.

of OTR and watched video clips of how to use it, and Mr. Smith practiced delivering questions to obtain a rate of at least three questions per minute. The intervention required the teacher to: "a) cue students to reply to the questions, b) allow adequate wait time for all students to respond, c) present the next problem to the students, and d) provide feedback" (p. 273).

Before the intervention was implemented (the baseline condition), the researcher observed a typical lesson taught by Mr. Smith and measured the following variables: Bree's disruptive behavior, correct responses, and on-task behavior, as well as Mr. Smith's rate of questioning. During baseline, Bree's median percentage of on-task behavior was 34%, median rate of disruptive behavior was 1.9 incidents per minute, and a median rate of correct responses of 0.025 per minute. Bree had a low percentage of on-task behavior, a high rate of misbehaviors, and a low rate of correct responses. Mr. Smith's rate of questioning during baseline was approximately one question per minute.

As part of the intervention, Mr. Smith used choral responding of science definitions rather than his typical question-and-answer format for reviewing definitions. He was able to increase his OTR rate so that students could respond at least three times per minute. During the intervention condition, the researcher observed Bree's on- and off-task behavior and number of correct responses. As Mr. Smith increased his rate of OTR, Bree's performance improved as well. Her median percentage for on-task behavior increased to 67% (almost double from the baseline condition), the median rate of disruptive behavior decreased to 0.25 per minute, and correct responses increased to 0.90 per minute.

Although Mr. Smith's use of OTR was highly successful, it will not solve all of Bree's problems; however, it is a refreshing alternative to using threats or punishments to try to improve Bree's behavior (and likely much more successful in doing so). It also adds to Mr. Smith's repertoire of instructional and behavioral strategies. This is a tool that will help him think about how to use effective instructional practices as part of managing behavior in the classroom.

Improving Academic Outcomes for Students with Behavior Disorders

Sutherland, Alder, and Gunter (2003) conducted a particularly interesting study that focused on a population of students who are among the most difficult to teach, those identified with emotional and behavioral disorders (EBD). Additionally, they wanted to examine how the strategy affected an entire class rather than measuring the outcomes of only one student, as discussed in the preceding study. The setting was a special day class of nine students (eight boys and one girl) ranging in age from about 8 to 12 years old. The teacher was a young man (26 years old) relatively new to teaching with just 2 years of experience. He was completing a master's degree program in emotional disturbance. The elementary school was located in an urban area, and about 70% of students received free or reduced-price lunches.

Before the intervention (increasing the teacher's rate of OTR) started, the researcher observed the teacher during math class, which consisted of teacher-led instruction in which the teacher called on students who raised their hands combined with independent seat work. Then (during baseline) the researcher collected the frequency of OTR and praise statements presented by the teacher. In addition, students' on-task behavior (time sampled in 1-minute intervals in rotating quadrants), number of disruptive behaviors, and number of correct responses were collected.

After collecting baseline data, the researcher completed the following steps with the teacher: (1) had the teacher predict his OTR per minute; (2) shared a graph that included the baseline data of the teacher's rate of OTR; (3) briefly discussed the benefits of using OTR and provided examples of what it looked like; (4) set a goal of three OTR per minute; and (5) showed the teacher how to graph his rate of OTR daily. Before each observation session started, the researcher reminded the teacher of the criterion level of three OTR per minute and, at the end of each observation, shared the rate of OTR the teacher had achieved. At the very end of the intervention, the teacher's graphs of his daily OTR rate were collected.

The study's design requires four phases. The first comes before the intervention starts when data are collected on typical teacher and student performance (Baseline A1). Then the intervention starts, and the teacher uses the specified strategies and receives feedback from the researcher (Intervention B1). In the third phase, no feedback is provided, but data are still collected (Withdrawal A2). The final and fourth phase is exactly the same as the second phase (Intervention B2), in which the teacher receives feedback on his or her use of the strategy. The pattern across these different phases—referred to as an ABAB withdrawal design (Gast & Ledford, 2014)—is what allows the researcher (and the consumer of the research) to decide how effective the intervention was in achieving the desired student outcomes.

In this investigation, the increase in OTR did positively affect all the variables (teacher praise, time on task, disruptive behavior, and number of correct responses) compared with the baseline condition. The biggest changes were in the average on-task percentage (from 55% during baseline to 79% during intervention) and the decrease in the average rate of problem behaviors (from nearly three during baseline to less than two in the last intervention phase). The rate of teacher praise and the number of correct responses only increased slightly; however, the intervention required little training and was of short duration, so this is not surprising. Even the slight increase, however, had a positive effect. The researchers hypothesize that a transactional relation may occur when using OTR: when students respond correctly and are more engaged, the teacher praises more frequently. In turn, the praise motivates students to be on task and avoid problem behaviors. In essence, the negative interaction cycle between students and teachers can be changed to a more positive interaction cycle. This is a subtle but important point. As teachers use a host of strategies (such as the ones explained in this book) that promote positive interactions, the synergy created may have a multiplicative effect that is more than the sum of its parts.

Using Choral Responding to Increase Student Participation

Haydon and Hunter (2011) conducted another interesting study looking at differences in student engagement during whole-group instruction depending on whether students responded in unison or used a more typical single-student responding format. This study is interesting because both conditions used OTR (choral and single-student responding conditions) and showed improvements over the baseline conditions (when OTR was not used), but the researchers wanted to know whether unison responding resulted in even higher gains.

The study took place in an urban school in the Midwest with approximately 500 students. Ninety percent of the student population was eligible for free or reduced-price lunches, and the school had a high transience rate (over 50%). The setting was a seventh-grade health class of 20 students. The teacher was in her fourth year of teaching and in her early 30s.

The researchers looked at the rate of OTR during baseline and the two conditions (single-student responding and unison responding). They also looked at other teacher variables, including the number of redirections (prompts from the teacher to the students to be on task) and praise statements. In order to determine whether the conditions increased on-task behavior, correct responses, and test scores, two student participants were observed: James, who had difficulty paying attention and staying on task, and Jerod, who did not have attentional problems. Neither student had a disability, but James was chosen to see whether the intervention would work for a student with high distractibility. Jerod was chosen to see whether OTR (in either condition) would have an impact on typically achieving students. When observing the students, the researchers looked at their on-task behavior and the number of correct responses. They also compared students' scores on tests that followed baseline and each condition.

The teacher's typical routine was to provide a lecture combined with a question-and-answer format. Multiple-choice questions were displayed on the overhead or whiteboard and students were randomly called on to answer a question. The single-student responding condition differed slightly in that the teacher increased the number of multiple-choice questions presented per minute, waited 5 seconds, randomly called on a student to respond, and then offered feedback on whether or not the response was correct. In this condition, James and Jerod had two OTR per session. In the unison condition, the first two steps were the same, but instead of calling on individual students, all students were asked to show either one, two, three, or four fingers corresponding to their multiple choice answer (a, b, c, or d).

Results showed that OTR in either condition was effective in improving both students' engagement, and unison responding may have offered slightly greater benefits. First, the teacher reduced the number of redirects (reminding students to be on task) from approximately 2 per minute during typical instruction to less than 1 per minute (and even 0 during the first intervention phase) when using either OTR strategy. The teacher increased the number of praise statements from 0 during typical instruction to approximately 1 per minute during the unison OTR.

The improvements in teacher behavior (fewer redirects and more positive feedback), in combination with increased OTR, positively affected the behavior of both student participants. James, the easily distracted student, had significant improvement in his on-task behavior. During typical instruction, he had an on-task rate of approximately 20%. This improved to 68% in the single-student response condition and to as much as 100% in the unison condition. Jerod demonstrated a similar pattern. Both students also showed improvement in the number of correct responses offered in class, as well as an increase in test scores. In fact, scores for James were 40% during typical instruction, near 66% during single-student response, and 70% during unison response. Jerod also showed improvement, with scores of 80%, 93%, and 100%, respectively. James and Jerod were each able to improve by an entire letter grade.

The researchers administered a social validity survey asking the teacher and students their opinions of the intervention. All felt it was beneficial, and the teacher noted it was easy to implement. The study demonstrates how a teacher can more effectively cover material with relatively little planning or energy, as student scores improved in the OTR condition. It also promoted good student behavior, which in turns fosters a positive classroom climate. In this case the intervention also had practical significance because it produced a substantial change in the academic outcomes for the two students. An intervention that can raise the course grade by an entire letter is noteworthy, as it has tangible, and beneficial, implications for students.

Summary

These studies (and others, shown in Table 2.1) illustrate how the use of OTR can diminish the number of behavioral incidents in a classroom whether the focus is on an individual student or an entire class. In each instance, when the teacher restructured the lesson to provide students with more opportunities to respond to academic content, on-task behavior improved. Not only was the strategy effective in a general education setting, but it was also effective for students identified for special education services due to their behavioral challenges. The studies also demonstrate how easy it was to use the strategy. Intensive training was not required in any of the interventions. Once the researcher reviewed the basic criteria, the teacher was ready to implement it. The most powerful aspect of implementation was having teachers review their performance, as it helped them maintain the criterion number of OTR. We encourage the reader interested in learning more about

OTR to see a recent systematic review of the literature conducted by Common and colleagues (2015).

Benefits and Challenges

OTR is a strategy with many benefits and few challenges. We discuss these briefly in this section.

Benefits

OTR offers an instructional format that is efficient but also engaging because it facilitates participation of all students. Content or skills can be reviewed with the entire class while still ensuring that students are taking part in the activity. It requires relatively little preparation and can be used for a wide variety of lessons across all grade levels.

Studies listed in this chapter demonstrating its effectiveness ranged from preschool (Godfrey, Grisham-Brown, Schuster, & Hemmeter, 2003) to middle school (Haydon & Hunter, 2011). More specifically, use of OTR is instrumental in decreasing off-task behaviors, thereby increasing academic performance. Empirical studies indicate it is effective for students with (Haydon et al., 2009) and without (Haydon et al., 2010) disabilities, including those with very challenging behavior (Sutherland et al., 2003).

Challenges

Although it is easy to learn the technique, initially it will require more advance preparation than a traditional lesson because a sufficient number of prompts or questions have to be created before beginning the lesson (see Sutherland & Wright, 2013). There may also be a gentle learning curve while becoming comfortable with a rapid pace of instruction. Ideally, students are presented with a minimum of three OTR per minute, so the teacher must practice moving through a lesson quickly to ensure the pace has sufficient momentum but is not so rapid that students are lost (Kounin, 1970). Finding an optimal rate of pacing is more difficult than many teachers anticipate, particularly new teachers. Yet OTR is a good strategy for understanding one's competence in this area because the strategy requires you be aware of your pacing and adjust it as necessary.

It is also important to monitor student performance while delivering the lesson to ensure students are accurately responding to a large percentage of the prompts. If there are too many incorrect responses, it may mean the difficulty level should be lowered or that students need a different type of lesson or practice session to gain more familiarity with the concepts. Despite these challenges, OTR is worth the effort when weighing the cost of preparation against the results.

Implementing Increased OTR in Your Classroom: Checklist for Success

Before beginning with OTR, it is useful to consider how the strategy will fit with the choice of other instructional models, such as cooperative learning, direct instruction, and technologically mediated lessons. This preliminary step is important because effective instruction relies on a host of practices used to reach specific goals. Students require different levels of support and scaffolding to master a skill or concept, so a mix of instructional models is critical. OTR should complement your instructional mix.

Preparation for OTR includes steps that occur before the lesson takes place (considering and preparing the content), as well as during instructional delivery (Sutherland & Wright, 2013). See Table 2.2 for the implementation checklist of each of the steps described in detail next.

- **Step 1: Identify the lesson content to be taught and the instructional objective.** The first step in using OTR is to identify the lesson content and its instructional objective: review of facts, practice of skills, and so forth. Also to be considered is whether the skill is entirely new to the student or whether he or she is already familiar with it. For example, direct instruction is a good choice for teaching students about the concept of multiplication, whereas OTR works well for practicing multiplication facts. However, OTR could be used with new material if the student has mastery of the prerequisite skills. Perhaps students have read a new story, but the teacher would like to review students' literal comprehension of the text. OTR would be an appropriate strategy in this instance.

- **Step 2: Prepare a list of questions, prompts, or cues related to the content.** Once the content is identified, questions or prompts about it are developed. It is simple to create questions for some content, such as practicing various math facts. All that is necessary is a sheet containing a list of the math facts to be reviewed;

TABLE 2.2. Implementation Checklist for Success: Opportunities to Respond (OTR)

- Step 1: Identify the lesson content to be taught and the instructional objective.
- Step 2: Prepare a list of questions, prompts, or cues related to the content.
- Step 3: Determine the modality by which the content will be delivered.
- Step 4: Determine the modality by which students will respond.
- Step 5: Explain to students how the format works and the rationale for using it.
- Step 6: Conduct the lesson with a minimum of three opportunities to respond per minute using either single-student or unison responding.
- Step 7: Respond to student answers with evaluative and encouraging feedback.
- Step 8: Offer students an opportunity to give feedback.

for instance, a table of multiplication problems. Other content may require more preparation. For example, if you are reviewing an entire science unit, then carefully reading the unit and choosing salient vocabulary, concepts, and facts, as well as deciding on their format, is necessary. One possible format could be presenting a definition or concept and having students respond with the appropriate term. Another is displaying statements and having students indicate whether they are true or false. As the technique is used more frequently, lessons can be saved and used in subsequent years or for multiple classes. The number of questions prepared will depend on the length of the instructional period. Most of the empirical literature recommends three OTR per minute (Sutherland & Wehby, 2001), so that figure can be used as a basic guideline for how many questions to prepare (multiply the number of minutes in the instructional period by 3).

• **Step 3: Determine the modality by which the content will be delivered.** After an adequate number of questions or prompts have been prepared, the next step is to decide how to present them. Teachers often present verbally, but it is important to decide on the method that best matches the complexity of the content, as well as other environmental factors. For example, if the classroom is large with many students, a visual presentation format using an electronic projector or an overhead document camera can be more effective. Noise will be less of a factor, and students will not have to strain to hear the teacher. If presenting to a small group, a verbal presentation may be the most efficient and feel the most interactive. Depending on the contextual factors, some presentation formats will be preferable to others.

• **Step 4: Determine the modality by which students will respond.** There are a variety of choices available of ways for students to respond. The literature indicates that both single-student and unison responding OTR are better than a non-OTR format, although unison responding may be more effective (Haydon et al., 2010; Haydon & Hunter, 2011). This choice will also be influenced by whether you are using a whole-class, small-group, or individual format. Students could answer in a number of ways: verbally, with a gesture (thumbs up, thumbs down), using a personal response system (PRS; clickers), with stackable communication cups (green [agree], yellow [undecided], or red [disagree]), using an electronic format (tablets or iPads), holding up premade response cards, or writing their responses on mini-whiteboards or chalkboards. Begin by using the format that requires the least preparation when first learning to use the strategy. Additional response formats can be tested in various content areas once both the teacher and students are familiar with the general procedure. Another consideration is student age. With younger students, a simple response format is probably better, such as thumbs up or down or choral responding, as it will require fewer materials and less time. Older students may prefer use of a PRS, and many systems now use mobile technology so students are able to use their own cell phones as a response device. A final consideration is to think about students with disabilities or other learning challenges. The response format should not interfere with a student's ability to provide an answer. For example, students with learning disabilities may have difficulty rapidly writing down an answer on a whiteboard even though they may know the correct answer. These students may have an easier time responding with gestures or by using response cards.

• **Step 5: Explain to students how the format works and the rationale for using it.** A brief explanation to students about the procedure and how they are expected to behave during the lesson is essential. Once students are familiar with the format, explanations will no longer be necessary, but providing them initially is a proactive move to reduce confusion and make students feel more comfortable. Explain the content to be covered, the presentation format, and how students are expected to respond. Also explain the pace will be rapid, maximum participation is expected, and the correct answer will be provided after students answer but that it is fine if they have offered incorrect responses. Be clear about whether students will respond individually when you call on them (or cue them in some manner) or whether the whole group is responding. Students should also be reminded about expectations for noise level and when it is appropriate to speak out.

• **Step 6: Conduct the lesson with a minimum of three opportunities to respond per minute using either single-student or unison responding.** When conducting the lesson, remember to keep the pacing rapid, with a minimum of three OTR per minute. Once the session is initiated, present the item, cue the students for a response, confirm accurate responses and correct inaccurate answers, and praise participation. Two areas to be aware of during the lesson are whether all students are engaged and participating and whether they know the correct answers. If students are not adequately participating, it may be necessary to rethink either the presentation or the response format. If students are having difficulty with correct responding, it may be additional review or reteaching is needed. Also to be examined is whether the content is a match for the strategy. However, becoming familiar with using the strategy will take a few sessions. Measuring certain aspects of the strategy's impact, such as participation rate, correct responding, and on-task behavior, can be done using an ABAB design, as discussed in the next section of the chapter.

• **Step 7: Respond to student answers with evaluative and encouraging feedback.** As students offer answers, the teacher should indicate whether they are correct or not. Depending on whether OTR is used whole group, small group, or individually, feedback can be addressed to the entire group or to an individual student. An important part of any lesson is that students receive feedback that helps them improve their skill or knowledge. Evaluative feedback offered in a supportive manner (with praise or encouragement) is an essential part of using OTR effectively. Responses might sound something like this: "Yes, 2×9 is 18" or "No, that is not correct, 4×9 is 36, not 45, but let's try again." Teachers frequently struggle with balancing the appropriate amount of encouragement to keep a student motivated or feeling positive without offering unrealistic or undeserved praise. Some teachers feel more comfortable with providing overall feedback that focuses on malleable factors such as effort: "I appreciate everyone's participation effort today." It is also fine to offer an individual private encouragement at a later time: "I noticed how hard you were trying today and how many times you participated. That was good work." It is easy to overlook what a strong impact a student's feelings have on his or her willingness to be engaged, and teachers sometimes think it is unfair or indulgent to provide too much praise. However, offering sincere, behavior-specific feedback on what students are doing well, even if they do not have the correct answer, can help a student become more productive and experience fewer behavior incidents. Also, the use of the schoolwide reinforcement system (e.g., positive behavior intervention and support [PBIS] tickets) can be intermittently paired with behavior-specific praise (BSP) when working in tiered systems of support. Preparing the types of verbal support you can offer students will improve the flow of the lesson and the speed of the pacing. Other chapters in this book address providing corrective feedback and BSP, which are complementary strategies to OTR.

• **Step 8: Offer students an opportunity to give feedback.** Finally, seeking input as to what teachers, students, and (in some cases), parents thought about the strategy can be very helpful. Soliciting their input on the goals, procedures, and outcomes to see what they thought (a point developed in the next section) can provide information that can be used to continually improve and expand a teacher's repertoire of low-intensity strategies to support strong instruction and limit behavior challenges. As is discussed in other chapters, it may not be practical to ask students what they think of each lesson, but it may be manageable to ask for input at the end of some lessons or at the end of several days of using a variety of strategies to increase OTR.

Examining the Effects: How Well Is It Working?

Testing the Strategy: Design Considerations

When implementing OTR, it is important to collect data on student performance to know how well this strategy is working. In many of the studies featured in this book, researchers have used single-case methodology to "test" the intervention effects. This is a particularly useful design approach for teachers, as it is highly flexible and very practical. It can be used with any of the strategies introduced in each chapter.

It is important to use an experimental design such as an ABAB or multiple baseline across settings, tasks, or students to establish a functional relation between the introduction of the intervention and changes in student performance (Gast & Ledford, 2014). In other words, this design helps determine whether or not the intervention worked. This information is helpful to both general education and special education teachers for a variety of reasons. The first, of course, is it allows you to evaluate the effectiveness of your instruction. With this information, you can decide how to adjust your instructional practices so they work better for your students. Second, members of the comprehensive, integrated, three-tiered (CI3T) team or members of professional learning communities (PLCs) can use these data to determine how students are responding to these low-intensity supports. Before moving on to student-focused Tier 2 (e.g., Check-In/Check-Out, behavior contracts, or self-monitoring strategies) or Tier 3 (e.g., functional assessment-based interventions; Umbreit, Ferro, Liaupsin, & Lane, 2007) supports, we want to be certain we have examined the extent to which teacher-driven strategies (e.g., OTR) have been effective in addressing students' needs (academically, behaviorally, and/or socially). Using an experimental design is one way to show whether or not this has occurred. We recommend these teams (e.g., CI3T and PLC) be composed of a range of individuals, including general and special education teachers, as they each bring unique talents. For example, as special education teachers are a critical resource for implementing and delivering specialized intervention, they can assist general educators with evaluating strategy implementation, as well as carefully measuring the effects of any given intervention for a particular student, as is demonstrated in Box 2.1. This is especially critical when focused on more intensive supports, such as functional assessment-based interventions, that require careful monitoring of students' performance (e.g., academic engagement, disruption). The ability to use single-case methodology is a critical skill in assessing the effectiveness of Tier 2 and 3 supports.

These designs begin with a baseline phase during which data on student performance are collected (referred to as the A phase), then the intervention is introduced for the first time (B), while still collecting data on student performance using the same data collection method used during the baseline phase (see Figure 2.1 in Box 2.1). Although it is tempting at this point to say the intervention was effective, two more replications are needed to be certain the intervention was responsible for the change and not something else. One demonstration (e.g., the change from A to B phases) along with two other replications can provide evidence that the introduction of the strategy produced the changes (the shift from B to A and then A to B; Gast & Ledford, 2014).

Although some designs, such as the ABAB design, require removal and then reintroduction of the intervention, it is also possible to explore a functional relation using a multiple baseline across setting design. This means the strategy is used in different settings, such as a different instructional period (math instead of reading) or a different physical location (playground instead of the lunchroom).

Making Certain the Strategy Is in Place: Treatment Integrity

In addition to using an experimental design to test the intervention, collecting treatment integrity data helps determine the extent to which the intervention is being implemented as planned. Figure 2.2 in Box 2.1 is an example of a treatment integrity checklist for OTR. Although there are many different ways to collect treatment integrity data, one way is to have the teacher collect these data each day by indicating the degree to which each intervention component was implemented as planned for each student. For example, in Figure 2.2, each item is a completed using a 3-point Likert-type scale as follows: 0 = *not in place*, 1 = *partially in place*, or 2 = *completely in place*. Each day the items are summed, divided by the total number of points possible, and divided by 100 to obtain a percentage of implementation for each student. These data can be used to interpret intervention outcomes (see Box 2.1). In addition, behavior component checklists not only determine the level of implementation but also serve as a prompt or reminder to implement each step.

Using an outside observer to collect treatment integrity data for approximately 25% of the sessions in each phase is recommended. An additional observer is important for establishing the accuracy of the data collected.

Examining Stakeholders' Views: Social Validity

Finally, in addition to collecting information on student performance and implementation (treatment integrity), it is important to understand how stakeholders felt about the intervention goals, procedures, and intended outcomes. Figure 2.3 in Box 2.1 is an example of a measure examining preschoolers' perceptions of the social validity of OTR.

It is important to obtain all stakeholders' views —the teacher, student, and parent—ideally before the intervention begins and again at the conclusion of the first "test." If social validity is low at the onset of the intervention, then it is wise to provide additional training to increase people's knowledge of the strategies, as well as their confidence in using the strategy prior to implementation. In theory (and in some instances in actuality; see Lane, Kalberg, Bruhn, et al., 2009), the opinions of those implementing and participating in the intervention may predict the extent to which the interventions are implemented as planned. In essence, a socially valid intervention is likely to be put in place with a high degree of integrity, leading to improvements in student performance that maintain over time and in new settings and with new people.

BOX 2.1. A Hypothetical Illustration of OTR in a CI3T Model

Little Flowers Preschool has used a schoolwide program for several years. They adopted the PeaceBuilders® program for preschoolers, which emphasizes six principles of cooperation and kindness through a series of lessons and activities: help others, right wrongs, praise people, notice hurts, seek wise people, and give up put-downs. This was a main component of their comprehensive, integrated, three-tiered (CI3T) model of prevention. Teachers, parents, staff members, and administrators alike participate in various aspects of the schoolwide program. Little

Flowers believes it is an important element in maintaining a school climate that helps their students flourish. In addition to fostering students' social and emotional development, Little Flowers used a curriculum that emphasized play-based activities and a rich literacy program. All teachers took pride in each element of their CI3T model, as they felt it provided a strong foundation for success as the students entered kindergarten.

Ms. Garcia, the lead teacher for the 4-year-old classroom, was trying to increase the participation of one of her students, Gabriel, as she felt it would help him gain confidence in the classroom setting. Although Gabriel had a gentle disposition and was not disruptive, he was shy and did not participate unless called on directly, and even then he was slow to offer an answer. When Ms. Garcia administered the Systematic Screening for Behavior Disorders (SSBD, 2nd ed.) screener during the second month of school, Gabriel exceeded normative criteria for internalizing behaviors. Ms. Garcia wanted to have Gabriel participate independently and more frequently. She decided to use opportunity to respond (OTR) and target the read-aloud time, as it would be simple to have students respond in unison with the use of response cards. This would also make it easier for Gabriel to participate, as he would only have to hold up the appropriate response card when cued.

Support	Description	Entry criteria	Data to monitor progress	Exit criteria
OTR	Increase OTR during read-aloud time using response cards	Systematic Screening for Behavior Disorders (SSBD, 2nd ed.): Exceeded normative criteria for internalizing behaviors in Stage 2	*Student performance:* Percentage of Gabriel's responses to teacher requests or prompts (number of times Gabriel used the response card to respond to teacher requests or prompts divided the number of OTR × 100) *Treatment integrity:* Component checklist *Social validity:* Student-completed survey	Two weeks of increased participation during read-aloud (85% response rate for 8 reading sessions)

Preparing for and Delivering OTR: The Intervention

• **Step 1: Identify the lesson content to be taught and the instructional objective.** Ms. Garcia identified read-aloud as a good place to build Gabriel's confidence, as it was a daily activity with a routine she and the students followed consistently. This would give them plenty of opportunities to practice and revisit the skill. The objective of the lesson was to have students identify the characters in the story.

• **Step 2: Prepare a list of questions, prompts, or cues related to the content.** Ms. Garcia thought ahead to the books she would introduce that week and made a list of the characters in each one. For each story she would read, she prepared a list of questions to which the correct answer would be the name of one of the story's characters.

• **Step 3: Determine the modality by which the content will be delivered.** It was easy to prepare for the delivery modality, as Ms. Garcia was going to use the routine she always did, in which she verbally asked the students questions about each of the characters. She made sure she had her list of questions ready for each story so that the pacing of the lesson would be appropriately rapid.

• **Step 4: Determine the modality by which students will respond.** Rather than call on one student at a time to answer questions verbally, Ms. Garcia prepared sets of "character cards." She cut out and pasted an illustration of each character on a rectangular piece of card stock. Each child had a set of characters for the story they would be reading that day. When she asked her questions, students could hold up the card with the appropriate character.

• **Step 5: Explain to students how the format works and the rationale for using it.** At the beginning of the read-aloud, Ms. Garcia explained to the students they would be using the "character cards" to respond to her questions about the story. She told students that using the cards would give everyone a chance to participate. All they had to do was hold up the card with the picture of the character she was asking about. Ms. Garcia emphasized that this would be a fun way to show what they knew about the book.

• **Step 6: Conduct the lesson with a minimum of three OTR per minute using either single-student or unison responding.** Before reading the story, Ms. Garcia briefly introduced each of the characters and then passed out a set of response cards to each of her students. She gave them chance to look through the cards and get used to holding them. Then, throughout the reading of the story, Ms. Garcia would pause and ask the questions from her list, such as: "Which character are we talking about?" or "Who was feeling happy?" The story took approximately 10 minutes to read, and Ms. Garcia reached her goal of asking 30 questions during the lesson.

• **Step 7: Respond to student answers with evaluative and encouraging feedback.** Once all students held up their response cards, Ms. Garcia indicated whether they had identified the correct answer. She offered corrective feedback when a student answered incorrectly: "I can see how you may have thought that, Samantha, but it was the little boy who received a kite as a holiday present." Evaluating student answers and offering encouragement and corrective feedback was done quickly.

• **Step 8: Offer students an opportunity to give feedback.** After 3 days of incorporating the OTR strategy, Ms. Garcia asked the students if they liked using the response cards and would like to use them again.

Looking at How Well OTR Worked

Although Ms. Garcia thought the OTR strategy would encourage all students to answer more questions, she particularly wanted to know how well it was working for Gabriel. Ms. Garcia could have looked at on-task behavior or correct responses, but she decided to keep it simple and focus only on the number of times Gabriel offered a response during each read-aloud session.

Ms. Garcia began by looking at Gabriel's participation during baseline (A1 in Figure 2.1, before she started using OTR). Each day during read-aloud, she counted the number of times Gabriel offered an answer to her questions, converted that number into a percentage (the number of responses divided by the number of OTR and multiplying the quantity by 100), and then graphed Gabriel's percentage daily. Figure 2.1 shows the results of Ms. Garcia's ABAB design, where she calculated Gabriel's participation (percentage of responses) each day during read-aloud time for 4 weeks. During baseline (Baseline A1, the first week), Gabriel's daily percentage ranged from a low of 5% to a high of 25%. When Ms. Garcia began using the OTR strategy (OTR B1), Gabriel had a dramatic increase in participation, with his percentage of responses increasing to a high of 90%. In the next phase (Baseline A2), when the intervention was withdrawn, Gabriel's percentage of responses was again low. In the final phase (OTR B2), his percentage of responses rose again with reintroduction of the strategy. OTR increased Gabriel's willingness to participate during read-aloud time.

While Ms. Garcia implemented the strategy, she used the Treatment Integrity Checklist in Figure 2.2 so she could be sure she completed each step, especially as she was just learning to use the technique. Each day, right after the lesson, she checked off each of the steps she had performed and calculated her percentage. Ms. Garcia had a high rate of implementation. She rarely had below 100%, but occasionally she had forgotten one step.

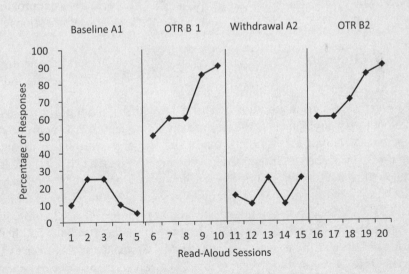

FIGURE 2.1. Examining the effects: Percentage of times Gabriel used the response card to respond to teacher request or prompts divided by the number of OTR multiplied by 100 during read-aloud time.

TREATMENT INTEGRITY CHECKLIST: OPPORTUNITIES TO RESPOND

Date: _____   Start time: _____   End time: _____   Total time: _____

Notes: _____

0 = *not in place*, 1 = *partially in place*, or 2 = *completely in place*

Item	Rating		
1. Did I identify the instructional objective?	0	1	2
2. Did I prepare a list of questions/prompts in advance?	0	1	2
3. Did I choose an appropriate presentation format?	0	1	2
4. Did I decide on how students will respond and prepare accordingly?	0	1	2
5. Did I explain to students how to respond to the questions/prompts?	0	1	2
6. Did I reach a presentation rate of at least three OTR per minute?	0	1	2
7. Did I respond to student answers with evaluative and encouraging feedback?	0	1	2
8. Did I offer the student an opportunity to give feedback?*	0	1	2
TOTAL			
$(N \div [14]) \times 100 =$			%

*Step 8 does not need to be done daily, but occasionally.

FIGURE 2.2. Making certain the strategy is in place: Treatment integrity checklist used by Ms. Garcia to monitor the extent to which each step was put in place as planned.

From *Supporting Behavior for School Success: A Step-by-Step Guide to Key Strategies* by Kathleen Lynne Lane, Holly Mariah Menzies, Robin Parks Ennis, and Wendy Peia Oakes. Copyright 2015 by The Guilford Press. Permission to photocopy this figure is granted to purchasers of this book for personal use only (see copyright page for details). Purchasers can download a larger version of this figure from *www.guilford.com/lane4-forms*.

Ms. Garcia was curious to know what the students thought of the strategy, so she created a very simple social validity measure (see Figure 2.3) appropriate for preschoolers. Although Ms. Garcia thought the students were likely to say they enjoyed the activity, she was interested in knowing whether they liked the response cards enough to keep using them. She sat down with each student individually, reminded him or her of the character cards they were using during read-aloud, and then asked the two questions on her social validity measure. Overwhelmingly, students enjoyed using the response cards. Given the students' feedback and her own evaluation of Gabriel's increased participation, Ms. Garcia felt it was worthwhile to have tried OTR. Not only did it help Gabriel, but it also turned out to be an easy way to increase all students' engagement in the read-aloud lessons. Ms. Garcia thought it might be a strategy they could add to their schoolwide plan, as it was an effective technique for supporting students' success in their academic skills.

SOCIAL VALIDITY FORM: OPPORTUNITIES TO RESPOND

Date: _____

Student: _____

Before we get started . . . What do you think?	☹ No, not really	☺ Yes, definitely
1. Do you think you would enjoy using the character card during read-aloud time?		
2. Do you have any questions about how to use the cards?		

Date: _____

Student: _____

Now that you have tried it . . . What do you think?	☹ No, not really	☺ Yes, definitely
1. Did you enjoy using the character card during read-aloud time?		
2. Would you like to use the character cards again?		

FIGURE 2.3. Examining stakeholders' views: Social validity form developed by Ms. Garcia to examine her preschool children's views on using the character cards during read-aloud time and in the future.

From *Supporting Behavior for School Success: A Step-by-Step Guide to Key Strategies* by Kathleen Lynne Lane, Holly Mariah Menzies, Robin Parks Ennis, and Wendy Peia Oakes. Copyright 2015 by The Guilford Press. Permission to photocopy this figure is granted to purchasers of this book for personal use only (see copyright page for details). Purchasers can download a larger version of this figure from *www.guilford.com/lane4-forms*.

Summary

OTR is an easy-to-use strategy that enhances whole-class instruction but can also be used for small-group and individual instruction (Sutherland & Wright, 2013). It is a technique that effectively reduces off-task behavior while requiring relatively little preparation and requires no special materials. One of its most powerful benefits is it can be used to intervene with an individual student while still addressing the academic needs of the entire class. Part of the difficulty in working with students who have challenging behaviors is doing so while having sole responsibility for an entire class. Of course a variety of strategies will have to be relied on when supporting students with disruptive behaviors; no single approach will be sufficient. However, employing strategies that allow teachers to address a particular student's needs while working with the rest of the class is critical. OTR, and other strategies introduced in this book, provide teachers the flexibility to do both.

CHAPTER 3

A Look at
Behavior-Specific Praise

Creating a positive school climate and safe classroom environments where students feel connected with caring adults can begin with the simple act of acknowledging students' appropriate behavior. Acknowledging appropriate behavior, or "catching" students being good, can take many forms. One of the easiest ways of doing this is through the use of praise contingent on appropriate behavior. The form of praise that has proven to be most effective is behavior-specific praise (BSP), or praise statements that include reference to the specific behavior for which the student is being recognized (Brophy, 1981; Sutherland, Wehby, & Copeland, 2000).

Research on the effectiveness of teacher praise dates back to 1968, when researchers saw a functional relation between increased rates of praise and decreased rates of inappropriate behavior (Madsen, Becker, & Thomas, 1968). Similarly, increased rates of praise resulted in increased rates of appropriate behavior and task engagement for disruptive students in general education classrooms (Hall, Lund, & Jackson, 1968). These findings are not surprising given the relationship between student and teacher behavior is reciprocal, meaning that teachers affect the behavior of their students and vice versa. Further, acknowledging appropriate behavior is integral to the process of teaching new behaviors and increasing students' use of or maintaining existing behaviors.

Using praise statements is most likely a part of every teacher's repertoire of behavioral strategies, as it is a readily available classroom resource. However, research suggests that it is greatly underutilized and most often used in the form of general praise rather than BSP (Walker, Ramsey, & Gresham, 2004. Praise can be more effective when (1) it is behavior-specific rather than more general praise and (2) teachers use strategies to intentionally increase their rate of BSP and target their delivery of BSP to identified students (Thompson et al., 2012). These minor adjustments to praise delivery can result in improvements in students' behavior, as evidenced by research in a variety of settings (i.e., general education classrooms, special education classrooms, and self-contained settings) and across the grade span (e.g., Fullerton, Conroy, & Correa, 2009; Hawkins & Heflin, 2011; Kennedy & Jolivette, 2008). This chapter highlights some of these research findings, as well as outlining how to effectively deliver BSP and how to maximize the use of BSP in the classroom.

What Is BSP?

Praise statements can be categorized as either general or behavior specific. General praise statements are statements that acknowledge appropriate behavior but do not specifically state what behavior has been performed. For example, statements such as "good job," "way to go," or "great work" are statements that acknowledge something appropriate has occurred but do not specifically recognize the desirable behavior that a student has displayed. BSP statements are statements that praise the student and clearly state what desirable behavior has been performed, such as, "Bob, great job showing your work on your math homework," or "I appreciate how you pushed in your chair on the way to line up for lunch. That keeps the walkways safe." These statements can be in reference to students' behavior during both academic (first example) and nonacademic (second example) activities. Further, BSP statements can be used to acknowledge the appropriate behavior of an individual student or multiple students (e.g., a small reading group, the class as a whole). In addition to linking the statement to a specific behavior, there are other essential components to consider when delivering BSP statements, such as providing feedback, being sincere, reflecting the student's skill level, and evaluating effectiveness (Haydon & Musti-Rao, 2011).

First, consider the impact of the BSP statement. The statement should provide students with feedback on their performance of a given task (Sutherland et al., 2001). If a student enters the classroom quietly and begins his morning work, which is a posted schoolwide expectation, we want to acknowledge him for doing so using BSP to increase the likelihood the behavior will occur again. This both serves to reinforce his appropriate responding and provides instructional feedback that he has adequately met the expectation for entering the class in the morning. The topic of instructional feedback is further explored in Chapter 5.

Second, it is important to be sincere (Marchant & Anderson, 2012). Students are perceptive and will know when they have genuinely made their teachers proud or when a teacher is acknowledging their behavior out of habit or routine. Every teacher has his or her own teaching style that reflects his or her personality. Some teachers function as cheerleaders for their students, interacting with students with great enthusiasm. For others, this persona is not natural or does not fit their personalities, as they have a more subdued affect. Regardless of personality, all teachers can deliver BSP effectively as long as they use it with sincerity.

Third, BSP should be reflective of the students' present skill levels (Haydon & Musti-Rao, 2011; Marchant & Anderson, 2012). For example, a teacher may want to use BSP with a student learning a new behavior by acknowledging students for completing a partial aspect of the behavior (e.g., entering the classroom quietly), then reinforcing successive approximations of the behavior (e.g., beginning morning work within 2 minutes of entering the classroom quietly) until the student has mastered the new behavior (i.e., beginning morning work immediately upon entering the classroom quietly). Similarly, students who have already mastered a target skill can be acknowledged periodically to ensure they maintain or build fluency with that behavior.

Fourth, as with any classroom strategy, the effectiveness of BSP should be evaluated. Given BSP is a form of positive reinforcement (i.e., it is added to a student's environment to increase the likelihood of that particular behavior occurring in the future), it can be determined whether or not the use of BSP increases the behavior for which the student is being praised (Haydon & Musti-Rao, 2011). Moreover, you can determine whether behavior is improving as a result of praise. Formal methods of evaluation are discussed later in this chapter.

Finally, if you are working in a school with a tiered system of supports, such as positive behavior intervention and support (PBIS; Sugai & Horner, 2002b), response to intervention (RTI; Fuchs & Fuchs, 2006), and comprehensive, integrated, three-tiered (CI3T; Lane, Kalberg, & Menzies, 2009) models of prevention, then BSP can be used as a mechanism for reinforcing students for meeting schoolwide expectations. For example, if there is an expectation that students show responsibility, teachers can look for opportunities to "catch" students engaging in responsible behaviors in the classroom (e.g., "Steve, thank you for turning in your assignment on time"; "Barbie, I love how you remembered to clean up your area after our science lab"). BSP can also be paired with a token such as a PBIS ticket to improve the effectiveness of a school- or classwide token economy system. BSP is critical when allocating tickets in these systems, and it defines for students why they are receiving the reinforcer (ticket or token). Each student who receives a ticket should understand clearly which expectation was met, thereby increasing the future probability of the behavior occurring.

Why Is BSP Effective?

There are several reasons why BSP statements are more effective than general praise statements (Brophy, 1981; Sutherland et al., 2000). First, when students are learning a new behavior (e.g., a kindergarten student learning how to appropriately walk to the lunchroom, a high school student learning how to write a lab report), they may not realize what behavior they have done well if they only hear statements such as "good job" instead of "nice work listing all the lab materials we used." Second, students who do not have a history of school success, such as those with and at risk for behavior problems, may not understand what desirable behavior they have displayed when an adult says "good job," as they have not yet learned how to consistently meet expectations in school.

BSP is an effective strategy because it can be added to any classroom with minimal effort, as it is not limited to a particular subject area or age level. It is also cost free and time efficient, making it a good technique for noninstructional settings as well as the classroom. For example, it can be quickly and easily used in the hallway, on the playground, or on a field trip, as it requires no special materials, just knowledge of how to use BSP correctly. It is an unobtrusive strategy and will not draw undue attention to an individual student (e.g., Kennedy, Jolivette, & Ramsey, 2014). It can also be paired with other strategies to increase their effectiveness. For example, research demonstrates that using BSP with rates of opportunities to respond (OTR; discussed in Chapter 2) results in better outcomes (Sutherland et al., 2000).

BSP is a simple strategy that can be used to increase the ratio of positive to negative instructional feedback. It is recommended that students receive instructive feedback at a rate of four positive to every one negative (4:1 ratio; Myers, Simonsen, & Sugai, 2011; Stichter et al., 2009). For every correction or redirect, a student should be recognized four times for appropriate behavior. This ratio is important to remember when considering students with challenging behaviors or those requiring frequent academic feedback. These students may feel overwhelmed when the majority of feedback they receive is corrective (i.e., negative). In keeping with a 4:1 ratio, this means acknowledging students' appropriate responding more frequently than offering negative feedback.

Finally, BSP is most effective when it is delivered consistently and immediately following the desired behavior (Marchant & Anderson, 2012). An acronym to help you remember how to use BSP correctly is IFEED-AV, which stands for Immediately, Frequently, Enthusiasm, Eye Contact, Describe, Anticipation, and Variety (Rhode, Jenson, & Reavis, 1992). *Immediately* refers to the behavior principle that reinforcement is stronger when delivered as soon as a behavior has occurred. *Frequently* refers to the frequency with which we should acknowledge students using BSP. Although this will be tailored based on the need of the learner, always consider the 4:1 ratio of positive to negative and the fact that students need increased feedback when learning new behaviors. *Enthusiasm* refers to the authenticity and gusto with which BSP is delivered. *Eye contact* is a reminder to look students in the eye when delivering BSP in an effort to make them feel special. *Describe* is a reminder to make sure praise statements are behavior specific and describe the behavior the student completed appropriately. *Anticipation* is a reminder to build excitement in the classroom using BSP to motivate students to engage in desired behaviors. Finally, *variety* refers to the fact that BSP statements used in the classroom need to be varied so that the same statements are not repeated over and over again.

Supporting Research for BSP

Research examining the effectiveness of BSP has been conducted across the grade span in a variety of settings, including general education classrooms, special education classrooms, and special education schools. Following are several key examples to illustrate how BSP can be used to improve student behavioral outcomes. For the interested reader, additional applications are described in Table 3.1.

Increasing Preschool Students' On-Task Behavior during Transitions in Inclusion Classrooms

Fullerton et al. (2009) worked with four preschool teachers (one male, three females) with associate's degrees to improve their rate of BSP in four inclusion preschool classrooms across two university-based early childhood centers. These teachers identified four male students for participation because they were exhibiting problem behaviors that interfered with engagement in the classroom but were otherwise typically developing. Teachers completed the Caregiver–Teacher Report Form (Achenbach, 1991), and all four students were found to have increased rates of attention problems. In addition, one child also had increased aggression, and another also had increased emotional reactiveness and anxious/withdrawal behavior. Each teacher identified noncompliance as being a behavior of primary concern and identified a transition activity during which the student was likely to be noncompliant (e.g., transition from a whole-class activity [circle time] to a small-group activity; transition from small-group activity to circle time). At the beginning of the study, students ranged from 2 to 4 years of age. Each classroom had at least two teachers (as many as four) and served anywhere from 24 to 40 students.

They used a multiple-baseline design across teacher–student pairs to examine the impact of BSP. During baseline, transition activities were observed until a stable pattern of responding was observed. Then teachers were trained when the students were not present to deliver BSP to their target students in the classroom. During this training, researchers met with teachers individually for approximately 90 minutes. As a part of the training, teachers were presented with a training booklet containing the following components: definitions of appropriate and inappropriate behaviors of the target child, explanations of how to use BSP, and examples of general praise and BSP statements. Researchers reviewed this material with each teacher and conducted two verbal checks for understanding (with 80% accuracy or better). The researcher then showed the teacher a video of the target student from baseline observations, and together they discussed opportunities where BSP could be used. Next, teachers identified five BSP statements, which the researcher

TABLE 3.1. Supporting Research: BSP

Authors and journal	Students	Intervention setting	Intervention	Measures	Design
Sutherland, Wehby, & Copeland (2000) Effect of varying rates of behavior-specific praise on the on-task behavior of students with EBD (JEBD)*	1 male teacher; 9 5th-grade students (7 males, 2 females)	Self-contained classroom for students with EBD	Teachers discussed their baseline rates of BSP and general praise and set goals for improvement	*Dependent variables:* 1. Non-BSP 2. BSP 3. On-task behavior *Social validity:* Not assessed	Withdrawal
Reinke, Lewis-Palmer, & Martin (2007) The effect of visual performance feedback on teacher use of BSP (BM)	3 female teachers; 6 third-grade students (5 males, 1 female) with disruptive behaviors	Three general education third-grade classrooms	Group consultation on BSP and visual performance feedback to monitor progress	*Dependent variables:* 1. Teacher praise 2. Academic engagement 3. Disruption *Social validity:* Assessed using a Likert-type scale	Multiple baseline across teachers
Kennedy & Jolivette (2008) The effects of positive verbal reinforcement on the time spent outside the classroom for students with emotional and behavioral disorders in a residential setting (BD)*	2 sixth-grade students (1 male, 1 female) with EBD	Three most problematic classrooms for each student in a residential facility	Trained teachers to add one (Phase I) and two (Phase II) positive statements above their baseline rates	*Dependent variables:* Time spent outside of the classroom *Social validity:* Assessed using a Likert-type scale	Multiple baseline across settings with embedded phases
Rathel, Dragsow, & Christle (2008) Effects of supervisor performance feedback on increasing preservice teachers' positive communication	2 female preservice teachers	Elementary classrooms for students with EBD	Preservice teachers were provided specific written performance feedback on BSP delivery	*Dependent variables:* 1. Positive teacher comments: BSP for academic behaviors, BSP for social behaviors, non-BSP, nonverbal approval of student behavior 2. Negative teacher comments: verbal teacher corrections for	Multiple baseline across preservice teachers

(continued)

41

TABLE 3.1. (continued)

Authors and journal	Students	Intervention setting	Intervention	Measures	Design
behaviors with students with emotional and behavioral disorders (JEBD)				academic behavior, verbal teacher corrections for social behavior, and nonverbal disapproval of student behaviors *Social validity:* Assessed using a Likert-type scale	
Fullerton, Conroy, & Correa (2009) Early childhood teachers' use of specific praise statements with young children at risk for behavioral disorders (BD)*	4 teachers (1 male, 3 females); 4 male preschool students with challenging behaviors	Transition between tasks in four inclusion classrooms at two university-based early childhood centers	Teachers trained to deliver BSP to a specific student	*Dependent variables:* 1. Teacher: behavior-specific and nonspecific praise 2. Student: engagement and compliance *Social validity:* Assessed using a Likert-type scale	Multiple baseline across teacher-student pairs
Duchaine, Jolivette, & Fredrick (2011) The effect of teacher coaching with performance feedback on behavior-specific praise in inclusion classrooms (ETC)	3 teachers (1 male, 2 females; 1 special ed teacher, 1 general ed.) and 62 students (34 males, 28 females; 4 with EBD)	Three math inclusion high school classrooms	Teacher coaching to deliver BSP and set personal goals for improvement over baseline rates	*Dependent variables:* 1. Student: on-task behavior 2. Teacher: behavior-specific praise *Social validity:* Assessed using a Likert-type scale	Multiple baseline across teachers
Hawkins & Heflin (2011) Increasing secondary teachers' behavior-specific praise using a video self-modeling and visual performance feedback intervention (JPBI)	3 teachers (1 male, 2 females); 3 self-contained high school classrooms for students with EBD	Morning and afternoon work in a self-contained day school for students with EBD	Visual performance feedback and video self-modeling on BSP statements	*Dependent variables:* 1. Student: on-task behavior 2. Teacher: behavior-specific praise, non-behavior-specific praise statements, reprimands *Social validity:* Assessed using a Likert-type scale	Multiple baseline across teachers with embedded withdrawal design

Study	Sample	Setting	Intervention	Dependent variables	Research design
Myers, Simonsen, & Sugai (2011) Increasing teachers' use of praise with a response-to-intervention approach (ETC)	4 female teachers	Urban middle school (7th-grade self-contained, 5th-grade inclusion, 6th-grade general education, and 7th-grade general education classes)	Response-to-intervention model of teacher training: Tier 1 = Schoolwide Positive Behavior Support training, Tier 2 = weekly meeting on BSP, Tier 3 = feedback following weekly meetings (prompts, scripts).	*Dependent variables:* 1. Teacher: BSP, general praise, negative interactions 2. Student: academic engagement, off-task, disruptions *Social validity:* Assessed using a Likert-type scale	Multiple baseline across teachers
Allday et al. (2012) Training general educators to increase behavior-specific praise: Effects on students with EBD (BD)	4 female teachers and 7 students (6 males, 1 female; grades K–2, 6; 3 with EBD; 4 with challenging behaviors/ referred for special education services)	Four general education classrooms (three elementary and one middle school)	Teachers were trained to better use BSP in the classroom and received performance feedback every third day via email.	*Dependent variables:* 1. Student: on-task behavior 2. Teacher: verbal interactions with students (behavior-specific praise, generic praise, behavior-specific correction, generic correction, target student praise, target student correction) *Social validity:* Assessed using a Likert-type scale	Multiple baseline across teachers; teachers trained to deliver BSP
Kennedy, Jolivette, & Ramsey (2014) The effects of written teacher and peer praise notes on the inappropriate behaviors of elementary students with emotional and behavioral disorders in a residential school (RTCY)	8 second-through fourth-grade students with EBD (7–11 years of age)	Self-contained art classroom in a residential facility	Teacher praise notes: Teacher provided a BSP note to each student prior to group work time in response to their behavior during the first portion of the class. Peer praise notes: Peers provided a BSP note to a peer of choice prior to group work time in response to their behavior during the first portion of the class.	*Dependent variable:* Duration of inappropriate behavior (defined for each student through the functional-behavioral assessment process) *Social validity:* Assessed using a Likert-type scale	Alternating treatment design

Note: In terms of treatment integrity, many authors reported the strategy (BSP) as a dependent variable, reporting interobserver agreement. BD, *Behavioral Disorders;* BM, *Behavior Modification;* ETC, *Education and Treatment of Children;* JEBD, *Journal of Emotional and Behavioral Disorders;* JPBI, *Journal of Positive Behavior Interventions;* RTCY, *Residential Treatment for Children and Youth;* *indicates full text is available through Google Scholar.

recorded on limited cards for the teacher to post in a visible location and use in the classroom. Following each intervention observation, the researcher provided written feedback (via a note or email) to each teacher with specific comments on her or his performance in the session.

Upon the introduction of the intervention, BSP statements increased for all teachers during the targeted transition activity. General praise statements also increased for two teachers and remained stable for the other two teachers. Engagement for all four students both increased and stabilized (became more predictable). A generalization activity (e.g., transitioning from outside play to inside, from teacher-directed activity to cleanup, from snacks to quiet reading), selected by the researcher and not shared with the teacher, was also evaluated twice during baseline and twice during intervention. In the generalization activity, BSP increased for all teachers. General praise increased for one teacher, remained stable for two teachers, and decreased for one teacher. Engagement increased for all four students during the generalization probes.

Following the intervention, teachers completed a social validity questionnaire on which they were asked to rate the intervention on a 5-point Likert-type scale. The mean of the responses was 4.75, suggesting overall acceptability of the intervention. Three of the four teachers rated the intervention as very helpful, with the fourth rating it as helpful.

Increasing Teachers' Use of BSP in Self-Contained Classrooms

Hawkins and Heflin (2011) investigated the effectiveness of BSP in three self-contained high school classrooms for students with EBD. Participants were three (one male with a bachelor's degree, two females with master's degrees) special education teachers with 2–7 years of teaching experience. The three classrooms served 27 students (ages 14–19) with IQs ranging from 40 to 95. Each classroom had two paraprofessionals who supported classroom activities but did not participate in the study directly.

Dependent variables in the study included teacher use of BSP, general praise, and reprimands. Student on-task behavior was not used as a dependent variable because student engagement was consistent with engagement levels expected in general education settings during baseline data collection (i.e., 75%–85%; Walker & Severson, 1992). A multiple-baseline design across participants with an embedded withdrawal design was used to determine whether there was a functional relation between the intervention and the teachers' use of BSP, general praise, and reprimands. This design involves a staggered start of the intervention (e.g., intervene with participant 1, observe stability, intervene with participant 2) and then a withdrawal and reintroduction of the intervention to demonstrate that the intervention (and not other factors) was responsible for a change in behavior. Following baseline, the researcher met with the teachers for 10 minutes prior to each data collection session. During these 10-minute sessions, the researchers reviewed the teachers' performance from the previous session(s) using visual performance feedback and video self-modeling. The visual performance feedback portion of the intervention involved the researcher presenting the teachers with graphs of their data and providing feedback on their frequency of BSP. Video self-modeling involved the teachers viewing videos of their previous use of BSP. Videos were edited to highlight effective use of BSP and to facilitate a brief viewing session. The researchers also modeled the use of BSP as they reviewed the videos with the teachers.

The intervention resulted in an increase in the rate of BSP for all three teachers, with a decrease observed during the embedded withdrawal phase that increased again when the intervention was reintroduced. Similarly, teachers' rate of reprimands decreased during intervention phases. Results were maintained at a follow-up evaluation 10 days after the end of the second intervention phase. Teachers completed a social validity rating of the intervention, noting that they felt BSP was an effective strategy and that they would use it with other students. Two of the teachers noted that seeing video feedback was helpful.

Increasing Time Spent Inside the Classroom in a Residential Facility

Kennedy and Jolivette (2008) explored the use of BSP in a 24/7 residential facility where students with and at risk for EBD receive educational and therapeutic services. Students were referred to this facility because they had been unsuccessful in more traditional settings and a residential facility was determined to be the least restrictive environment. Participants were two sixth-grade students (one male, one female) who were identified because they met the criteria of having a high number of in-school suspensions or removal from the classroom because of inappropriate behavior. Additionally, the students had to have a history of attention-seeking behaviors. This second criteria helped identify students who were more likely to be reinforced by BSP and positive interactions with the teacher. Student identification was based on teacher nomination, an archival record review, and a functional behavioral assessment interview.

Once students were identified, researchers evaluated data on in-school suspensions and removal from the classroom to determine each student's three most problematic classrooms. A multiple-baseline design across settings (female = language arts, math, reading; male = language arts, science, social studies) with two changing criterion phases was used for each student. This involves staggered introduction of the intervention in each setting. Once the intervention was introduced, new goals were set for each criterion (adding one and, later, two praise statements). During baseline, teachers self-monitored their use of positive and negative verbal statements to each target student. In phase 1, they set a goal of adding one verbal praise statement to their baseline levels. In phase 2, they set a goal of adding two verbal praise statements to their baseline levels. The intervention was introduced in each class period in a staggered fashion. Both students had a significant reduction in the amount of time spent outside the classroom (i.e., a reduction in inappropriate behaviors resulting in their removal from the classroom).

In addition to the reduction in time spent outside class, the teachers and unit supervisors (students' foster parents while at the facility) rated the intervention as highly socially valid, noting the positive impact it had on student performance. Teachers also stated that they intended to continue use of the intervention, which was evidenced by maintenance follow-ups with levels of praise consistent with phase 2.

Summary

This research illustrates how one simple strategy can have a tremendous impact on the behavior of students. Sometimes the easiest way to change a student's behavior is to first change the teacher's behavior. The three studies outlined here used a variety of strategies to increase teachers' use of BSP, including video self-modeling, visual performance feedback, and goal setting. These three studies also showed that BSP can be increased with feedback presented in person, written, or via a digital recording. Similarly, these studies demonstrated that when BSP increases, the rate of reprimands decreases, which is encouraging given that a 4:1 ratio of praise to corrective feedback is recommended for effective classroom management. Table 3.1 contains a list of additional studies that illustrate the relationship between an increase in teacher BSP and improved student responding in a variety of settings across the K–12 continuum.

Benefits and Challenges

BSP is a strategy that is easily implemented in any classroom. There are several benefits and potential challenges to consider when using BSP as an instructional strategy.

Benefits

A number of effective strategies have been used to increase teachers' use of BSP statements across a variety of classroom settings (i.e., general education, special education, and residential) across the grade span (i.e., preschool to high school). These strategies include teacher coaching (Duchaine, Jolivette, & Fredrick, 2011), delivering BSP to target students (Fullerton et al., 2009), performance feedback in writing (Rathel, Drasgow, & Christle, 2008) or via email (Allday et al., 2012), visual performance feedback (Reinke, Lewis-Palmer, & Martin, 2007), video self-modeling (Hawkins & Heflin, 2011), adding BSP statements to their baseline rate of BSP (Kennedy & Jolivette, 2008; Sutherland et al., 2000), and using praise notes from both teachers and peers (Kennedy et al., 2014). This variety of strategies for increasing teacher use of BSP is promising and is further evidence of the flexibility with which BSP can be added to any classroom setting.

Teachers' use of increased BSP has been associated with a decrease in negative feedback and general praise statements (Allday et al., 2012). Researchers have also reported improvements in the quality of teacher–student interactions and classroom climate associated with increased BSP (e.g., Hawkins & Heflin, 2011). BSP has been used to increase desirable classroom behaviors, such as compliance (Fullerton et al., 2009), engagement (Fullerton et al., 2009; Myers et al., 2011; Reinke et al., 2007), and on-task behavior (e.g., Allday et al., 2012; Duchaine et al., 2011; Hawkins & Heflin, 2011; Sutherland et al., 2000). Likewise, BSP has also been used to decrease disruption (Myers et al., 2011; Reinke et al., 2007), off-task behavior (Myers et al., 2011), time spent outside the classroom (Kennedy & Jolivette, 2008), and the duration of inappropriate behavior (Kennedy et al., 2014).

Challenges

It is important to note that no single strategy is effective for all students all of the time. One way to increase the effectiveness of BSP is to consider the function of a student's behavior: What are students trying to access (positive reinforcement) or avoid (negative reinforcement)? (See Chapter 9 for additional information on function.) Students who seek access to teacher attention are most likely to be responsive to BSP, but other students may also respond to BSP, as everyone appreciates having their hard work recognized. However, some adjustments may need to be considered to address student behavior that serves a different function. Students who seek access to peer attention may be more responsive to BSP when it is delivered by a peer. In this instance, teachers may want to train students to deliver BSP statements to one another. For students who seek access to tangible items or escape from (avoidance of) tasks, the teacher may want to allow them to earn rewards, such as school supplies or homework passes, in conjunction with receiving BSP. As we discussed previously, in a school with a CI3T framework, BSP can be paired with a PBIS ticket. These can be accrued or cashed in to purchase an item that aligns with the function of the student's behavior.

A similar consideration is to evaluate a student's preferred method of praise. Some students may enjoy the recognition that comes with receiving BSP publicly in the classroom. Other students may prefer to receive BSP in private or quietly so that it does not draw the attention of others. Kennedy et al. (2014), in a follow-up to their earlier investigation on BSP, found that praise notes (from both teachers and students) could be used to acknowledge the behavior of students who preferred private recognition and that BSP notes resulted in decreases in inappropriate behaviors. The nice thing about BSP is that it is flexible enough to meet the needs of diverse students, as long as we understand their preferred form of reinforcement or pay close attention to the effect BSP has on student behavior.

The most important thing to remember when implementing BSP is that it is the teacher's behavior that changes first. Research has shown that teachers are less likely to interact with students who display behavior challenges, regardless of whether students are identified as at moderate or high risk (Van Acker, Grant, & Henry, 1996), possibly because their teaching efforts are met with defiance or misbehavior. Teachers themselves then engage in escape/avoidance behavior (Wehby, Symons, Canale, & Go, 1998). Fortunately, the use of BSP can be pivotal in eliminating or reducing this dynamic. The steps for using BSP are detailed next, and a checklist is provided in Table 3.2.

Implementing BSP Strategies in Your Classroom: Checklist for Success

In the following sections, we offer a step-by-step approach for using BSP. The steps are also provided in Table 3.2 as an implementation checklist. A hypothetical illustration of how these steps can be used in a CI3T model at the elementary level is provided in Box 3.1, including a step-by-step approach to delivering BSP. These steps are designed to increase the rate and quality of BSP statements with a little preplanning.

• **Step 1: Evaluate current rates of general and behavior-specific praise (BSP).** Before delivering BSP, consider evaluating your current rate of general and behavior-specific statements in the classroom (Sutherland et al., 2000). This can be done in several ways. For example, a peer, instructional coach, or paraprofessional could observe you during a set period or activity. This practice is great for professional development, and teachers can take turns providing feedback (i.e., they observe you, and then you observe them). If you do not have access to a partner for observations, you could audio- or video-record yourself and listen to the recording for the specific examples of praise statements and how frequently they occur. You also can keep track of praise statements using *in vivo* observations in which you mark instances of BSP by moving a paper clip from one pocket to another

---

TABLE 3.2. Implementation Checklist for Success: BSP

- Step 1: Evaluate current rates of general and behavior-specific praise (BSP).
- Step 2: Identify behaviors to reinforce.
- Step 3: Practice delivery of BSP.
- Step 4: Observe student behavior.
- Step 5: Provide BSP.
- Step 6: Monitor BSP delivery.
- Step 7: Seek student input.

Note. Based on Stormont and Reinke (2009).

every time you deliver a BSP statement. Regardless of which method you choose, consider collecting data on the number and type of praise statements you naturally make. If possible, determine whether there is a pattern in which students receive praise statements. Any and all of this information is valuable in the next steps in the BSP delivery process (Stormont & Reinke, 2009).

• **Step 2: Identify behaviors to reinforce.** The next step in delivering BSP is to plan ahead to target the behaviors to reinforce (Fullerton et al., 2009). It may seem natural to acknowledge all good behavior; however, planning ahead to acknowledge specific behaviors ensures that they will be noticed. It may be easiest to start out with only a couple of behaviors, such as task completion or quiet voices. School-wide and classwide data can help determine which behaviors to target. For example, if there is a high level of office referrals for vandalism or destruction of property, you can offer BSP to students who use school materials and facilities responsibly. In a CI3T model, the target behaviors could be the schoolwide expectations (or one target expectation). Similarly, if the school's CI3T model involves a character education program (e.g., Positive Action; *www.positiveaction.net*), BSP could be used to reinforce students who display the skills taught as part of the lessons. Teachers have many responsibilities, so identifying the target behavior in advance will help make sure this effective strategy is used systematically and consistently.

It is also important to consider using BSP with particular students. As previously discussed, students whose behavior results in less positive interactions with adults may benefit the most from BSP. For this reason, you may want to choose target students to receive BSP. Research has shown that even when target students are selected, teachers' BSP delivery increases with all students (Reinke et al., 2007), perhaps because the awareness of BSP delivery increases. BSP can be tailored for target students by focusing on behaviors they need support with or by considering a student's skill level and acknowledging him or her for behaviors that fall within his or her ability level.

• **Step 3: Practice delivery of BSP.** The next step is to prepare for BSP delivery. To begin, it is helpful to script out examples of BSP that can be used in the classroom. For example, if you want to acknowledge students who are being respectful, think of several ways in which students show respect and write out statements that acknowledge these behaviors. This step is especially important if you do not currently use BSP, are using BSP at a low rate, or if using BSP feels unnatural or inauthentic (Myers et al., 2011). This step can be completed very quickly, but it is helpful because it allows you to think of the feedback you want to provide students beforehand and not have to produce behavior-specific comments on the spot. This also provides an opportunity to think of ways to acknowledge student behavior that are sincere and reflect your personality. Once potential BSP statements are scripted, you may want to practice saying them before actually using them in a classroom. This step may be omitted if you are already comfortable using BSP;

however, scripting and practice are great ways to improve your BSP delivery. If you are more experienced and comfortable using BSP in the classroom, scripting and practice can be used to help develop new BSP statements, so that students remain encouraged by the variety of BSP feedback they receive. During this time, think about whether or not you want to deliver BSP to the class as a whole or to individual students. Based on students' preferences, will you deliver BSP loudly for all students to hear or more privately while standing directly beside the students and speaking in a low tone of voice? Considering these things outside of the class will help better anticipate the needs of your students.

• **Step 4: Observe student behavior.** Once the initial or preparation steps are completed, you are all set to put BSP into practice in the classroom (or setting of choice). Begin by closely observing all students, watching for the identified behaviors. An alternative is to focus on specific students to see whether they are using the target behaviors. As a reminder, depending on the skill level of the students or the stage in which they are learning a new behavior, it is important to recognize partial completion or successive approximations of a target behavior (Cooper et al., 2007). This serves as a teaching tool to shape the behavior into what you want it to look like. One way to do this is through active supervision of student activities. Active supervision is another effective classroom management strategy that is discussed in more detail in Chapter 4. Active supervision is actively attending to student behavior using strategies such as teacher proximity, so that you can provide them with appropriate feedback. Just like opportunities to respond (OTR; Chapter 2), there is a reciprocal complementary relation between BSP and active supervision. The more aware you are of student behavior, the more likely you are to acknowledge appropriate responding.

• **Step 5: Provide BSP.** Once a student is engaged in appropriate behavior (i.e., "caught being good"; meeting expectations), deliver the BSP statements immediately following the behavior. Immediacy is an important component of BSP and part of what makes it so effective, as it helps students learn the connection between appropriate responding and the receipt of BSP (Cooper et al., 2007). If you are making praise statements to one target student, stand in close proximity, make eye contact, and/or say the student's name so he or she is aware of being recognized.

During this time, also consider the function of the student's behavior and whether private or public formats are preferred. As previously discussed, options such as peer BSP (peer attention as positive reinforcement), BSP paired with the opportunity to earn a homework pass (negative reinforcement from academic tasks), or PBIS tickets saved to shop in the school store (tangible items as positive reinforcement) can make BSP an effective strategy for students other than those motivated by teacher attention. Likewise, if BSP is paired with a PBIS ticket or some other token system, provide the BSP and ticket simultaneously so students understand why they have earned the ticket and learn the connection between correct responding and earning tickets.

- **Step 6: Monitor BSP delivery.** To increase use of BSP, consider adopting a method of self-monitoring. The purpose of monitoring teacher behavior is two-fold. First, self-monitoring will help you gather data on your frequency (rate = frequency divided by time) of BSP delivery. If you or a partner collected data on your BSP delivery prior to planning (i.e., your baseline levels), then you can compare whether your BSP delivery rate has increased (Sutherland, Copeland, & Wehby, 2001). There are several methods for monitoring that can be adapted while teaching. As previously mentioned, paper clips can be moved from your left pocket to your right every time a BSP statement is delivered. You can also use a golf counter, which is a small handheld device that can be clicked every time a BSP statement is delivered. These can be purchased for a nominal amount at any sporting goods or office supply store. Further, several electronic programs are available online, as well as applications for smartphones that can track classroom behavior for teachers and multiple target students.

Second, self-monitoring can serve as a prompt to deliver BSP. Wearing a MotivAider® (*www.difflearn.com/product/MotivAider*), which is a small electronic device that can be clipped to a pocket or collar and programmed to pulse at regular or random intervals, can help with self-monitoring. Similarly, interval timers, commonly used for exercise and available as stand-alone tools or as applications on smartphones, can be set to pulse every few minutes. This is an effective prompt to observe student behavior and acknowledge students who are responding appropriately.

- **Step 7: Seek student input.** As a final step, it is important to provide students with opportunity to give feedback on the intervention, as social validity (see the next section) can impact the success of an intervention (Lane, Kalberg, Bruhn, et al., 2009). As noted in the section on challenges, some students may respond differently to receiving BSP, especially in a public forum. Therefore, it is essential to obtain student feedback to determine whether our classroom practices are successful. Furthermore, you may want to consider obtaining feedback from all stakeholders: students, teachers, paraprofessionals, and parents.

Here we have outlined steps for implementing BSP statements, but it is important to remember that BSP can be delivered effectively in a matter of seconds. Practicing these steps can lead to fluency when using them in the classroom. Once you are comfortable with using BSP, it can easily be added to all classroom and instructional activities to increase student engagement and decrease inappropriate behaviors. This helps establish a supportive and positive classroom environment, which in turn builds positive relationships between teachers and students (Stormont & Reinke, 2009). BSP is also an effective strategy for parents to use at home. As we strive to increase collaboration between home and school and communication between teachers and parents, BSP is one strategy that can be easily shared with parents to help them acknowledge their child's academic and social behaviors at home.

Examining the Effects: How Well Is It Working?

Testing the Strategy: Design Considerations

When implementing BSP, it is important to collect data on student performance to know how well this strategy is working. In many of the studies featured in this book, researchers have used single-case methodology to "test" the intervention effects. This is a particularly useful design approach for teachers, as it is highly flexible and very practical. It can be used with any of the strategies introduced in each chapter.

It is important to use an experimental design such as an ABAB or a multiple baseline across settings, tasks, or students to establish a functional relation between the introduction of the intervention and changes in student performance (Gast & Ledford, 2014). In other words, this design helps determine whether or not the intervention worked. This information is helpful to both general education and special education teachers for a variety of reasons. The first, of course, is it allows you to evaluate the effectiveness of your instruction. With this information, you can decide how to adjust your instructional practices so they work better for your students. Second, members of the CI3T team or members of professional learning communities (PLCs) can use these data to determine how students are responding to these low-intensity supports. Before moving on to student-focused Tier 2 (e.g., Check-In/Check-Out, behavior contracts, or self-monitoring strategies) or Tier 3 (e.g., functional assessment-based interventions; Umbreit et al., 2007) supports, we want to be certain we have examined the extent to which teacher-driven strategies (e.g., BSP) have been effective in addressing students' needs (academically, behaviorally, and/or socially). Using an experimental design is one way to show whether or not this has occurred. We recommend these teams (e.g., CI3T and PLC) be composed of a range of individuals, including general and special education teachers, as they each bring unique talents. For example, as special education teachers are a critical resource for implementing and delivering specialized intervention, they can assist general educators with evaluating strategy implementation, as well as carefully measuring the effects of any given intervention for a particular student, as is demonstrated in Box 3.1. This is especially critical when focused on more intensive supports, such as functional assessment-based interventions, that require careful monitoring of students' performance (e.g., academic engagement, disruption). The ability to use single-case methodology is a critical skill in assessing the effectiveness of Tier 2 and 3 supports.

These designs begin with a baseline phase during which data on student performance are collected (referred to as the A phase), then the intervention is introduced for the first time (B), while still collecting data on student performance using the same data collection method used during the baseline phase (see Figure 3.1 in Box 3.1). Although it is tempting at this point to say the intervention was effective, two more replications are needed to be certain the intervention was responsible for the change and not something else. One demonstration (e.g., the change from A to B phases) along with two other replications can provide evidence that the introduction of the strategy produced the changes (Gast & Ledford, 2014).

Although some designs, such as the ABAB design, require removal and then reintroduction of the intervention, it is also possible to explore a functional relation using a multiple baseline across setting design (as shown in Box 3.1). This means the strategy is used in different settings, such as a different instructional period (math instead of reading) or a different physical location (playground instead of the lunchroom).

Making Certain the Strategy Is in Place: Treatment Integrity

In addition to using an experimental design to test the intervention, collecting treatment integrity data helps determine the extent to which the intervention is being implemented as planned. Figure 3.2 in Box 3.1 is an example of a treatment integrity checklist for BSP. Although there are many different ways to collect treatment integrity data, one way is to have the teacher collect these data each day by indicating the degree to which each intervention component was implemented as planned for each student. For example, in Figure 3.2, each item is a completed using a 3-point Likert-type scale as follows: 0 = *not in place*, 1 = *partially in place*, or 2 = *completely in place*. Each day the items are summed, divided by the total number of points possible, and divided by 100 to obtain a percentage of implementation for each student. These data can be used to interpret intervention outcomes (see Box 3.1). In addition, behavior component checklists not only determine the level of implementation but also serve as a prompt or reminder to implement each step.

Using an outside observer to collect treatment integrity data for approximately 25% of the sessions in each phase is recommended. An additional observer is important for establishing the accuracy of the data collected.

Examining Stakeholders' Views: Social Validity

Finally, in addition to collecting information on student performance and implementation (treatment integrity), it is important to understand how stakeholders felt about the intervention goals, procedures, and intended outcomes. Figure 3.3 in Box 3.1 is an example of a measure examining one elementary student's perceptions of the social validity of BSP.

It is important to obtain all stakeholders' views—the teacher, student, and parent—ideally before the intervention begins and again at the conclusion of the first "test." If social validity is low at the onset of the intervention, then it is wise to provide additional training to increase people's knowledge of the strategies, as well as their confidence in using the strategy prior to implementation. In theory (and in some instances in actuality; see Lane, Kalberg, Bruhn, et al., 2009), the opinions of those implementing and participating in the intervention may predict the extent to which the interventions are implemented as planned. In essence, a socially valid intervention is likely to be put in place with a high degree of integrity, leading to improvements in student performance that maintain over time and in new settings and with new people.

BOX 3.1. A Hypothetical Illustration of BSP in a CI3T Model

Mrs. Arnold is a general education teacher at Reedy River Elementary, a suburban elementary school currently implementing a comprehensive, integrated, three-tiered (CI3T) model of prevention. As part of their CI3T plan, they use an SRA/McGraw-Hill reading curriculum for all students, a positive behavior intervention and support (PBIS) plan to support behavior, and Second Step (Beland, 1992), an evidence-based social skills and violence prevention curriculum for elementary schools. Mrs. Arnold teaches fifth grade to 28 students, three of whom receive special education services according to the Individuals with Disabilities Education Improvement Act (IDEA, 2004) and two of whom receive Tier 2 academic supports through the school's CI3T model. During one of the fifth-grade team's professional learning community meetings, Mrs. Arnold noted three of her fifth graders, Bob, Barbie, and Steve, were all struggling both academically and behaviorally. All three students had received rankings of 2 or 3 (yellow level) in the areas of Reading and Motivation to Learn on the Social Skill Improvement System—Performance Screening Guide (SSiS-PSG; Gresham & Elliott, 2008a). In addition, their most recent reading curriculum-based measurement (CBM) benchmarking assessment had placed them in the 25th percentile. Mrs. Arnold knew she needed to motivate all three students to participate in the daily *Corrective Reading—Comprehension* (Engelmann et al., 1999) lessons, as their engagement was low.

Support	Description	Entry criteria	Data to monitor progress	Exit criteria
Behavior-specific praise (BSP)	BSP statements acknowledge the student and clearly state what desirable behavior has been performed	Ranking of 2 or 3 on Reading and Motivation to Learn on the SSiS-PSG (Gresham & Elliott, 2008a)	*Student performance:* • Academic engagement (percentage of intervals during which each student was academically engaged in reading instruction) • Work completion *Treatment integrity:* Component checklist *Social validity:* Student-completed survey	Ranking of 4 or 5 on Motivation to Learn on the SSiS-PSG (Gresham & Elliott, 2008a)

Mrs. Arnold decided to adopt a strategy to increase her use of behavior-specific praise (BSP) statements during *Corrective Reading* lessons. Mrs. Arnold worked through the seven-step process as follows. These steps can also be found in Table 3.2.

Preparing for and Delivering BSP: The Intervention

•**Step 1: Evaluate current rates of general and behavior-specific praise (BSP).** Mrs. Arnold began by evaluating her current use of BSP during reading lessons. She kept a golf counter in her hand during reading lessons and clicked it each time she made a BSP statement directed at either academic ("Great job identifying the key words in the passage") or social ("Nice job, quietly waiting your turn") behaviors. She noticed that her current rate was quite low (two to three praise statements during the 30-minute lesson). She set a goal to double her highest rate of BSP praise statements (six) and decided to initially focus on providing BSP to only one of her target students, Bob.

• **Step 2: Identify behaviors to reinforce.** Because all three of her target students received low scores in the Motivation to Learn scale of the SSiS-PSG and displayed low rates of academic engagement, she decided to provide BSP statements that focused on class participation and appropriate responding during the reading lesson, which were also defined in the schoolwide expectation matrix developed as part of their PBIS framework. She reviewed her school's CI3T behavioral expectation matrix and highlighted some of the behaviors under the expectation of "Show Your Best Effort," such as: have all assigned materials, participate to the best of your ability, keep your eyes on the teacher, and follow directions the first time. She decided to watch for Bob to display any of these behaviors so that she could provide him with BSP.

• **Step 3: Practice delivery of BSP.** Mrs. Arnold was disappointed in her current level of BSP delivery during reading, so she decided to spend some time preparing praise statements in advance. She wrote out ways she could acknowledge Bob for showing his best efforts—for example, "Bob, thank you for following directions and turning to page 3" and "I like the way you have a pencil, paper, and your workbook on your desk."

• **Step 4: Observe student behavior.** The next day, Mrs. Arnold proceeded with the reading lesson, paying careful attention to Bob's behavior so that she could "catch" him displaying one of the behaviors she had identified. She used the expectation matrix hanging in her classroom to remind her of which behaviors she should watch for. She also used increased opportunities to respond (OTR) and active supervision and proximity to facilitate this process.

• **Step 5: Provide BSP.** Since Mrs. Arnold had decided to focus BSP delivery on a target student, she tried to vary the ways in which she delivered praise to Bob. She would sometimes kneel beside his desk and provide BSP in a soft tone of voice that only he could hear. Other times, she provided BSP statements from the front of the room but used his name and made eye contact so he knew she was acknowledging him.

• **Step 6: Monitor BSP delivery.** Given her initial rates of BSP were low, Mrs. Arnold decided she needed a reminder to provide BSP statements, so she purchased an interval timer from a sporting goods store and set it to pulse every 2 minutes to remind her to provide BSP. This would allow her to exceed her goal of 6 BSP statements in 30 minutes.

• **Step 7: Seek student input.** Finally, after implementing BSP for a few weeks, Mrs. Arnold asked each student how he or she felt about this extra support. She had also asked their initial opinions before beginning this low-intensity support so she could make sure they would be comfortable with the praise, and then later to see whether BSP met their expectations.

Looking at How Well BSP Worked

Mrs. Arnold decided to collect data on academic engagement (referred to as academic engaged time; AET) and work completion (percentage of engagement) for Bob, Barbie, and Steve to see how they responded to this low-intensity support. She clearly defined AET so that any outside observer would understand what was meant by being academically engaged, including both examples and non-examples.

- **Label.** Academic engaged time (AET).
- **Definition.** AET refers to engaging in instructional tasks as requested by the teacher.
- **Examples.** Examples of AET include: eyes on the teacher, peer contributing to lesson, or assigned materials/smartboard; in designated area of the room; following teacher directions within 5 seconds of prompt; gathering class materials (e.g., getting a piece of paper from a binder); raising hand and quietly waiting to be called on; asking relevant questions; sitting up straight.
- **Non-examples.** Non-examples of AET include: nonacademic talk with peers; complaining about a task; sighing or making inappropriate noises; not following teacher direction within 5 seconds of prompt; getting out of seat without permission during instruction; doodling; sleeping; putting head down without working; daydreaming (staring off into other parts of the classroom).

AET was collected using a momentary time-sampling procedure in which Mrs. Arnold used her interval timer set to 2-minute intervals to prompt her to observe each student's behavior and note whether or not he or he was engaged. Prior to collecting data, Mrs. Arnold practiced this process with a practicum student, Miss Seelig, assigned to her classroom for two mornings a week. During both practice and actual data collection sessions, Miss Seelig also wore an interval timer. Once they were in agreement on how to interpret the AET definition for all target students, Miss Seelig would collect data with Mrs. Arnold twice a week for reliability purposes. The two would collect data on the same time schedule, starting their timers simultaneously, but would not look at one another's ratings until the end of the session.

Figure 3.1 shows Bob's, Barbie's, and Steve's AET. Once Mrs. Arnold noticed a marked, immediate improvement in Bob's behavior (change in level) as a result of delivered BSP, she began delivering BSP to Barbie, and finally to Steve. Mrs. Arnold became so adept at delivering higher rates of BSP that when she started delivering BSP to Barbie, she continued to deliver BSP at a high rate to Bob, and so on. By trying it out with one student at a time, Mrs. Arnold was able to determine that it was the introduction of BSP with a target student that improved his or her behavior during reading rather than other factors (e.g., the chapter being taught, changes to the schoolwide discipline plan, seasonal changes in student behavior). When you compare rates of AET for each student prior to the implementation of BSP, you see a marked increase for each student. For example, if you look at Bob's data, you will notice that he was engaged 50% or less of the time. Once Mrs. Arnold increased

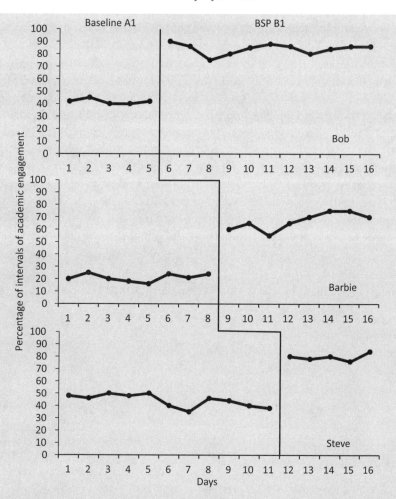

FIGURE 3.1. Examining the effects: Percentage of intervals during which each student was academically engaged in reading instruction.

her delivery of BSP, his AET improved to an average of 80% of the time when the intervention was in place.

In addition to collecting information on AET, Mrs. Arnold also collected data on work completion (not graphed in Figure 3.1). Work completion was evaluated using a daily report card on which Mrs. Arnold evaluated the assigned instruction task, with scores ranging from 0 to 100% completion. All three students had a marked increase in work completion once the intervention was introduced.

To make certain the intervention was happening as planned, either Mrs. Arnold or Miss Seelig completed a daily Treatment Integrity Form (see Figure 3.2 for treatment integrity data on BSP delivery). Each day they recorded whether the intervention component was *not in place* (0), *partially in place* (1), or *fully in place* (2). These data were very important, as they help to interpret how students responded to BSP. For example, it would be expected that AET was much lower during baseline when Mrs. Arnold was not implementing her plan to increase her rate of praise.

Prior to the beginning and at the end of the intervention, Mrs. Arnold and Miss Seelig decided to see what the students thought about receiving BSP during reading lessons. They asked all three target students to rate five short statements about their experience (see Figure 3.3). All students enjoyed receiving BSP during reading and felt that it helped them do better in school. In addition, their scores following the intervention increased from their opinions of the intervention before it was in place.

Mrs. Arnold noticed that over time, providing BSP to all students became habit during reading lessons, for both herself and Miss Seelig. She found she was often delivering BSP prior to the reminders from the interval timer. Her use of BSP also generalized to other activities both in and outside of the classroom.

TREATMENT INTEGRITY CHECKLIST: BEHAVIOR-SPECIFIC PRAISE

Setting: ☐ Classroom: _____   Observer: ☐ Primary: _____

        ☐ Other: _____   ☐ Secondary: _____

Date: _____   Start time: _____   End time: _____   Total time: _____

Notes: _____

0 = not in place, 1 = partially in place, or 2 = completely in place

Item	Rating		
1. Did I identify target behaviors and/or students to acknowledge using BSP?	0	1	2
2. Did I prepare to deliver BSP prior to the lesson (i.e., scripts completed, delivery practiced, additional reinforcers gathered)?	0	1	2
3. Did I observe students for the target behavior (or a portion/approximation thereof)?	0	1	2
4. Did I provide a praise statement that acknowledged a specific target behavior and was administered immediately following the target behavior?	0	1	2
5. Did I self-monitor my use of BSP?	0	1	2
TOTAL			
$(N \div [10]) \times 100 =$			%

FIGURE 3.2. Making certain the strategy is in place: Treatment integrity checklist used by Mrs. Arnold to monitor the extent to which each step was put in place as planned.

From *Supporting Behavior for School Success: A Step-by-Step Guide to Key Strategies* by Kathleen Lynne Lane, Holly Mariah Menzies, Robin Parks Ennis, and Wendy Peia Oakes. Copyright 2015 by The Guilford Press. Permission to photocopy this figure is granted to purchasers of this book for personal use only (see copyright page for details). Purchasers can download a larger version of this figure from *www.guilford.com/lane4-forms*.

SOCIAL VALIDITY FORM: BEHAVIOR-SPECIFIC PRAISE

Before we get started, tell me what you think about BSP . . .	☹ Strongly disagree	☺ Strongly agree
I would like to receive BSP for meeting classroom expectations.		
Receiving BSP would help me get more work done.		
I think that receiving BSP could help improve my grades.		
Receiving BSP would help other students in my class/school.		
I think that receiving BSP will make school a happier place to be.		

Total _____/30 (Total Possible) × 100 _____% Acceptability

Now that you've received BSP in the classroom, tell me what you think about it. . . .	☹ Strongly disagree	☺ Strongly agree
I liked receiving BSP for meeting classroom expectations.		
Receiving BSP helped me get more work done.		
I think that receiving BSP helped improve my grades.		
Receiving BSP would help other students in my class/school.		
I think that receiving BSP made school a happier place to be.		

Total _____/30 (Total Possible) × 100 _____% Acceptability

FIGURE 3.3. Examining stakeholders' views: Social validity form developed by Mrs. Arnold to examine students' views on BSP.

From *Supporting Behavior for School Success: A Step-by-Step Guide to Key Strategies* by Kathleen Lynne Lane, Holly Mariah Menzies, Robin Parks Ennis, and Wendy Peia Oakes. Copyright 2015 by The Guilford Press. Permission to photocopy this figure is granted to purchasers of this book for personal use only (see copyright page for details). Purchasers can download a larger version of this figure from *www.guilford.com/lane4-forms*.

Summary

BSP is a strategy that can easily be added into a classroom routine. Since BSP is a form of reinforcement, it is likely to increase students' engagement and participation in the classroom. BSP is cost free and takes minimal time to implement. It can be used anywhere in the school building where a teacher and student are present. BSP can be used to create a positive and supportive school climate and improve relationships between teachers and students. BSP packs a big punch for a strategy that can be implemented in seconds!

CHAPTER 4

A Look at Active Supervision

Student safety is a top priority of teachers and administrators, making supervision an integral part of school life. Supervising students looks different depending on age and grade level, but in general schools make it a point to have all students under adult observation to ensure that they are not engaged in or exposed to dangerous or harmful behavior. Teachers have an extra concern with respect to instructional considerations: not only are they cognizant of safety issues, but they also want students to be productive and to complete assigned tasks. Engaged academic time translates directly to improved behavior and academic outcomes (Gettinger & Walter, 2012); so, for teachers, supervision is a strategy that promotes success in both areas.

The research on active supervision has its beginnings in the 1970s. One early study looking at how teachers managed problem behavior showed there were no systematic differences in how less effective and more effective teachers addressed behavior infractions; what differed was how they managed their classrooms to prevent problems from occurring in the first place (Kounin, 1970). It turned out that a key strategy of more effective teachers was that they regularly monitored activity in the classroom. Teachers placed themselves where they could easily see students and made it clear they were aware of how engaged students were with various tasks.

Active supervision is something teachers perform every day; however, it is easy to forget just how powerful a strategy it is and not use it as effectively as possible. Active supervision must be both frequent and systematic. Using it this way is critically important in promoting positive behavior, especially when teachers pair it with reminders about the type of behavior they want to see. This chapter discusses how to maximize the use of active supervision in the classroom, as well as in

61

unstructured areas such as the cafeteria, playground, and hallways (e.g., De Pry & Sugai, 2002; Haydon, DeGreg, Maheady, & Hunter, 2012; Johnson-Gros, Lyons, Griffin, 2008). Teachers often report that behaviors from unstructured periods spill over into the classroom and make it difficult to establish a calm and orderly environment. When students know their teacher is actively looking for smooth performance of regular routines (e.g., sitting down and taking out materials for the next activity, working independently) and the teacher calmly reminds them how to perform those tasks (e.g., quietly and quickly), students will get to work more quickly and be productive for longer periods of time.

What Is Active Supervision?

Active supervision is the use of "specific and overt behaviors (scanning, escorting, interacting) designed to prevent problem behavior and promote rule-following behavior" (Colvin, Sugai, Good, & Lee, 1997, p. 346). It is even more effective when used with explanations (also called *precorrections,* a topic addressed in Chapter 7) about the behavior expected in the particular context. Active supervision is easier to implement if basic routines and procedures are already in place. For example, students must know what the expectations are in regard to lining up, making transitions to other settings or activities, or getting materials, just to name a few. They must also be aware of the teacher's expectations for other classroom events, such as when it is acceptable to talk among themselves and when to listen, what voice level is suitable for different instructional groupings, and when it is permissible to get materials or sharpen a pencil. When working in a school with a schoolwide positive behavior intervention and support (PBIS) framework or comprehensive, integrated, three-tiered (CI3T) models, then these expectations are established and present in the expectation matrix.

Active supervision has several distinct elements (De Pry & Sugai, 2002; Haydon & Scott, 2008). First, after establishing expectations for desired behavior performance, the teacher moves among students to prompt the expected behavior by reminding students of her or his presence. Second, the teacher (or supervising adult) frequently scans the setting, whether it is a classroom, elementary playground, middle school cafeteria, or high school hallway, to assess students' performance and monitor interactions. Third, the teacher interacts positively with students, offering reminders about the expected behavior (precorrection), as well as brief prompts to make sure they stay on task and avoid engaging in troublesome behaviors. Prompts can be either verbal or nonverbal. Many teachers have a repertoire of gestures, smiles, and signals they use to communicate with students. Nonverbal cues are especially helpful when you do not want to interrupt the flow of the students' activity. It is a good idea to use a precorrection at the start of an activity to cue students to expected behavior. As discussed in Chapter 7, precorrection involves reminding students of, and sometimes reteaching them, the desired behavior (e.g., "Just a gentle reminder, one of the ways we demonstrate responsible behavior on the playground is waiting our turn while we check out equipment"). Fourth, the teacher reinforces desirable behaviors or, in everyday language, lets students know their hard work and good behavior is appreciated. Finally, when necessary, a teacher provides corrections (indicates a student is misbehaving and reminds him or her of what is expected behavior) in an effort to help students be successful. Active supervision sounds amazingly easy, but teachers manage literally hundreds of interactions a day, so implementing active supervision consistently and frequently until it is second nature requires forethought and practice.

Two essential elements of active supervision are proximity and reinforcement. A few points about each follow.

Proximity

Use of proximity is an important component of active supervision, as it is one of the most powerful reminders that a teacher is aware of what students are doing. However, it is important not to allow proximity to escalate situations in which students feel angry. Proximity can easily be interpreted as a threat if a teacher violates a student's sense of personal space. Moving too close to students when they feel upset can trigger an intense negative response that results in an emotional outburst or physical aggression. Proximity should only be used as a proactive cue to remind students to get to work, not as a form of intimidation.

Reinforcement

Teachers sometimes balk at using reinforcement, preferring students to be intrinsically rather than extrinsically motivated. Yet most of us are motivated in some degree by extrinsic forces (getting paid for going to work), and the two are not mutually exclusive. The goal is to establish routines and expectations that, in time, require little in the way of external reinforcement. Initially, reinforcement can help cement those routines into place. Also, it is reasonable to let students know when you appreciate their work and effort. This is part of learning how to participate in society, and good work deserves recognition. Of course some students will require more overt reinforcement before they easily perform required tasks. (See Chapter 3 for information on how to use behavior-specific praise [BSP].) Although acknowledging that this can be frustrating, it is still more effective to motivate students through positive interactions than through punishment or reprimands (Mooney, Ryan, Gunter, & Denny, 2012).

Although the elements of supervision are introduced later in this chapter as though they are linear, in practice they are recursive and happen throughout the activity period. Each piece of the strategy should be used, but not necessarily in a lockstep fashion. For some teachers, the strategy may initially include using behaviors that feel unfamiliar, such as precorrections and prompts; however, they are well worth trying. For other teachers, using proactive strategies will not be unfamiliar or uncomfortable, but using them systematically and as a complete package may be new.

Why Is Active Supervision Effective?

Teachers who anticipate potential difficulties and proactively avert them are more successful in reducing negative behavior incidents and improving achievement. Active supervision rests on this same assumption—preventing problems from occurring or escalating is more efficient and productive than addressing them after they have occurred (Colvin, 2004). In behavioral terms, the focus is on an antecedent-based intervention instead of a consequence-based intervention. Rather than thinking problematic behavior is the moral failing of a particular student, teachers (and school systems as a whole) need to have routines and structures in place to avoid problem behavior, especially when many behaviors are a result of overcrowding and a lack of personalization (Jackson, 1990), combined with inadequate supervision. It is analogous to businesses that use safety procedures to protect their workforce. Businesses recognize their employees will have fewer accidents when the workplace itself has been made safe. In addition, many businesses realize they create safer work conditions when they alert workers to unsafe practices. Schools can do the same by systematically using procedures that avert problems while at the same time reminding students about the prosocial behaviors they need to use—in essence, PBIS (Sugai & Horner, 2006).

Classrooms are places where a great deal of activity is carried out by many people at the same time. Often, classrooms are not overly large, which adds to the challenge of creating a productive learning atmosphere. So a good teacher not only teaches but also manages the flow of movement and work in a very particular context. This requires several skills, one of which Kounin (1970) called "with-itness." Teachers who have this sense of with-itness are adept at monitoring the classroom and identifying problems in advance. Equally important, students know the teacher is mindful of what they are doing. This signaling of awareness is critical because it prevents problems from occurring. Students are less likely to engage in problem behavior when the teacher is watching and aware of their actions. Closely related to with-itness is another skill Kounin referred to as "overlapping," or the ability to do more than one thing at once. This, too, is an essential skill, as teachers are constantly performing more than one task at a time: helping one student while giving directions to the entire class, or working with a small group while monitoring the rest of class as they work independently.

The demands of managing a busy classroom require that even when a teacher is juggling two or more activities at the same time, she or he must keep a close eye on the class and communicate either verbally or nonverbally that she or he is aware of students' activities—in other words, use with-itness and overlapping. A teacher who consistently performs this type of active supervision sends the powerful message to students that he or she cares what they do and about the choices they make in the classroom. Teachers who are oblivious to what students are doing, either because they are inattentive or because they have not mastered the ability to supervise two things at once (actively supervising the entire class while interacting with a single student), send an altogether different message to students: that it is fine to be off task because no one is monitoring their work. Constant monitoring could be thought of as oppressive, but it can also be thought of as a way to demonstrate interest and caring. Teachers who care are cognizant of their students' actions and are interested in their well-being, not just academically, but behaviorally and socially as well.

Supporting Research for Active Supervision

Studies examining active supervision cover a range of interventions, including reducing high levels of minor problem behaviors, improving students' interactions during recess, decreasing tardiness to class, increasing time on task, and improving the overall behavior of individual students. Next we discuss a few studies to = provide illustrations of how active supervision can be a powerful strategy. For the interested reader, additional studies are presented in Table 4.1.

Reducing High Rates of Minor Classroom Misbehavior

De Pry and Sugai (2002) worked with a general education teacher of 20 years' experience to reduce the number of minor behavioral incidents in a sixth-grade classroom. They included talking out of turn, not following the teacher's directions, eating in class, and getting out of one's seat without permission. The researchers reviewed the elements of active supervision with the teacher in a 30-minute meeting and then observed her use of them during a 45-minute class over several weeks. The intervention also consisted of a daily data review in which the teacher was provided with a graph depicting the rates of problem behavior and was taught how to analyze the data in order to use the strategy of supervision more effectively during the next observation period. This opportunity for reflection was important, as it provided the teacher the opportunity to consider how the strategy was working and how to use it in a way that produced results.

Prior to the intervention, the teacher typically lectured from the front of the room. She was asked to incorporate the following approach during instruction: "(a) move around the classroom while teaching, (b) scan the classroom being sure to attend to all areas of the room, (c) interact with students verbally and non-verbally about academic content and expected social behavior, and (d) reinforce students when they demonstrate expected academic and social behaviors" (De Pry

TABLE 4.1. Supporting Research: Active Supervision

Authors and journal	Students	Intervention setting	Intervention	Measures	Design
Colvin, Sugai, Good, & Lee (1997) Using active supervision and precorrection to improve transition behaviors in an elementary school (SPQ)	$N = 475$ students, 42 staff members (24 certified, 18 classified, and 1 principal); 77% free and reduced-price lunches; elementary (grades K–5)	Entering the school building, moving from the classroom to the cafeteria, and leaving the school building	Precorrection and active supervision strategies 1. Defined expected behaviors: walk, keep hands and feet to self, use a quiet voice 2. Schoolwide discipline team taught strategies (15 minutes) 3. Active supervision: move around, look around, interact with students 4. Precorrection: remind students of expected behaviors just before entering the transition area	*Dependent variables:* 1. Setting characteristics (number of supervisors, number of students) 2. Supervisor behavior (escorting, scanning, interacting) 3. Student behavior (frequency of problem behavior: running, pushing, shouting, sliding, throwing, other rule violations) *Treatment integrity:* Not measured (addressed as a limitation) *Social validity:* Not measured	Multiple baseline design across the three settings
Lewis, Colvin, & Sugai (2000) The effects of precorrection and active supervision on the recess behavior of elementary students (ETC)	$N = 475$ students, 42 staff members (24 certified, 18 classified, and 1 principal); 44% free and reduced-price lunches; elementary (grades K–5)	Recess on an elementary school playground	Precorrection 1. Identified problem behaviors exhibited by students at recess 2. Identified expected or replacement responses for problem behaviors 3. Printed rules and expectations for recess were reviewed with students 4. Students were precorrected regarding rules and expectations prior to being released for the playground for recess Active supervision (15-minute meeting) 1. Move around 2. Look around 3. Interact with students	*Dependent variables:* 1. Students' problem behavior 2. Playground monitor supervision behavior *Treatment integrity:* Programmed for, but not measured *Social validity:* Not measured	Multiple baseline design across groups

Study	Participants/Setting	Setting	Intervention	Measures	Design
De Pry & Sugai (2002) The effect of active supervision and precorrection on minor behavioral incidents in a sixth-grade general education classroom (JBE)*	$N = 26$ sixth-grade students, 1 teacher with 20+ years of experience; elementary (grades 4–6)	Elementary general education social studies class	Package: Instructionally based intervention 1. Active supervision: circulate while teaching, scan to attend to all areas, interact with student verbally and nonverbally, and reinforce demonstrations of expected academic and social behavior as part of instruction 2. Precorrection: instructional prompt before students entered a context in which a problem behavior was likely to occur 3. Daily data reviews between teacher and researcher each morning (5–10 minutes)	*Dependent variable:* Minor behavioral incidents (partial interval recording; IOA 85%) *Treatment integrity:* Assessed by an outside observer *Social validity:* Assessed using a Likert-type scale	ABAB withdrawal design
Oswald, Safran, & Johanson (2005) Preventing trouble: Making schools safer places using positive behavior supports (ETC)	$N = 950$ students, rural small-town middle school (grades 6–8)	Middle school; hallway behavior during transitions to lunch	Instructional plan for teaching hallway behaviors; positive behavior intervention package included: 1. Positive practice 2. Precorrection 3. Verbal praise 4. Reinforcement 5. Correction of inappropriate behavior 6. Active supervision 7. Discussion with students 8. On-time dismissal	*Dependent variable:* Frequency counts of target behaviors (running, jumping, cursing, kicking, pushing, screaming/loud noises; nontraditional IOA) *Treatment integrity:* Not measured (addressed as a limitation) *Social validity:* Not measured	Mixed-model analysis
Johnson-Gros, Lyons, & Griffin (2008) Active supervision: An intervention to reduce high school tardiness (ETC)	$N = 450$ students, 34 teachers; 58% free and 11% reduced-price lunches; rural high school (grades 9–12)	Rural high school hallways (tardies)	Active supervision (30-minute training) 1. Arrive at designated post on time 2. Remain in post area throughout the entire transition periods 3. Moving towards groups of congregated students in post area 4. Physically escorting students throughout the entire transition area 5. Scanning the transition area 6. Interacting with students using brief nonverbal gestures throughout the transition period	*Dependent variable:* Tardies to three instructional periods, tardy discipline data (number of referrals for tardiness per week) *Treatment integrity:* Procedural integrity form with operational definitions of active supervision (momentary time sampling) *Social validity:* Not measured (addressed as a limitation)	Multiple baseline

67

(continued)

TABLE 4.1. (continued)

Authors and journal	Students	Intervention setting	Intervention	Measures	Design
Tyre, Feuerborn, & Pierce (2011) Schoolwide intervention to reduce chronic tardiness at the middle and high school levels (PSF)	N = 355 students; 98% Native American; 100% reduced-price lunches; rural high school (grades 7–12)	Tribal middle and high school	1. Explicit teaching of expectations 2. Active supervision 3. Consistent implementation of consequences	*Dependent variable:* Tardies and unexcused absences *Treatment integrity:* Implementation checklist *Social validity:* Not measured	AB, non-experimental
Haydon, DeGreg, Maheady, & Hunter (2012) Using active supervision and precorrection to improve transition behaviors in a middle school classroom (JEBPS)	N = 534 students; 90% free or reduced-price lunches; high transiency; urban district, middle school (grades 6–7)	Seventh-grade health class in middle school; transitioning in from lunch in the cafeteria	Precorrection Active supervision Explicit timing procedure B: Active supervision + precorrection C: Active supervision + precorrection + timing procedure	*Dependent variables:* 1. Teachers' redirections 2. Number of minutes during transition *Treatment integrity:* Checklist completed by outside observer *Social validity:* Teacher-completed Likert-type scale	ABCBC + maintenance phase

Note. IOA, interobserver agreement; ETC, *Education and Treatment of Children*; ISC, *Intervention in School and Clinic*; JBE, *Journal of Behavioral Education*; JEBPS, *Journal of Evidence-Based Practices for Schools*; PSF, *Preventing School Failure*; SPQ, *School Psychology Quarterly*; *indicates full text is available through Google Scholar.

& Sugai, 2002, p. 259). Just as importantly, she was explicitly taught and asked to use precorrection and reinforcement. The teacher learned to recognize when students did not have the behavioral skills she was looking for (also referred to as acquisition or skills deficits; Gresham & Elliott, 2008b). She then took a few moments to teach the desired behavior.

By using active supervision as a low-intensity intervention, the teacher lowered the rates of misbehavior. Overall, the average number of behavioral incidents dropped as much as 40% when the strategies of precorrection, prompting, and active supervision were used. One particularly impressive feature of this intervention is that it demonstrates that even experienced teachers can improve their practice by consciously and systematically paying attention to the mechanics of a particular practice or strategy. In addition, the teacher, in a social validity report, agreed the intervention was effective and that she would use it again.

Increasing Learning Time in Middle School

In a recent study, Haydon, DeGreg, Maheady, and Hunter (2012) looked at how a middle school teacher addressed problems that negatively affected instructional time as students transitioned from lunch to her class. Misbehavior included students blocking the classroom doorway, taking too long to get to their seats, and not being ready with appropriate materials at their desk. The school was located in an urban area and had a transient rate of over 50%. The teacher's health class was composed of 20 seventh-grade students.

The teacher's usual procedure was to use threats, consequences, and office discipline referrals to motivate students to get to their seats more quickly. In a 25-minute session, the researchers taught the teacher how to use precorrection and active supervision strategies to reduce transition time. She also had an opportunity to model the strategies to ensure she would use them correctly in the classroom.

The intervention required a combination of active supervision and precorrection. When using the strategy, the teacher met students at the door, reminded them to walk into the room quietly, keep their hands and feet to themselves, and take a seat. After providing the precorrection, the teacher scanned the room and offered verbal and nonverbal prompts on the expected behaviors, as well as verbal prompts to students who were following directions. Then, during a second intervention phase, they added a timing procedure which involved using a timer set to 2 minutes to cue the students as to how long they were taking. Results were dramatic. When all strategies were used together (precorrection, active supervision, and timer), transition times decreased from 10 minutes to under 2 minutes, and verbal redirects (asking or reminding students to be ready at their seats) were reduced from an average of 10 per session to an average of 1. Additionally, social validity measures indicated that the teacher thought the strategies were helpful and easy to implement. Not only was the intervention effective, but it was also socially valid from the teacher's perspective.

Using Active Supervision (and Precorrection) to Improve Transition Behaviors

Active supervision is not simply a classroom strategy; it is an important element of ensuring safety in less structured school areas such as the playground, cafeteria, hallways, and bus loading zone. In fact, a majority of behavior issues start outside of the classroom and are a concern because they negatively affect learning when students have difficulty transitioning from non-classroom activities to academic tasks inside the classroom. Some schools may have less consistent supervision outside the classroom when personnel other than teachers are responsible for monitoring students. Overall behavior is better when expectations and procedures are consistent across school settings.

In a rural area of the Pacific Northwest, Colvin et al. (1997) used active supervision and precorrection in an elementary school to improve transition behaviors as students moved from instructional to noninstructional settings. The school, which served 475 students from kindergarten through fifth grade, had 42 staff members. Approximately 77% of the students qualified for either free or reduced-cost lunches (see Table 4.1).

The staff was particularly concerned with three transition periods. The first was in the morning, when students entered the building and crossed through a courtyard into their respective classrooms. The second problem transition was at lunchtime, when students left their classrooms for the cafeteria, and the final period of difficulty occurred at the end of the day, when students exited the building. Some of the problems during these transitions were "running, pushing, hitting, yelling, screaming, and crossing prohibited areas (e.g., gardens and shrubbery areas)" (p. 348).

Staff members attended two brief trainings: one 15-minute meeting and one 10-minute meeting. Staff members were instructed to remind students of the school's expectations before the transition occurred (a precorrection), as well as during the transition period. The expectations were to walk, to keep hands and feet to oneself, and to use a quiet voice. The trainers modeled the active supervision elements for staff members, which included (1) moving around, (2) visually scanning the designated area, and (3) interacting with students. Staff members watched brief role plays in which trainers provided both negative and positive examples of how active supervision and precorrection should be conducted.

The researchers collected three types of data in this study. The first thing they looked at was the setting itself. They noted how many staff members and students were present in an area during a transition. Second, they documented the type of actions the staff used, including scanning, interacting, and escorting (physically accompanying students during the transition). Finally, the frequency of student behaviors was monitored. These included running, pushing, shouting, sliding, and throwing, as well as any other rule violation.

Before the intervention began, high levels of problem behavior were observed during all three transitions. When students entered in the morning, the average number of behavior problems was 40 during the 5-minute transition period. Transitioning to lunch and leaving the school building had somewhat fewer incidents, at 25 and 23, respectively, per session. Once staff engaged in active supervision, problem incidents in the first transition period were reduced to an average of only 8 per session. Similar declines were observed during lunch, with an average of 15 incidents, and when exiting school, with an average of 9 incidents. The study demonstrates how a brief training dramatically increased staff members' effectiveness in supervising students. Requiring staff to use precorrection and active supervision greatly decreased student misbehavior. This type of supervision is instrumental in establishing a safe and calm school environment, which translates directly into improved student behavior.

Reducing Class Tardiness through Active Supervision in Middle and High School

In a secondary school struggling with a high number of tardies, Tyre, Feuerborn, and Pierce (2011) examined the use of schoolwide active supervision to address the problem. The combined middle and high school had a significant and pervasive problem with students arriving late to classes throughout the day. The school was located in Washington State and was composed almost completely (97%) of students from Native American tribes. There were 355 students in grades 7–12.

Teachers and administrators were concerned with the negative impact tardiness was having on instructional time. Large numbers of students were arriving to class as late as 15 minutes. Tardies averaged 60 per day. Not only did the problem affect the students who arrived late, but it also had a detrimental effect on the rest of the class when instruction was interrupted by the latecomers. To tackle this problem, a school site team developed a plan to increase supervision in the hallways between class periods to encourage students to arrive to class on time. In addition to active supervision, the staff developed three lessons about expectations for arriving to class. A schedule was developed for delivering the lessons to ensure all students were aware of the expectations. Both administrators and teachers took part in the active supervision between classes. The administrative team circulated through the halls during the passing period and the first 5 minutes of class. Teachers without an instructional period were assigned zones, which included hallways, restrooms, and other areas students passed through or congregated. They moved throughout their zones reminding students to get to class on time. Teachers with an instructional period waited at the doors of the classrooms to greet students as they arrived. When the tardy bell rang, teachers immediately shut the door and began instruction. Students who arrived late to class received a consequence depending on the number of tardies they had accumulated.

Although the main component of the program was active supervision, the staff also used precorrection and prompting (the lessons informing students of the on-time expectations and the reminders about not being late during the passing period) and consequences. The program had an immediate and positive effect on the number of tardies. In the first month of implementation, there were only 22 tardies. Over the next 18 months, tardies ranged from a low of 13 to a high of 26 (still considerably lower than before the program), with an average of 20 a month. While the school staff continued to work on refining and enhancing their use of active supervision to decrease tardiness, they were able to quickly and efficiently use existing school resources to create a program that addressed the very specific needs of their school community.

Summary

These studies illustrate just how powerful simple strategies can be when implemented conscientiously in a range of settings. Whether one is an experienced or a beginning teacher, understanding the discrete elements of the strategy and using them consistently in classrooms will result in improved classroom management and, as a result, increased learning time. When these strategies are applied in non-instructional areas, they offer students an opportunity to enjoy interactions with both peers and adults in a safe, respectful manner. Table 4.1 offers a list of studies that illustrate other applications of this strategy across the K–12 continuum.

Benefits and Challenges

Active supervision is fundamental to good classroom management. Although it is simple to use, there are a few considerations to keep in mind.

Benefits

Active supervision is a powerful tool for reducing problem behaviors in classrooms, as well as other school contexts, including the playground, cafeteria, hallways, and bus loading areas, so it is a critical aspect of schoolwide positive behavior support. In addition to improving time spent on task, it can be leveraged to target specific problems, such as bullying and tardiness (e.g., Johnson-Gros et al., 2008; Ttofi & Farrington, 2011). Because supervision is an essential part of school safety, all school personnel foster a safe environment when they actively supervise students, but they should be supported in how to do so effectively.

Challenges

Despite its ubiquity and effectiveness, supervision can be difficult to perform consistently. Although all teachers and school personnel can learn to be good at supervision, some have a better innate ability to monitor student activity—Kounin's "with-itness." Teachers constantly have their attention divided, so a critical part of supervision is developing one's ability to multitask. Finally, understanding the purposes of precorrection, prompting, and reinforcing and using those skills accurately are requisites for effective and active supervision. Teachers who struggle in the shift from a reactive to a proactive stance may be able to monitor student activity, but they are unlikely to shape the critical prosocial behaviors students need for both school and life. Fortunately, teachers and other staff members on site can learn how to implement active supervision strategies by following the steps (see Table 4.2) detailed next.

Implementing Active Supervision Strategies in Your Classroom: Checklist for Success

In the following sections, a step-by-step approach for implementing active supervision is detailed. These steps are also listed in Table 4.2, the Implementation Checklist; and a hypothetical illustration of how these steps can be used in a CI3T model at the middle school level is provided in Box 4.1.

- **Step 1: Identify the activity or transition period that would benefit most from active supervision.** The first step in deciding how to use active supervision is to reflect on the different types of instructional and transition activities that occur throughout the school day. You may want to rate how trouble-free you perceive these activities to be and focus on those that require more attention to run smoothly. For example, a major activity that sets the tone for the entire day or class period is when students first enter. Are students purposeful and focused as they get ready to begin their work for the day, or is the atmosphere chaotic or overly social? Similarly, transitions that occur during instructional periods such as group work and independent assignments should be scrutinized.

TABLE 4.2. Implementation Checklist for Success: Active Supervision

- Step 1: Identify the activity or transition period that would benefit most from active supervision.
- Step 2: Ensure that the routine for the target activity is familiar and understood by students. If not, routines and expectations must be established.
- Step 3: Provide the cue or prompt to begin the activity.
- Step 4: As the activity unfolds, scan and monitor the area.
- Step 5: Signal your awareness of students' actions through proximity, prompts, and nonverbal communication.
- Step 6: Manage infractions and off-task behavior efficiently: privately, in a businesslike way, and with opportunities for positive interactions.
- Step 7: At appropriate intervals and at the end of the activity or transition, reinforce students' good behavior with positive comments and gestures.
- Step 8: Provide students with an opportunity to give feedback.

Any time students move from one activity to other, active supervision should be used. This includes movement from one physical location to another, as well as preparing materials for a different activity. In addition to transitions, think about each instructional period and evaluate how successfully it is managed. A simple 3-point Likert-type rating scale can help assess each area. For example, a 3 is assigned when students are on task and orderly and the activity (or transition) runs smoothly. A score of 2 indicates students understand what to do and most are on task and orderly. A score of 1 is assigned when students take their time getting to work and problems frequently erupt.

Activities that score a 1 should definitely be considered for improvement. Those rating a 2 might benefit from some reflection to determine whether active supervision would improve student engagement. And although a score of 3 is excellent and requires no attention, it is equally worthwhile to reflect when practices are successful.

• **Step 2: Ensure that the routine for the target activity is familiar and understood by students. If not, routines and expectations must be established.** Of course, a critical prerequisite is whether the use of effective routines and procedures for common activities and events is in place. In a school that has a PBIS or CI3T model of prevention, expectations for classroom behavior are specified in the expectation matrix posted in the classroom and are taught at the beginning of the year. If a school does not use a PBIS or CI3T schoolwide plan, teachers need to establish their own expectations. Most teachers have classroom rules, but they should also have procedures in place for everyday occurrences, including lining up, gathering materials, putting away books, handing out papers, and sharpening pencils. Until students are aware of the teacher's expectations of how these activities are performed, it is unrealistic to expect to see them occur with the frequency most teachers desire. When teachers model how they expect the activities to be carried out, it is extremely effective in helping students perform them fluently and accurately.

• **Step 3: Provide the cue or prompt to begin the activity.** Once an instructional period has been identified and routines are in place, the elements of supervision can be considered: monitoring, prompting, and reinforcing prosocial behavior. For example, a common classroom activity is independent reading. Students frequently read text under the supervision of the teacher; however, the quality and effectiveness of this activity varies greatly. In some classrooms this is an opportunity to do nothing while pretending to look at the page, and in other classrooms students may not even pretend to read but use it as a time to socialize or be off task. In classrooms in which teachers actively supervise, chances are much greater that students are genuinely engaged in their reading and using the time productively.

When beginning the activity, provide reminders on how it should be carried out (precorrection). This reminder should be brief and to the point. For example, in the case of the independent reading activity, the teacher would say: "Please read quietly in your seats without talking to others for the next 20 minutes." In this case, students would already know how to get their books and whether or not they should have their journals or any other materials available to help them complete the activity.

• **Step 4: As the activity unfolds, scan and monitor the area.** After giving the instructions to take out the necessary materials and begin reading, the teacher looks about the room to ensure that everyone is on task and whether any students need assistance. There will undoubtedly be students who need help in getting started or transitioning, and this is where monitoring and prompting immediately come into play. The teacher walks about the room as she observes students getting ready. With eye contact, smiles, and nods, she quickly communicates her expectations as she helps students get settled. The teacher deliberately communicates that she is monitoring by walking about the room and assisting individual students.

Remember, this communication is critical, particularly when first establishing classroom routines and then when reviewing them to be sure they are still working effectively. Monitoring is an unmistakable cue that the teacher expects students to be on task. If one supervises without communicating awareness of students' actions, behavior problems are more likely to occur. Monitoring and scanning are also how a teacher is able to anticipate and head off problems before they occur.

If students are engaged in an independent activity, the teacher will most likely work quietly with an individual student or a small group while the class is reading. However, it is crucial to be aware of the class despite having one's attention focused on another instructional group. This can be difficult. One scans the room periodically, with an eye for potential trouble areas. Although all students and areas of the classroom must be monitored, teachers will be aware of which students must be supervised more carefully and can prompt them. Students should be in a teacher's sight at all times, so bookcases and other pieces of furniture should be positioned strategically.

• **Step 5: Signal your awareness of students' actions through proximity, prompts, and nonverbal communication.** Before, during, and at the end of an activity, the teacher offers precorrections and prompts. Sometimes teachers are reluctant to do so, as they believe students should already know what is expected of them. However, it is worth the time and energy to support students with the use of precorrections and prompts as they reduce behavior problems (see Chapter 7). Even when students do know what to do, precorrections and prompts help them focus. (Precorrections are the reminder of what the expectations are for a particular activity before it begins, and prompts are gentle cues to remain on task.)

Precorrections and prompts also provide opportunities to interact with students in a positive manner and offer an instructional approach to behavior—teaching and reteaching what is expected to help students be successful in all settings (Faul, Stepensky, & Simonsen, 2012). These encouraging and constructive encounters with students enhance the climate of your classroom. Developing a productive classroom climate can feel elusive, but prompting and reinforcing is a concrete way to do so. Prompting is another way to signal the teacher's awareness, which is what makes the supervision an *active* rather than a passive approach. For example, reminding a student who appears off task to refocus on his or her work is a common example of how teachers use prompts. Of course a supportive tone and choice of words is essential in making it clear that the reminder is a prompt and not a reprimand.

Returning to the independent reading example, a teacher might prompt the whole class after 10 minutes by saying in a low voice, "I appreciate how quietly everyone is reading." Alternatively, she or he may choose not to use a verbal prompt and instead get up and walk about the room. If a student is off task, it is tempting to reprimand or assign a consequence, but a student may comply more readily if you first redirect with a gentle reminder to get back to work. The combination of monitoring and prompting reminds students that the teacher is checking to see that they are on task and engaged with their assignment. This is effective in the moment, but it also works for future sessions because students understand that the teacher is continually looking for and supporting a high level of engagement. It is also a way to communicate that support is always available when needed.

• **Step 6: Manage infractions and off-task behavior efficiently: privately, in a businesslike way, and with opportunities for positive interactions.** Sometimes it will be necessary to provide corrective feedback to a student who is not adhering to expectations, but this should be done in a calm and respectful manner. First decide whether it is necessary to address the misbehavior immediately. If it can be effectively managed later, it is less disruptive to the rest of the class. Sometimes this is not possible. In cases in which a student is engaged in off-task behavior or violating a rule (and cannot be easily redirected), something that must be addressed immediately, it should be managed with the least amount of disruption as possible. Any corrective action should be delivered in a businesslike manner—no anger, loud voice, or communicated exasperation. It is also important to avoid embarrassing a student. Corrective action should be brisk so it does not disrupt the flow of the activity taking place and is not so drawn out that the student feels humiliated. Do not engage in a conversation with the student (this can be done later in a less public setting), as you do not want to be drawn into an argument; simply state the infraction and then follow the procedure in place for administering the consequence. Allow the student to return to the class activity as soon as is possible.

• **Step 7: At appropriate intervals and at the end of the activity or transition, reinforce students' good behavior with positive comments and gestures.** Finally, teachers must remember to reinforce the good behavior they see by telling students their work, focus, and efforts are noticed. A thank-you at the end of the class session stating what most students did well (see behavior-specific praise [BSP], discussed in Chapter 3) is appropriate: "Students, I noticed most of you read silently and seemed to enjoy your time reading. Thank you for staying focused on your reading materials." Some school sites use tickets or tokens paired with BSP. A brief "thank you" and a smile may be all that is needed. Either way, sincerity is important. Excessive enthusiasm is not necessary, but the reinforcer must be authentic to be meaningful to students. Sometimes teachers are reluctant to give praise, thinking it indulges students, but many people (students and adults!) appreciate having their efforts recognized. When students make a genuine effort, it is appropriate to say something positive about it, and it is effective in promoting the prosocial behavior teachers work so hard to develop in their students.

• **Step 8. Provide students with an opportunity to give feedback.** With many instructional strategies, it is useful to ask students their opinion of the technique and whether it helped them learn. This information can improve a teacher's effectiveness. However, active supervision is slightly different because it is not only a strategy, but it is a teacher's responsibility to ensure students' safety by being aware of what students are doing. It might be more informative to ask an administrator for feedback on your use of active supervision or to ask students and/or parents whether they feel the classroom is adequately supervised and provides a feeling of safety. This is a slightly less direct approach typically used when determining what others think about the use of a particular strategy. See Figure 4.3 in Box 4.1 for an example of asking students their opinion of active supervision during lunchtime.

Examining the Effects: How Well Is It Working?

Testing the Strategy: Design Considerations

When implementing active supervision, it is important to collect data on student performance to know how well this strategy is working. In many of the studies featured in this book, researchers have used single-case methodology to "test" the intervention effects. This is a particularly useful design approach for teachers, as it is highly flexible and very practical. It can be used with any of the strategies introduced in each chapter.

It is important to use an experimental design such as an ABAB or multiple baseline across settings, tasks, or students to establish a functional relation between the introduction of the intervention and changes in student performance (Gast & Ledford, 2014). In other words, this design helps determine whether or not the intervention worked. This information is helpful to both general education and special education teachers for a variety of reasons. The first, of course, is it allows you to evaluate the effectiveness of your instruction. With this information, you can decide how to adjust your instructional practices so they work better for your students. Second, members of the CI3T team or members of professional learning communities (PLCs) can use these data to determine how students are responding to these low-intensity supports. Before moving on to student-focused Tier 2 (e.g., Check-In/Check-Out, behavior contracts, or self-monitoring strategies) or Tier 3 (e.g., functional assessment-based interventions; Umbreit et al., 2007) supports, we want to be certain we have examined the extent to which teacher-driven strategies (e.g., active supervision) have been effective in addressing students' needs (academically, behaviorally, and/or socially). Using an experimental design is one way to show whether or not this has occurred. We recommend these teams (e.g., CI3T and PLC) be composed of a range of individuals, including general and special education teachers, as they each bring unique talents. For example, special education teachers are a critical resource for implementing and delivering specialized intervention; they can assist general educators with evaluating strategy implementation, as well as carefully measuring the effects of any given intervention for a particular student, as is demonstrated in Box 4.1. This is especially critical when focused on more intensive supports, such as functional assessment-based interventions, that require careful monitoring of students' performance (e.g., academic engagement, disruption). The ability to use single-case methodology is a critical skill in assessing the effectiveness of Tier 2 and 3 supports

These designs begin with a baseline phase during which data on student performance are collected (referred to as the A phase), then the intervention is introduced for the first time (B), while still collecting data on student performance using the same data collection method used during the baseline phase (see Figure 4.1 in Box 4.1). Although it is tempting at this point to say the intervention was effective, two more replications are needed to be certain the intervention was responsible for the change and not something else. One demonstration (e.g., the change from A to B phases) along with two other replications can provide evidence that the introduction of the strategy produced the changes (the shift from B to A and then A to B; Gast & Ledford, 2014).

Although some designs, such as the ABAB design, require removal and then reintroduction of the intervention, it is also possible to explore a functional relation using a multiple baseline across setting design. This means the strategy is used in different settings, such as a different instructional period (math instead of reading) or a different physical location (playground instead of the lunchroom).

Making Certain the Strategy Is in Place: Treatment Integrity

In addition to using an experimental design to test the intervention, collecting treatment integrity data helps determine the extent to which the intervention is being implemented as planned. Figure 4.2 is an example of a treatment integrity checklist for active supervision. Although there are many different ways to collect treatment integrity data, one way is to have the teacher collect these data each day by indicating the degree to which each intervention component was implemented as planned for each student. For example, in Figure 4.2 in Box 4.1, each item is completed using a 3-point Likert-type scale as follows: 0 = *not in place*, 1 = *partially in place*, or 2 = *completely in place*. Each day the items are summed, divided by the total number of points possible, and divided by 100 to obtain a percentage of implementation for each student. These data can be used to interpret intervention outcomes (see Box 4.1). In addition, behavior component checklists not only determine the level of implementation but also serve as a prompt or reminder to implement each step.

Using an outside observer to collect treatment integrity data for approximately 25% of the sessions in each phase is recommended. An additional observer is important for establishing the accuracy of the data collected.

Examining Stakeholders' Views: Social Validity

Finally, in addition to collecting information on student performance and implementation (treatment integrity), it is important to understand how stakeholders felt about the intervention goals, procedures, and intended outcomes. Figure 4.3 in Box 4.1 is an example of a measure examining middle school students' perceptions of the social validity of active supervision before and after implementing the strategy.

It is important to obtain all stakeholders' views —the teacher, student, and parent—ideally before the intervention begins and again at the conclusion of the first "test." If social validity is low at the onset of the intervention, then it is wise to provide additional training to increase people's knowledge of the strategies, as well as their confidence in using the strategy prior to implementation. In theory (and in some instances in actuality; see Lane, Kalberg, Bruhn, et al., 2009), the opinions of those implementing and participating in the intervention may predict the extent to which the interventions are implemented as planned. In essence, a socially valid intervention is likely to be put in place with a high degree of integrity, leading to improvements in student performance that maintain over time and in new settings and with new people.

BOX 4.1. A Hypothetical Illustration of Active Supervision in a CI3T Model

Cahuilla Valley Middle School was in its first year of implementing a comprehensive, integrated, three-tiered (CI3T) model of prevention. It had adopted a program called Responding in Peaceful and Positive Ways (RIPP; Meyer, Farrell, Northup, Kung, & Plybon, 2000), designed to help students choose nonviolent strategies for dealing with conflict and to improve their interactions with one another. The school included sixth, seventh, and eighth grades, and the preceding few years had seen increasing incidences of fighting, rule violations, and bullying. There was also concern that sixth graders were ill equipped for the transition to middle school. After careful research, the staff decided to use RIPP, spent a year preparing for the new program, and began implementation in September. They believed it would be a strong complement to their newly established schoolwide rules and strong focus on academic outcomes.

Just a few months into the school year they were already seeing good results with noticeably fewer fights and an improved school climate; however, the eighth-grade teachers had a new concern. They noticed that the eighth-grade students were taking too long to transition from the lunch court to their classrooms. On some days, nearly 20% of students were late to class. And once students arrived in the classroom, they took several minutes to get to work. Issuing detention slips to late students did not seem to improve matters, so the eighth-grade teachers met during their Professional Learning Community (PLC) time to tackle the problem.

After discussing the problem, the eighth-grade PLC felt that active supervision combined with precorrection would encourage students to arrive to class on time. There were several contributing factors to the problem. One was that there was inadequate supervision at the end of the lunch period. Supervisors watched for problems but did not help clear the lunch court. Another was a lack of a clear schoolwide expectation about arriving to class on time. Some teachers imposed consequences, some did not, and others felt it took too much energy to address the problem on their own. Finally, teachers had started to wait until all students arrived, which further exacerbated the issue because more students were tardy when they saw that it did not matter if they were late.

Because they needed to implement active supervision in the cafeteria and the hallways, as well as in the classroom, the eighth-grade PLC met with the lunch supervisors and the principal to work out a plan.

Support	Description	Entry criteria	Data to monitor progress	Exit criteria
Active supervision	Active supervision, precorrection, and prompting in the cafeteria during lunch and the transition to the next class	Percentage of students tardy to class following lunch exceeded 10% of the student body during a 1-week period. ODRs after lunch were three or more per day for a 1-week period.	*Student performance:* • Timely arrival to class after lunch • Appropriate behavior in cafeteria and class *Treatment integrity:* Component checklist *Social validity:* Student-completed survey	No planned exit criteria; new procedures incorporated for the full academic year

Preparing for and Delivering Active Supervision: The Intervention

• **Step 1. Identify the activity or transition period that would benefit most from active supervision.** The PLC had already identified the transition from lunch to the classroom as a critical period. By working with the lunch supervisors and the principal, they were able to address the entire transition from its beginning in the lunch court to its end in the classroom.

• **Step 2. Ensure that the routine for the target activity is familiar and understood by students. If not, routines and expectations must be established.** Eighth-grade language arts teachers agreed to deliver a 15-minute lesson on the expectations for leaving the lunchroom promptly and arriving at the next class before the tardy bell rang. They reminded students of the importance of being present for the entire class time, as well as how arriving late negatively impacted their peers. Teachers modeled hearing the tardy bell, throwing away their trash, packing up their things, and heading off to class. Although students thought this was amusing, it provided a visual they would think of when they heard the warning bell ring and would remind them they were expected to leave the lunch court in a timely manner. Teachers also emphasized that instruction would begin the moment the bell rang indicating the start of class. Because all students had a language arts class on their schedule, it was the ideal class in which to provide the lesson. Teachers gave the lesson for 2 consecutive weeks, making slight changes so that it would not seem overly repetitive.

• **Step 3. Provide the cue or prompt to begin the activity.** The cue to begin the activity was a new 1-minute warning bell. The principal agreed to institute this additional bell to facilitate the active supervision strategy. A second bell rang to indicate the beginning of the passing period and gave notice that students should be actively leaving the lunch court.

• **Step 4. As the activity unfolds, scan and monitor the area.** Once the first warning bell rang, lunch supervisors, the principal, and the assistant principal moved throughout the cafeteria prompting students to begin cleaning up. They used humor and gentle voices, as they wanted to keep the tone friendly, not punitive. When the second bell rang, supervisors and administrators reminded students how many minutes they had to get to class. At the same time, teachers stepped outside their classroom doors and made sure students were aware of their presence. However, 1 minute before the tardy bell rang, teachers returned to their classrooms so they would be ready to start instruction.

• **Step 5. Signal your awareness of students' actions through proximity, prompts, and nonverbal communication.** As students left the lunchroom and walked down the halls to class, all adult supervisors made eye contact, gave thumbs-up, or smiled at students as they reminded them to get to class on time. When there was 1 minute left, supervisors motioned to the clocks on the walls or watches on their wrists to indicate the passing period was almost over.

• **Step 6. Manage infractions and off-task behavior efficiently: privately, in a businesslike way, and with opportunities for positive interaction.** A procedure was worked out in advance for students who were roughhousing or violating rules. Their names were recorded, and they were given a referral to meet immediately with the dean in her office. Because this was preplanned, the dean would be ready and waiting to receive students. Referrals were to be given out quickly, with as little interaction as possible. Students who were still in the hallways after the bell rang were also given a referral slip but were directed to class. Their referral required them to meet after school with a counselor once they had received two referral slips.

• **Step 7. At appropriate intervals and at the end of the activity or transition, reinforce students' good behavior with positive comments and gestures.**

As students entered their classrooms, teachers said hello and thanked them for getting to class before the bell rang. Once the tardy bell rang, teachers immediately started the lesson.

•**Step 8. Provide students with an opportunity to give feedback.** The eighth-grade PLC was interested in seeing what students thought about active supervision during the transition from lunch to the classroom, but they also wanted to know whether it changed students' perceptions about whether it was important to arrive to class on time. They created a short measure (see Figure 4.3) that helped them examine both these issues and asked students to complete it twice: before and after the strategy was introduced.

Looking at How Well Active Supervision Worked

The PLC knew it was important to collect data on the intervention because teachers and supervisors were dedicating quite a bit of energy and time to its planning and implementation. While they were still in the planning stages, the six PLC teachers decided to determine just how many students were arriving late to class, so for a 1-week period each teacher took a frequency count of the number of students who arrived after the bell rang. They also wanted to know how many discipline referrals were given during lunch and the passing period immediately after. These data were collected and maintained in the office, so the principal asked a counselor to find out those numbers.

Figure 4.1 shows the results of the ABAB withdrawal design the team used to examine the effectiveness of their active supervision strategy. To determine how it was working across the entire eighth grade, the teachers totaled the number of tardies earned for all eighth-grade students after lunch each day, and the attendance secretary computed the percentage of students tardy to class for each day (see Figure 4.1, Panel A). They also included the number of discipline referrals made for rule violations immediately after the bell rang signaling the end of lunch. These data are represented in Figure 4.1 in Panel B.

Visual inspection of the data collected suggested a functional relation between the introduction of this intervention and changes in tardiness and ODRs. During the baseline phase, the percentage of students tardy to class ranged from approximately 16 to 21% over a 1-week period, with a slight upward trend throughout the week. In the first week of the intervention, there was an immediate decrease in the percentage of eighth-grade students tardy to class that remained low and steady (range of approximately 7–9%). In the third week, when the intervention was withdrawn, tardiness increased to 16%, with an upward trend toward the end of the week. When the intervention was reintroduced, again the percentage of students tardy to class declined immediately and stayed quite low (less than 8% of students tardy to class each day of the 1-week period). The intervention also decreased the number of referrals for other problems (see Figure 4.1, Panel B). The staff thought this was tremendous progress and were sure they could even improve on it.

Panel A. Tardies

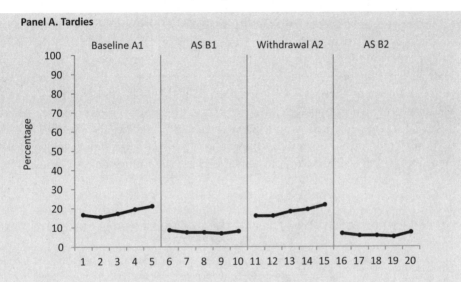

Panel B. Office Discipline Referrals (ODRs)

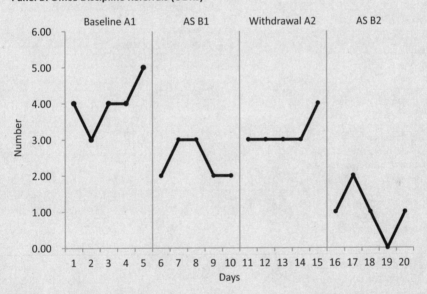

FIGURE 4.1. Examining the effects: Panel A depicts the percentage of eighth-grade students tardy to class after lunch each day. Panel B depicts the number of office discipline referrals (ODRs) earned each by eighth graders after the lunch bell. Although ODR data are typically presented in rate, we present them here in number earned for ease of interpretation (based on the assumption of no changes in student enrollment).

To ensure that everyone remembered each step of the strategy, the PLC had created simple Treatment Integrity Forms to use in the cafeteria and the hallway and another one for teachers (see Figure 4.2 for the form used in the cafeteria). They asked that during the first week of intervention, each participating staff member fill it out each day and then drop it in the assistant principal's box. The assistant principal arranged to have the data aggregated so they could see whether it was being implemented as they had planned. During the first week of intervention, implementation was a little uneven, and the combined daily average of treatment integrity for supervisors, teachers, and administrators ranged from a low of

TREATMENT INTEGRITY FORM FOR CAFETERIA SUPERVISORS AND ADMINISTRATORS: ACTIVE SUPERVISION

Supervisor/Administrator: Ms. Murphy

Scale: 0 = Not in place   1 = Partially in place   2 = Fully in place

Location: Cafeteria

	Session 1	Session 2	Session 3	Session 4	Session 5
Component	Monday 9/4/2015	Tuesday 9/5/2015	Wednesday 9/6/2015	Thursday 9/17/2015	Friday 9/18/2015
1. I continually scanned and monitored the lunch court.	1	1	1	2	2
2. I let students know I was present and aware of their actions by using verbal and nonverbal communication.	1	2	2	2	1
3. When the 1-minute warning bell rang, I circulated the lunch court and prompted students to clean up.	2	2	2	2	2
4. When the passing bell rang, I circulated the lunch court and reminded students it was time to leave for their next class.	2	2	2	2	2
5. I interacted with students in a friendly manner.	1	2	1	1	2
Percentage Session Integrity: (Total points earned/# points possible) × 100	70%	90%	80%	90%	90%

FIGURE 4.2. Making certain the strategy is in place: Treatment Integrity Form used by the eighth-grade professional learning community (PLC) to monitor the extent to which each step was put in place as planned. Ms. Murphy's scores for the first week of implementation.

66% to a high of 93%. By the last week, average implementation was much better, ranging from 93 to 97%. Figure 4.2 shows Ms. Murphy's completed Treatment Integrity Checklist. Her scores were averaged with those of the other adults monitoring implementation to obtain the overall implementation scores for each day.

The PLC was interested in knowing whether students' perceptions changed after the strategy was implemented, so as part of the lesson on expectations, the language arts teachers administered a very short survey that served as the social validity measure. They asked students to rate their agreement with the main elements of the plan using a 3-point Likert-type scale (shown in Figure 4.3, Panel A, with Henry's completed forms showing how an individual student completed the measure before the intervention began and again after the intervention had been tested). They surveyed students again after 2 weeks of full implementation, and one of the PLC members aggregated the data and reported the percentages for each of the items by time point (see Figure 4.3, Panel B). Interestingly, the teachers found that providing the lesson on expectations and using the strategy improved

SOCIAL VALIDITY FORM: ACTIVE SUPERVISION

Panel A

Active Supervision Survey I: Henry			
	Not at all	Somewhat	Definitely
It is important to arrive to class on time.	(0)	1	2
It would be helpful to have lunch supervisors remind me when it is time to clean up and get ready to go to class.	0	(1)	2
I think teachers should start class when the bell rings.	(0)	1	2
I would appreciate it if a teacher thanked me for arriving to class on time.	0	(1)	2

Active Supervision Survey II: Henry			
	Not at all	Somewhat	Definitely
It is important to arrive to class on time.	0	(1)	2
It is helpful to have lunch supervisors remind me when it is time to clean up and get ready to go to class.	0	1	(2)
I think teachers should start class when the bell rings.	0	1	(2)
I appreciate it when a teacher thanks me for arriving to class on time.	0	1	(2)

(continued)

FIGURE 4.3. Examining stakeholders' views: Social validity forms developed by the eighth-grade professional learning community (PLC) to examine individual students' (Panel A) and all eighth-grade students' (Panel B) views on active supervision.

Panel B

Preintervention Summary Sheet for Social Validity			
Active Supervision Survey II: Students			
	Percentages for all student responses *before* implementation:		
	Not at all 0	Somewhat 1	Definitely 2
It is important to arrive to class on time.	25%	46%	29%
It would be helpful to have lunch supervisors remind me when it is time to clean up and get ready to go to class.	62%	33%	5%
I think teachers should start class when the bell rings.	3%	23%	74%
I appreciate it when a teacher thanks me for arriving to class on time.	10%	5%	85%

Postintervention Summary Sheet for Social Validity			
Active Supervision Survey II: Students			
	Percentages for all student responses *after* implementation:		
	Not at all 0	Somewhat 1	Definitely 2
It is important to arrive to class on time.	4%	28%	68%
It is helpful to have lunch supervisors remind me when it is time to clean up and get ready to go to class.	7%	13%	80%
I think teachers should start class when the bell rings.	3%	23%	74%
I appreciate it when a teacher thanks me for arriving to class on time.	5%	10%	85%

FIGURE 4.3. *(continued)*

students' perceptions of all the items. For example, before the staff used active supervision, students did not think it was all that important to get to class on time, with only 29% of students indicating it was *definitely* (score of 2) important to be on time. This is compared with 68% who thought it was *definitely* important after introduction of the strategy. The responses also demonstrated that students thought it was helpful to have the lunch supervisors remind them it was time to clean up, with 80% *definitely* agreeing with the statement after the intervention. Students felt very positive about teachers thanking them for arriving to class on time, with 85% *definitely* agreeing and 10% *somewhat* agreeing that they appreciated it.

Although the eighth-grade teachers and supervisors had put in considerable effort and time using their active supervision strategy, they thought the payoff was well worth it. They were able to decrease the number of behavior incidents and to increase instructional time. The social validity measure seemed to demonstrate that students, too, appreciated the new approach. They also felt the strategy was an important enhancement to their schoolwide plan, which included their academic core plan, PBIS framework, and RIPP as their social skills component; collectively these strategies led to a noticeable improvement in school climate. They decided to keep this support in place for the balance of the school year.

Summary

Active supervision is an easy strategy to use that almost invariably results in improved student behavior, whether it is an increase in time on task or a reduction in misbehavior. It takes little time or effort for a teacher to prepare and implement, although deliberate reflection and a plan of action will result in quicker and better outcomes. Active supervision is also a foundational strategy in that it is used across settings; it is equally effective in instructional contexts such as the classroom and in less structured environments such as the cafeteria or playground. It can, and should, be used in a variety of settings by teachers, administrators, and support personnel. Active supervision, when implemented correctly, improves the quality of instructional time, rewards students who behave appropriately, improves adult and student interactions, ensures student safety, and shapes misbehavior into pro-social behavior: a powerful effect from a simple strategy.

CHAPTER 5

A Look at Instructional Feedback

As teachers have become focused on better understanding the relation between their instruction and student learning, the role of instructional feedback is increasingly more important. In this case, the function of feedback is twofold. First, when teachers create a learning context in which they are intentional about providing instructional feedback, the teacher gains important information on how students perceive instruction and respond to it; this guides the teacher in instructional planning (Hattie, 2009). Second, students benefit from getting specific feedback from teachers in several ways: clarifying misinformation, confirming and fine-tuning understandings, and restructuring current schemas (Butler & Winne, 1995). With benefits for teachers and students, instructional feedback has been shown to be one of the most powerful influences on student achievement (Hattie, 2009).

When teachers create intentional and frequent opportunities to provide specific instructional feedback, they are also creating a context in which they access immediate feedback on the effectiveness of their instructional choices on students' learning (Hattie, 2009). When their practices have the desired effects on student learning, teachers are more likely to continue to implement the practices, and this is particularly important for sustaining the use of new evidence-based practices (Burns et al., 2013). Conversely, when practices do not have the desired effect, teachers will seek new strategies to better address student needs. Teachers are, now more than ever, using data to make instructional decisions to improve educational outcomes for all students; instructional feedback provides one type of data for these decisions. Teachers' decisions include teaching strategies and practices for creating positive learning environments such as opportunities to respond (see Chapter 2); incorporating instructional choice (Chapter 8); pacing of instruction

(Brophy, 1979); type and amount of feedback (Kulik & Kulik, 1988); and differentiation of instruction and assessments (Tomlinson, 2005). These choices are made to best support student learning.

Instructional feedback has been suggested for developing self-regulated learners (Butler & Winne, 1995). Butler and Winne (1995) described self-regulated learning as a process in which students engage in and direct their own learning by setting goals, using past evidence to make decisions about strategies to employ in a learning task, taking steps to use the strategy, and monitoring the effect and adjusting as needed. Effective self-regulation includes the students' use of internal and external (e.g., from a peer, teacher, parent) feedback (Nicol & MacFarlane-Dick, 2006). Further, feedback delivered in a positive and instructive fashion can increase intrinsic motivation (Deci & Ryan, 2000) and persistence on future difficult tasks (Kamins & Dweck, 1999). In order for this feedback to enhance motivation, it should be related to autonomous behaviors applied to appropriately difficult tasks (Deci & Ryan, 2000); that is, tasks that provide optimal challenge and feedback (Lane, Menzies, Bruhn, & Crnobori, 2011; Stipek, 1993).

Within comprehensive, integrated three-tiered (CI3T) models of prevention, educators strive to create proactive, positive, and safe learning environments. The use of instructional feedback should be clearly understood within this context. Providing positive, instructive feedback can have positive effects on learning and engagement, whereas negative or punitive feedback will have the opposite effect (Deci & Ryan, 2000). Negative instructional feedback disrupts feelings of safety for students, reducing the likelihood that they will take instructional risks and make and learn from mistakes—all critical elements in learning (Hattie, 2009). Further, negative feedback or comments (also known as criticism) about the students "self" have been demonstrated to be attributed to ability, and may decrease motivation (Kamins & Dweck, 1999). The latter point should be of particular concern to early childhood teachers and parents, as young children interpret negative feedback to mean they are bad, and they exhibit patterns such as lack of effort in response to criticism (Kamins & Dweck, 1999). Therefore, positive and informative feedback is recommended. In this chapter we focus on the uses of positive and instructive feedback to support student engagement and learning.

What Is Instructional Feedback?

Instructional feedback is a teaching strategy for providing specific information to students about their performance with the purpose of clarifying misinformation, confirming and fine-tuning understandings, or restructuring current schemas (Butler & Winne, 1995). Instructional feedback should be used when students have a base of understanding of the new learning and are working toward proficiency and fluency. When students have not yet attained base knowledge, instruction is needed instead of feedback (Hattie, 2009; Kulhavy, 1977). Closely monitoring student data guides the teacher in deciding when feedback is appropriate and when reteaching is needed.

Delivered appropriately, feedback can provide incentive for a student to give more effort on future activities and tasks (Kulhavy & Wager, 1993). Whereas early theoretical work attempted to disentangle feedback from reinforcement, theoretical and practical applications continue to conceptualize feedback to include reinforcement, such as behavior-specific praise (BSP) related to effort or accomplishment, not to ability, which is not malleable (e.g., Alber, Heward, & Hippler, 1999; Harks, Rakoczy, Hattie, Besser, & Klieme, 2014). Generally, an understanding of feedback as "information provided by an agent (e.g., teacher, peer, book, parent, self, experience) regarding aspects of one's performance or understanding," that is, feedback as a " 'consequence' of performance," is used in this chapter (Hattie & Timperley, 2007, p. 81). The relation between reinforcement and feedback is further supported by the definition of praise as "feedback that is intended to be reinforcing" (Stichter et al., 2009, p. 69). We rely on the common conceptualization that instructional feedback produces learning by delivering content-related information and reinforcement that positively affects motivation, effort, and engagement (Butler & Winne, 1995; Kulhavy & Wager, 1993).

Feedback is a critical feature of the learning process, which consists of cues (e.g., teacher or parent prompts, directions, instructions), participation (e.g., action or response by the student), and feedback and/or reinforcement (e.g., response by the adult directed to the student; Heward, 1994; Lysakowski & Walberg, 1982; Miller & Dollard, 1941). Teachers and parents must keep in mind that few skills are learned by telling a student or child only one time. New knowledge, skills, and behaviors are acquired through instruction, practice, and feedback provided in a loop. This loop is applicable to academic, social, and behavioral domains, and within a supportive and positive environment students are guided to acquire knowledge, skills, and understandings (Sadler, 1989). CI3T models (as described in Chapter 1) provide a context in which this feedback loop can be implemented. The purpose of feedback is to close the gap between expected and current performance in any of the three domains (i.e., academics, behavior, and social skills). Further, feedback is only feedback when the learner has an opportunity to engage in an action in response to the feedback, as opposed to a teacher's or adult's evaluation of a student when no opportunity for change is expected on that particular task or behavior (e.g., final grade; Hattie & Timperley, 2007; Sadler, 1989).

For example, a teacher presents a new math concept to students in a whole-class format. After the introduction of new material, modeling, guided practice, and checking for understanding are done, the teacher provides the directions for completing the independent practice task with the new material. Independent practice is meant to increase the students' fluency with the new math concept; therefore, immediate and specific feedback is needed so that errors in learning do not become ingrained. Acknowledgement of correct responses allows students to proceed with confidence, and information connecting the new learning with previous learning is done individually for each student if needed. During independent practice, teachers should expect high levels of accuracy, and instructional feedback is essential to facilitate this success, in contrast to assessment when feedback is not provided.

Hattie and Timperley (2007) proposed a model for feedback focusing on three questions: "Where am I going? (What are the goals?), How am I going? (What progress is being made toward the goal?), and Where do I go next? (What activities need to be undertaken to make better progress?)" (p. 84). Effective instructional feedback provides information on the learning process and content acquisition instead of focusing on a correct response. Continuing with the example, long division is introduced and taught to fifth-grade students. Once students engage in independent practice, the teacher closely monitors the work students are doing. He recognizes a student who is accurately calculating the problems and states, "Jorge, you are using the four-step process we learned to accurately complete the problem." This feedback confirms Jorge's understanding of the task and encourages him to continue ("How am I going?"). This instructional feedback is focused on the process of the learning and not merely whether the student produced the correct answer (i.e., evaluative feedback). When the teacher observes a student with an error in the learning process, he states, "Celia, please write the acronym for the four-step process next to the problem and cross off each step as you complete it. That will help you keep the order of the steps" ("Where do I go next?"). The teacher then watches as Celia writes the mnemonic and works through the process. The teacher again provides feedback: "Celia, using the mnemonic helped you apply the process to solve the problem accurately." This example demonstrates process feedback to clarify Celia's misunderstanding by redirecting her to a support (i.e., the mnemonic) for her to be successful and independent. The praise for Celia is directed to her effort in applying the mnemonic to successfully solve the problem and not merely "getting the right answer."

This example illustrates verbal feedback on an academic task, but feedback may also be provided for behavioral and social performance and in multiple forms: (1) verbal (Fyfe, DeCaro, & Rittle-Johnson, 2014), (2) written (Harks et al., 2014), and (3) electronic (e.g., Blood & Gulchak, 2013). Further, feedback may also be provided by peers (Gan & Hattie, 2014).

Why Is Instructional Feedback Effective?

Instructional feedback is effective for a number of reasons. As previously described, it is widely accepted that instructional feedback serves multiple purposes, acting as a motivator and a reinforcer, as well as providing instructional information (Harks et al., 2014; Kulhavy & Wager, 1993; Pressey, 1927). Instructional feedback targets content learning and provides a cue for students to focus in on key processes, information, and concepts (Butler & Winne, 1995).

This teaching strategy is easy for teachers to implement during whole-group, small-group, or individualized instruction, requires no material resources, and is highly effective for increasing students' engagement and learning outcomes (Hattie, 2009). In addition, instructional feedback is a positive, proactive approach for correcting learning errors and supporting intrinsic motivation by confirming students' understanding, which contributes to feelings of competence (Harks et al., 2014; Ryan & Deci, 2000). When teachers are using active supervision (see Chapter 4) in the classroom, they are constantly monitoring students' engagement and performance. Using active supervision creates a context not only for supporting expected behaviors but also for allowing opportunities to deliver instructional feedback.

There are different theories as to why feedback is effective. One explanation for feedback's effect on achievement shows specific feedback offers learners support in correcting content and procedural misunderstandings (Harks et al., 2014). This feedback is most effective and positively perceived by students when it is compared with a criterion or the individual's previous performance. In contrast, when the feedback is provided by comparing the student's performance to those of peers, it can have a negative effect on performance (e.g., evaluation; Harks et al., 2014). As such, we recommend that feedback not be used to compare one student's performance to another student's performance.

Another theory states that instructional feedback confirming a student's understanding or providing specific information for how to proceed supports a student's sense of competence. Further, relating the progress to effort expended (and not ability) increases motivation by attributing the progress and learning to an unstable characteristic (and therefore one within the control of the student) as opposed to intelligence, which is considered to be stable and unchangeable by the student (Kamins & Dweck, 1999). For example, feedback regarding effort states, "You included all of the elements of the essay; you did a good job using the rubric to write your paper," rather than emphasizing aptitude, as in "You are so smart, your paper is well written and includes all the elements on the rubric."

Too often, students receive feedback that is critical in nature—telling them what they have done wrong, what behavior they should stop doing, or that their way of behaving is inappropriate. In essence, these actions by educators and parents serve to create doubt, lower self-confidence, and lower motivation to attempt difficult tasks, to name a few. This is particularly true for students with emotional and behavioral disorders (EBD) and learning disabilities (LD) who less often demonstrate learning performance and behavioral or social actions that naturally elicit teachers' positive feedback and praise (Alber et al., 1999). These are certainly not the outcomes teachers anticipate. Teachers and parents may improve outcomes for students by being intentional in the use of instructional feedback to increase motivation and persistence and to narrow the gap between expected and current performance. It is not surprising that studies of instructional feedback have focused on the use of feedback to support the learning of students with a range of abilities, as we discuss in the next section.

Supporting Research for Instructional Feedback

Studies examining instructional feedback have demonstrated the effectiveness of this intervention in increasing academic and behavioral outcomes for a range of students, including those with developmental disabilities, EBD, and autism, as well as typically developing students (e.g., Allday et al., 2012; Fyfe et al., 2014; Simonsen, Britton, & Young, 2010). In addition, instructional feedback has been examined in both elementary and high school in a wide range of instructional settings (see Table 5.1). This chapter highlights a few studies demonstrating how instructional feedback has been applied in a range of settings to support students.

Increasing On-Task Behavior in the General Education Classroom

Allday et al. (2012) worked with four female teachers in one middle school in the Midwest and two elementary schools in the Southwest to implement a form of positive instructional feedback to support student behavior: BSP. For each teacher, one or two students were identified as having challenging behaviors in the general education setting. Student participants were seven (six male, one female) students in kindergarten and first, second, and sixth grades. Of the participants, three were receiving special education services for EBD, and the remaining four had been referred to their schools' multidisciplinary evaluation team for challenging behaviors. The elementary students were observed during circle or center activities at the same time each day. The middle school students were observed during their on-campus learning time. Although target students were identified in each class, teachers were trained to deliver BSP to the entire class to increase the on-task behaviors of students with or at risk for EBD.

Data were collected on teachers' instructional feedback delivered to the entire class, including BSP, generic praise, behavior-specific correction, and generic correction. In addition, data were collected on interactions between the teacher and the target students (i.e., target student praise and target student corrections) and on the target students' on-task behavior. A multiple baseline across teacher participants was used to evaluate the effectiveness of the intervention. At the conclusion of baseline data collection, teachers were trained to better use BSP, as it has been found to be more effective than general praise (Sutherland, Wehby, & Copeland, 2000) and it is recommended that positive feedback be delivered more often than corrective/negative feedback (4:1 ratio). Training took place in the classroom via a 30- to 40-minute training session that included examples and definitions of BSP,

TABLE 5.1. Supporting Research: Instructive Feedback

Authors and journal	Students	Intervention setting	Intervention	Measures	Design
Sutherland, Wehby, & Copeland (2000) Effect of varying rates of behavior-specific praise on the on-task behavior of students with EBD (JEBD)	1 male teacher; 9 5th-grade students (7 males, 2 females)	Self-contained classroom for students with EBD	Teachers discussed their baseline rates of BSP and general praise and set goals for improvement	*Dependent variables:* 1. Non-BSP 2. BSP 3. On-task behavior *Treatment integrity:* Not measured *Social validity:* Not assessed	Withdrawal
Rathel, Drasgow, & Christle (2008) Effects of supervisor performance feedback on increasing preservice teachers' positive communication behaviors with students with emotional and behavioral disorders (JEBD)	2 female preservice teachers	Elementary classrooms for students with EBD	Preservice teachers were provided specific written performance feedback on BSP delivery	*Dependent variables:* 1. Positive teacher comments: BSP for academic behaviors, BSP for social behaviors, non-BSP, nonverbal approval of student behavior 2. Negative teacher comments: verbal teacher corrections for academic behavior, verbal teacher corrections for social behavior, and nonverbal disapproval of student behaviors *Treatment integrity:* Not measured *Social validity:* Assessed using a Likert-type scale	Multiple baseline across preservice teachers

Study	Sample	Setting	Independent variable	Dependent variables	Design
Simonsen, Britton, & Young (2010) School-wide positive behavior support in an alternative school setting: A case study (JPBI)*	Year 1: 39; year 2: 52; year 3: 53 students with disabilities (including ID, VI, ED, TBI, OHI, OI, ASD) ages 3–22 referred to the school for aggression	State certified non-public school for students with disabilities and behavioral needs	Baseline: Secondary and tertiary systems only (i.e., small-group and individualized supports) Intervention: schoolwide positive behavior support (establishing expectations, teaching expectations, teaching social skills [Second Step, Committee for Children, 2002], token economy system facilitated by weekly teachers' meetings and ongoing professional development (weekly staff meetings and *in vivo* coaching)	*Dependent variables:* 1. Teacher: climate data (opportunities to respond, positive feedback, negative or corrective feedback) 2. Student: index of serious incidents per month, distribution of incident reports *Treatment integrity:* Not measured *Social validity:* Not measured	Descriptive, single-subject case study (AB)
Allday et al., (2012) Training general educators to increase behavior-specific praise: Effects on students with EBD (BD)	4 female teachers and 7 students (6 males, 1 female; grades K–2, 6; 3 with EBD; 4 with challenging behaviors/ referred for special education services)	Four general education classrooms (three elementary and one middle school)	Teachers were trained to better use BSP in the classroom and received performance feedback every third day via email	*Dependent variables:* 1. Student: on-task behavior 2. Teacher: verbal interactions with students (behavior-specific praise, generic praise, behavior-specific correction, generic correction, target student praise, target student correction) *Treatment integrity:* Not measured *Social validity:* Assessed using a Likert-type scale	Multiple baseline across teachers; teachers trained to deliver behavior-specific praise (BSP)

(continued)

TABLE 5.1. (continued)

Authors and journal	Students	Intervention setting	Intervention	Measures	Design
Fyfe, DeCaro, & Rittle-Johnson (2014) When feedback is cognitively demanding: The importance of working memory capacity (IS)	64 2nd- and 3rd-grade children (19 males, 45 females)	Four general education classes across two schools (one public, one private)	Comparison of strategy (stated whether or not strategy had been completed accurately) and outcome (stated whether or not the answer was accurate) feedback	*Dependent variables:* Math equivalence assessment, working memory, cognitive load *Treatment integrity:* Not measured *Social validity:* Not measured	Pre-, posttest, maintenance
Gan & Hattie (2014) Prompting secondary students' use of criteria, feedback specificity and feedback levels during an investigative task (IS)	121 12th-graders (75 males, 46 females)	Six chemistry classes from three urban New Zealand secondary schools	Prompted and unprompted peer feedback on writing	*Dependent variables:* Science performance, specificity and level of feedback *Treatment integrity:* Not measured *Social validity:* Not measured	Pre-, posttest
Harks, Rakoczy, Hattie, Besser, & Klieme (2014) The effects of feedback on achievement, interest and self-evaluation: The role of feedback's perceived usefulness (EP)	146 9th-graders (76 males, 70 females)	Math classes in a German intermediate school	Comparison of grade-oriented (score in relation to other students) and process-oriented (general performance rating with up to six strengths) feedback	*Dependent variables:* Achievement change, calibration change, interest change *Treatment integrity:* Not measured *Social validity:* Adapted perceived usefulness scale	Pre-, posttest

Note. ASD, autism spectrum disorder; BD, behavioral disorders; BSP, behavior-specific praise; ED, emotional disturbance; EP, educational psychology; ID, intellectual disability; IS, *Instructional Science*; JEBD, *Journal of Emotional and Behavioral Disorders*; JPBI, *Journal of Positive Behavior Interventions*; MBI, multiple-baseline design; OHI, other health impairment; OI, orthopedic impairment; TBI, traumatic brain injury; VI, visual impairment; *indicates full text is available through Google Scholar.

including examples used by the teacher during baseline data collection. Teachers were also shown a graph of their baseline data and were asked to set a goal for improving their BSP use. Following the training, they received performance feedback via email after every third day of implementation/data collection, which included their performance, whether or not they had met their goal, and their students' performance.

All four teachers increased their rate of BSP following the very brief professional development session and intermittent feedback. As a result, all students displayed increased rates of on-task behavior, at levels consistent with those of their general education peers. Similarly, for many students, there were moderate to large correlations (some statistically significant) between teacher praise directed toward the target students and the students' on-task behavior. Three teachers demonstrated a decrease in the use of generic praise (e.g., "nice job"), as they were now making more BSP statements. Likewise, the use of behavior-specific corrective feedback by all four teachers decreased, as teachers were now making more BSP statements. Following the intervention, all four teachers rated the intervention as favorable or highly favorable using an 8-item social validity questionnaire rated with a Likert-type scale. Teachers also reported that they were likely or highly likely to tell other teachers about BSP and to use it in the future.

Using Strategy Feedback to Improve Students' Math Outcomes, Working Memory, and Cognitive Load

In an exploration of academic instructional feedback, Fyfe et al. (2012) evaluated the effects of two different types of instructional feedback, strategy feedback and outcome feedback. Strategy feedback is concerned with how the student obtained a given response (process) and involves stating the strategy the student used, accompanied by a statement on whether it was correct or incorrect. Outcome feedback is concerned with the accuracy of a response (product) and involves stating the student's answer accompanied by a statement on whether it was correct or incorrect.

Fyfe and colleagues (2012) randomly assigned the 64 second- and third-grade students to one of the two feedback conditions: strategy (5 males, 26 females) and outcome (14 males, 19 females). Students, participants from a larger study from eight general education elementary classrooms across two schools (one public, one private), were identified for the instructional feedback intervention if they scored < 80% on the pretest assessment. Even though random assignment was done at the student level, there were approximately the same numbers of students for both conditions in all classes. Fyfe and colleagues used a pre- and posttest design with a 2-week maintenance follow-up assessment.

Math equivalence was assessed using an assessment with multiple forms. Form A was administered at pretest, and Form B was administered at posttest and follow-up. Forms included items assessing procedure (assessment of correct strategy use), learning (similar to those used in lessons), transfer (different from lesson problems on key elements such as mathematical operation required), and concept (assessment of understanding of equations, equal sign). In addition, researchers evaluated students' working memory and cognitive load to see whether these two qualities affected the impact (i.e., was a moderator for) of instructional feedback on math equivalence. Working memory was assessed using the backward digit span task from the Wechsler Intelligence Scale for Children Working Memory Index (Wechsler, 2003). Cognitive load was measured using a three-item subjective assessment. First, students were asked to rate the difficulty of the items using a Likert-type scale. The next two items measured students' level of frustration when completing math equivalence activities.

Math equivalence was taught using a 12-problem lesson, including six problems with three (i.e., 10 = 3 + ____) or four addends and six problems with five addends. During the lesson, a researcher worked with students one-on-one. As students completed each problem, they were asked to report either their strategy or their outcome to the researcher, depending on which condition they had been randomly assigned to. Following the completion of each problem, the students received strategy or outcome feedback from the researcher and were prompted to move on to the next problem.

Results suggested that both types of instructional feedback improved math outcomes, which were maintained at a 2-week follow-up. The results also suggest that students with higher working memory benefited from strategy feedback for improved levels of conceptual knowledge, as well as transfer problems. Students with lower working memory performed higher following outcome feedback. These findings suggest that, although both forms of instructional feedback improved outcomes, students' working memory capacity may affect which type of feedback is most effective.

Increasing Task Engagement and Improving Academic Performance in an Inclusive Setting

Simonsen and colleagues (2010) examined the impact of schoolwide positive behavior intervention and support (PBIS) on teacher and student behavior at a state-certified nonpublic school for students with disabilities. Students were referred to the school because of aggressive behavior, as the school specialized in applied behavioral analysis techniques for improving students' behavior. The school consisted of students ages 3–22 with disabilities, including emotional disturbance, intellectual disabilities, orthopedic impairments, other health impairments, traumatic brain injury, and visual impairments. Enrollment ranged from 39 to 53 students over 3 years. Students were served at a student-to-staff ratio of 3:1, with some students requiring 1:1 support.

During baseline conditions, the school implemented only secondary (small group) and tertiary (individualized) interventions with no formal schoolwide plan for the supporting the behavior of all students. During the intervention, members of the school team participated in schoolwide PBIS training to develop expectations, as well as the procedures for teaching expectations. In addition, they adopted the Second Step program, a schoolwide social skills training curriculum (Committee for Children, 2002). Most teachers used a token economy system prior to PBIS training. As a part of the training, they were asked to incorporate praise for completing expected behaviors as a means of providing more frequent instructional feedback. To help facilitate the implementation of their schoolwide plan, clinical administrators provided weekly teacher meetings and ongoing professional development.

Researchers collected data on the school climate by measuring teacher behavior, including opportunities to respond (OTR; a stimulus or instruction designed to occasion a response; see Chapter 2), positive feedback (feedback designed to increase the future occurrence of a behavior), and negative feedback (feedback designed to decrease the occurrence of a future behavior). Researchers also collected data on student behavior to determine whether the schoolwide PBIS intervention was effective. Data were collected on the index of serious behavioral incidents (i.e., incidents requiring physical restraint or in which students left campus without permission), as well as the distribution (number of students with 0, 1–5, and 6+ incidents).

Results suggest that the schoolwide PBIS intervention did not improve the overall rates of OTR, positive feedback, and corrective feedback, as rates of OTR and positive feedback were already high and rates of corrective feedback were already low. What did change, however, was the content of the instructional feedback. Before PBIS, staff would praise students on different behaviors on an individual basis. After PBIS implementation, staff would tie instructional feedback to the schoolwide expectations. Schoolwide PBIS implementation resulted in decreases in serious behavioral incidents. The number of students with zero serious incidents increased from 70 to 83% from baseline to year 2 of the intervention.

Summary

These studies represent the variety of ways in which instructional feedback may be implemented in schools. In order to illustrate this variety, models of classroom-based behavioral and academic instructional feedback, as well as a schoolwide model of instructional feedback, have been provided. Table 5.1 presents other academic illustrations, including use of peer feedback in a high school science classroom (Gan & Hattie, 2014) and strategy and outcome-based feedback in ninth-grade math classes (Harks et al., 2012). Also detailed are behavioral examples, including increasing preservice teachers' use of BSP (Rathel et al., 2008) and teachers' use of BSP (Sutherland et al., 2000). In the next section we discuss some of the benefits and challenges associated with providing instructional feedback.

Benefits and Challenges

As discussed at the beginning of this chapter, instructional feedback offers several distinct benefits for students, as well as a few considerations. These are noted briefly in the sections that follow.

Benefits

Incorporating instructional feedback into daily activities provides benefits to both teachers and students by increasing engagement and learning (Hattie, 2009). Instructional feedback can be provided in large-group instruction through the use of clickers or other electronic voting systems (Blood & Gulchak, 2013), written peer feedback (Gan & Hattie, 2014), and increased OTR. It is also effective with small-group or individualized instruction such as targeted BSP for students with challenging behaviors (Allday et al., 2012).

In general, preparing for instructional feedback takes minimal additional time, as it can be done at the same time as regular academic planning. Teachers can review and then incorporate specific feedback relevant to the learning goals and practice opportunities being planned. New teachers and those teachers trying to shift from more negative types of feedback may find it easier to script out feedback phrases in advance. Scripting ideas allows for thoughtful phrasing that might be more difficult to come up with in the moment. However, once teachers' routines and habits for using positive instructional feedback are established, planning for and using the technique will become second nature. Positive instructional feedback creates a learning environment in which students feel safe to take instructional risks, learn from their mistakes, and develop a sense of self-regulated learning (Butler & Winne, 1995; Hattie, 2009). Specifically, feedback is directed at supporting students in demonstrating expected behaviors, improving academic outcomes, and increasing engagement (Kulhavy & Wager, 1993). Overall, increasing instructional feedback will support students' learning of academic content and skills, as well as prosocial behaviors and social interactions, and this is especially true for students with and at risk for disabilities who typically need additional assistance.

Challenges

Potentially, the most challenging part of using instructional feedback is in determining the best type of feedback to use and then carefully selecting the words. Feedback, when used for supporting students' acquisition of academic, behavioral, and social skills, can narrow the gap between current and expected performance (Hattie, 2009). However, when students receive feedback from adults within a criticizing context (or one that is perceived that way by the student), then the feedback can have the unintended consequence of decreasing the students' motivation, perseverance, and sense of self-efficacy (Deci & Ryan, 2000). This is not to say that teachers should not provide feedback for error correction; however, when answers, responses, or behaviors do not meet the expectations or goals, providing *instructional* feedback will improve performance (Gable, Hester, Rock, & Hughes, 2009). Therefore, teachers must carefully plan the delivery of the feedback they use.

Measuring the effectiveness of instructional feedback has methodological challenges given the differing types and schedules of feedback and the variety of ways feedback can be delivered (verbal, written, and electronic), as well as the specific context in which it is used. Hattie (2009), in his synthesis of the evidence, determined that feedback (as a global term for information provided to the learner to reduce the gap between current and expected performance) is an effective practice for improving achievement.

Given the importance of the benefits and relatively few challenges in using instructional feedback, we recommend this easy-to-use strategy in a range of settings to improve academic, behavioral, and social outcomes. The following section presents a step-by-step guide for successfully implementing instructional feedback in your classroom.

Implementing Instructional Feedback in Your Classroom: Checklist for Success

The following steps are also listed in Table 5.2 as an implementation checklist, and a hypothetical illustration of how these steps can be used in a CI3T model at the high school level is provided in Box 5.1.

TABLE 5.2. Implementation Checklist for Success: Instructional Feedback

- Step 1: Identify learning goals.
- Step 2: Provide instruction to meet established goals.
- Step 3: Provide clear directions and checks for understanding.
- Step 4: Plan opportunities for practice and feedback.
- Step 5: Implement active supervision and provide instructional feedback.
- Step 6: Provide time and direction for students to review work or have additional opportunities to practice.
- Step 7: Evaluate instructional practices.
- Step 8: Offer students an opportunity to give feedback on how instructional feedback is being offered.

Note. Butler and Winne (1995); Hattie (2009); Konrad, Helf, and Joseph (2011).

• **Step 1: Identify learning goals.** Teachers can begin by establishing learning goals. Establishing goals may be done solely by the teacher or with input from students. Goal setting is an important skill for developing self-determined behavior (Carter, Lane, Crnobori, Bruhn, & Oakes, 2011) and self-regulated learners (Lane, Harris, et al., 2011), so it is a beneficial activity for students. Teachers may take an instructional approach by teaching and modeling behavioral and instructional goals and then provide practice and feedback to students on goal setting.

Goals should be guided by learning standards, schoolwide behavioral expectations, and identified social competencies and should include performance measures. When a clear goal or purpose has been established, expected outcomes are shared with students. When students and teachers are clear on the expectation, confusion is reduced (Fisher & Frey, 2009). It is commonplace for teachers to post the learning goal or standard and begin the lesson by sharing the goal with students. Adding a clearly stated expected outcome provides clarity for students on how they will know if they have accomplished the intended goal. For example, "practice math facts with 80% or better accuracy."

Further, setting a goal for behavioral or social expectations is also important. If the teacher has planned for group work, goals focused on how the group will work together are needed. Teachers may choose to use the PBIS behavioral expectations for the classroom as a guide for setting the goal prior to beginning work: "Students please remember to show respect for each other and give your best effort during this work block." Similarly, teachers may choose to base these goals on the content addressed in the validated curriculum selected as part of the social skills component of the CI3T plan. Or teachers may select and set specific behavioral goals with a criterion. For example, a teacher may say, "Today I am watching for students focused on the practice activity and I expect you to demonstrate TIGER PRIDE as specified on the PBIS expectation matrix." Teachers are well versed in setting goals. To support students in becoming self-regulated learners, the setting of goals and monitoring progress through feedback should become explicit and intentional.

• **Step 2: Provide instruction to meet established goals.** Instructional feedback is used after instruction is presented. This may be any inquiry-based, direct, or explicit instruction that introduces specific content or skills.

In an academic context, this seems obvious. Teachers design specific, detailed lessons to engage students in learning in order to achieve instructional goals. However, less obvious and equally as important is for teachers to plan instruction related to behavioral and social skills (Lane, Oakes, & Magill, 2014). Engagement, study skills, interpersonal skills, and motivation are behaviors that facilitate academic skills (DiPerna & Elliott, 2002).

Within the context of CI3T models of prevention, students are taught the established behavioral expectations for all school settings (Lane, Menzies, et al., 2013). Setting lessons (e.g., expectations for the hallway, cafeteria, or classroom) are taught to all students schoolwide so that any adult in the building can provide

BSP, one type of instructional feedback. Similarly, schools select social skills or character development curricula targeted on specific school needs and engage students in instruction to learn these skills. Together the integrated framework establishes a safe, positive learning environment. Often the social skill of the week or month is revisited prior to engaging in instruction (e.g., before going into cooperative learning groups) to remind them of how to use this skill and why it will be helpful to do so.

The key is to provide instruction to all students in the areas of academics, behavioral expectations, and social skills (Lane, Kalberg, Bruhn, et al., 2009). Instruction across all domains should be considered to ensure that students have the opportunity for comprehensive skill development as part of the regular school day.

- **Step 3: Provide clear directions and checks for understanding.** After instruction but prior to independent practice with feedback, teachers provide clear directions about the expected activities—group work, project-based assignment, individual writing assignments, independent reading with a comprehension activity, physics lab, graphic design project, and the like. Directions provided both verbally and in writing better support all learners. For older students, teachers may provide scoring rubrics with expectations clearly articulated, task lists, or guides. For younger students, teachers may post models of completed projects, visual prompts, or task lists. For any grade level, teachers may use questions and student responses to check for understanding of directions. One simple strategy is to have green, yellow, and red cups on each table (or for each student). When directions are given, teachers can ask students to rate their understanding of the task. Green cups indicate clear understanding and readiness to proceed, yellow cups indicate the student has the general idea but needs some additional clarification, red cups indicate that they are unsure of how to proceed. Then students with green cups are asked to review the directions with the students with yellow cups displayed, and the teacher attends to students with red cups (after stopping to recognize and thank students with green for helping their peers; Lane, Eisner, et al., 2009). Teachers may also integrate technology using voting systems to assess readiness to proceed to the next task (Blood & Gulchak, 2009). Many strategies can be used to check students' understanding of the task; what is important is that teachers check for clarity before students begin the task.

- **Step 4: Plan opportunities for practice and feedback.** In Step 4, opportunities to practice the lesson objectives are planned. At times, adults may expect students to demonstrate proficiency with new learning immediately after instruction, when in fact students need opportunity to practice with feedback. Prior to instruction, errors in learning or difficulty demonstrating target skills are assumed to be an acquisition deficit, meaning the student has not acquired the behavior, skill, or knowledge (Gresham & Elliott, 2008b). However, once instruction has been provided, students may still (and should be expected to initially) demonstrate fluency deficits, meaning they need more practice to become proficient (Gresham & Elliott, 2007). Practice allows development of proficient and fluent behaviors, skills, or knowledge. For example, research tells us that students need to engage with new vocabulary up to 20 times before the word becomes part of their repertoire (Wolfe & Nevills, 2004). Similarly, students need to practice newly learned behaviors such as turn taking to establish the behavior as a habit.

Feedback is the mechanism that refines learning, and this occurs during practice. For example, if a student practices using a vocabulary word in an incorrect context, the teacher must provide clarification on the use of the word. If the teacher is using self-regulated strategy development for story writing and the student leaves out an element in his or her practice, then the teacher provides feedback to redirect the student to the mnemonic (Lane, Harris, et al., 2011). Feedback provides confirmation to students that they are on the right track. Error correction provides clarification and fine tuning and alerts the teacher when additional instruction is needed.

- **Step 5: Implement active supervision and provide instructional feedback.** After students are clear on the task or activity, teachers actively monitor students during the work time. Teachers are moving around the classroom, listening to student conversations during group work to assess understanding, asking questions for fine tuning, and providing instructional feedback (De Pry & Sugai, 2002). Active supervision (see Chapter 4) supports good student behavior, as well as providing opportunities for instructional feedback. The teacher stops frequently to engage with students as they practice. The feedback is focused on the instructional goal and is specific to the individual student's needs. For example, the teacher provides feedback related to the instructional goal: "Read your paper with a peer and listen for all parts of the essay using the TREE mnemonic" (see Project WRITE; Lane, Harris, Graham, Driscoll, et al., 2011). Focusing on the process instead of simply providing an evaluation (e.g., "you did not include a topic sentence") supports the learner in constructing meaning and provides evidence that can be more broadly applied than can evaluative feedback consisting only of right or wrong (Gan & Hattie, 2014).

- **Step 6: Provide time and direction for students to review work or have additional opportunities to practice.** Students need time to respond to the instructional feedback they are given. Returning to the idea of the feedback loop, learning occurs when students have an opportunity to apply the feedback and receive additional feedback. For learning to take place, the student must have an opportunity to take action (Hattie & Timperley, 2007; Sadler, 1989). Otherwise, the student receives the feedback and then may disregard it (a grade on a paper, or comment stating "rewrite this section") or forget it the next time it is needed.

Teachers are pressured to cover multiple subjects at a rapid pace with little time for reteaching and practice. Monitoring student performance on each learning goal or objective enhances planning for future instruction. Teachers who are actively supervising students and providing prompt feedback during the practice time will have the information needed to quickly adjust teaching methods and strategies. Compare this approach with a more traditional model of teaching— providing assignments and grading them after they are completed (maybe up to a week later). This time-delayed approach does not offer teachers the data they need to respond to student learning until it is too late (e.g., after they are onto the next topic or unit).

• **Step 7: Evaluate instructional practices.** Teachers have multiple evidence-based strategies and practices to support students' academic, behavioral, and social learning. Monitoring student progress by engaging in timely instructional feedback provides data on the effectiveness of the strategy chosen, the delivery of instruction, the amount of practice needed, the pacing, and the expected performance. If teachers observe that a large group of students has difficulty with the concepts or ideas, then reteaching is needed. Likewise, if, through instructional feedback, the teacher learns that only a small group of students is having trouble, then the teacher may pull that group together for additional practice (e.g., after school, during study hall, or while other students are engaging in enrichment activities; Frey & Fisher, 2011). Finally, if only a few students are having difficulty, then the teacher can assume the instruction was effective and provide supports for those few students—such as peer-assisted learning, targeted self-monitoring interventions, or additional Web-based practice with built-in corrective feedback (such as for vocabulary practice, reading comprehension, or math facts; see *www. quizlet.com*).

• **Step 8. Offer students an opportunity to give feedback on how instructional feedback is being offered.** Finally, allow students an opportunity to give input on how instructional feedback is being offered. In Figure 5.3 in Box 5.1, a sample social validity form is provided, offering one option for assessing students' view of this strategy before beginning and after the strategy is implemented for a period of time. This gives the students an opportunity to exert some control in their instructional day, which also fosters intrinsic motivation.

Examining the Effects: How Well Is It Working?

Testing the Strategy: Design Considerations

When implementing instructional feedback, it is important to collect data on student performance to know how well this strategy is working. In many of the studies featured in this book, researchers have used single-case methodology to "test" the intervention effects. This is a particularly useful design approach for teachers, as it is highly flexible and very practical. It can be used with any of the strategies introduced in each chapter.

It is important to use an experimental design such as an ABAB or multiple baseline across settings, tasks, or students to establish a functional relation between the introduction of the intervention and changes in student performance (Gast & Ledford, 2014). In other words, this design helps determine whether or not the intervention worked. This information is helpful to both general education and special education teachers for a variety of reasons. The first, of course, is it allows you to evaluate the effectiveness of your instruction. With this information, you can decide how to adjust your instructional practices so they work better for your students. Second, members of the CI3T team or members of professional learning communities (PLCs) can use these data to determine how students are responding to these low-intensity supports. Before moving on to student-focused Tier 2 (e.g., Check-In/Check-Out, behavior contracts, or self-monitoring strategies) or Tier 3 (e.g., functional assessment-based interventions; Umbreit et al., 2007) supports, we want to be certain we have examined the extent to which teacher-driven strategies (e.g., instructional feedback) have been effective in addressing students' needs (academically, behaviorally, and/or socially). Using an experimental design is one way to show whether or not this has occurred. We recommend these teams (e.g., CI3T and PLC) be composed of a range of individuals, including general and special education teachers, as they each bring unique talents. For example, special education teachers are a critical resource for implementing and delivering specialized intervention; they can assist general educators with evaluating strategy implementation, as well as carefully measuring the effects of any given intervention for a particular student, as is demonstrated in Box 5.1 This is especially critical when focused on more intensive supports, such as functional assessment-based interventions, that require careful monitoring of students' performance (e.g., academic engagement, disruption). The ability to use single-case methodology is a critical skill in assessing the effectiveness of Tier 2 and 3 supports.

These designs begin with a baseline phase during which data on student performance are collected (referred to as the A phase), then the intervention is introduced for the first time (B), while still collecting data on student performance using the same data collection method used during the baseline phase (see Figure 5.1 in Box 5.1). Although it is tempting at this point to say the intervention was effective, two more replications are needed to be certain the intervention was responsible for the change and not something else. One demonstration (e.g., the change from A to B phases) along with two other replications can provide evidence that the introduction of the strategy produced the changes (the shift from B to A and then A to B; Gast & Ledford, 2014).

Although some designs, such as the ABAB design, require removal and then reintroduction of the intervention, it is also possible to explore a functional relation using multiple baseline across setting designs. This means the strategy is used in different settings, such as a different instructional period (math instead of reading) or a different physical location (playground instead of the lunchroom).

Making Certain the Strategy Is in Place: Treatment Integrity

In addition to using an experimental design to test the intervention, collecting treatment integrity data helps determine the extent to which the intervention is being implemented as planned. Figure 5.2 in Box 5.1 is an example of a treatment integrity checklist for instructional feedback. Although there are many different ways to collect treatment integrity data, one way is to have the teacher collect these data each day by indicating the degree to which each intervention component was implemented as planned for each student. For example, in Figure 5.2, each item is a completed using a 3-point Likert-type scale as follows: 0 = *not in place*, 1 = *partially in place*, or 2 = *completely in place*. Each day the items are summed, divided by the total number of points possible, and divided by 100 to obtain a percentage of implementation for each student. These data can be used to interpret intervention outcomes (see Box 5.1). In addition, behavior component checklists not only determine the level of implementation but also serve as a prompt or reminder to implement each step.

Using an outside observer to collect treatment integrity data for approximately 25% of the sessions in each phase is recommended. An additional observer is important for establishing the accuracy of the data collected.

Examining Stakeholders' Views: Social Validity

Finally, in addition to collecting information on student performance and implementation (treatment integrity), it is important to understand how stakeholders felt about the intervention goals, procedures, and intended outcomes. Figure 5.3 in Box 5.1 is an example of a measure examining one elementary student's perceptions of the social validity of instructional feedback.

It is important to obtain all stakeholders' views—the teacher, student, and parent—ideally before the intervention begins and again at the conclusion of the first "test." If social validity is low at the onset of the intervention, then it is wise to provide additional training to increase people's knowledge of the strategies, as well as their confidence in using the strategy prior to implementation. In theory (and in some instances in actuality; see Lane, Kalberg, Bruhn, et al., 2009), the opinions of those implementing and participating in the intervention may predict the extent to which the interventions are implemented as planned. In essence, a socially valid intervention is likely to be put in place with a high degree of integrity, leading to improvements in student performance that maintain over time and in new settings and with new people.

BOX 5.1. A Hypothetical Illustration of Instructional Feedback in a CI3T Model

Miss Germer is a special education teacher at Verde Mission High School, where they implement a comprehensive, integrated, three-tiered (CI3T) model of prevention. As part of their CI3T plan, students engage in academic coursework designed to meet graduation requirements, use a positive behavior intervention and support (PBIS) plan, and address character development using the Walker Social Skills Curriculum—The ACCESS Program (Walker, Todis, Holmes, & Horton, 1988; teaching one lesson each week). Miss Germer and the general education teacher, Mr. Carroll, provide inclusive educational experiences for students with special needs. During one of the professional learning community (PLC) meetings, Miss Germer and Mr. Carroll noticed there were three ninth-grade students who scored in the moderate-risk range on the Student Risk Screening Scale (SRSS; Drummond, 1994) and also had low quiz and test grades. In addition, they had three to five tardies in their first-period Spanish class. Because one credit in a foreign language is needed for graduation, Miss Germer decided to observe in Mr. Carroll's Spanish class to offer strategies that Mr. Carroll might use to better engage these students.

Support	Description	Entry criteria	Data to monitor progress	Exit criteria
Instructional feedback	Specific information for students from a teacher or peer to confirm, fine-tune, clarify, and restructure current schemas. Verbal, written, or technology-based specific feedback on processes and progress	SRSS score in the moderate-risk range, or three assignment grades in any class at C or below	*Student performance:* • Homework, quiz, and test grades • Percentage of work completed *Treatment integrity:* Component checklist *Social validity:* Student-completed survey	Grade point average of 2.5 or higher; SRSS scores in the low-risk range

Miss Germer noticed that although the majority of the class seemed to quickly engage in the activities designed to provide practice (spoken and written), about a third of them did not. She made the following observations. First, instruction was well planned and clear directions were provided; however, no time was allotted to check for understanding beyond the "Any questions?" prompt. Miss Germer heard students whisper "What are we supposed to do?" after they were asked to begin work. Second, once the assignments were given, Mr. Carroll used that time to answer parent emails, grade assignments from other classes, and input grades. Therefore, he was unable to gauge students' understanding until he graded their practice papers. Mr. Carroll was continually frustrated that a third of the class did not seem to do well on assignments, and the problem was compounded by the fact that he frequently did not have this information until after they had moved on to the next unit. Therefore, Miss Germer recommended that Mr. Carroll consider a classwide instructional feedback strategy. They set a plan for seeing how the three students of concern, specifically, responded to this low-intensity support. Miss Germer thought this strategy would benefit not only these three students but also all the other students. In particular, she noticed that one student, Artie, who received special education services under the category of emotional disturbance, didn't seem to receive any response from Mr. Carroll beyond criticism (e.g., "Please stop disrupting the class." and "Do you need to work in the hall?").

Miss Germer worked through the eight-step process with Mr. Carroll as follows. These steps can also be found in Table 5.2.

Preparing for and Delivering Instructional Feedback: The Intervention

• **Step 1: Identify learning goals.** Miss Germer worked with Mr. Carroll to develop instructional goals to share with the students. He was clear on his learning objective but did not have a clear procedure for making sure students also knew the lesson's goal(s). Examples of goals they wrote were the following:

- Students will ask and answer questions related to travel in a Spanish-speaking country. Specifically, questions will be related to finding their desired location, checking into a room or hotel, asking for directions to a restaurant, and paying their bill. Students will work in pairs to ask and answer the five questions each and practice by writing the questions to apply to a travel brochure.
- Students will read and interpret a travel brochure written in Spanish. They will answer the questions they wrote in the previous activity as it relates to the reading. Students will complete the activity independently and turn in written responses.
- Students will work together completing activities in a way that values each student's contributions and completes the project within the time allotted—meeting expectations of "Be Respectful" and "Be Accountable."

• **Step 2: Provide instruction to meet established goals.** Next, Mr. Carroll reviewed his lesson plans to specifically account for instruction to support students in accomplishing the goals stated in Step 1. Although he typically thought of his role more in terms of academic outcomes, he began to see the role that the school-wide behavioral expectations played in students' class success. He built time in his lesson plan to review behavioral expectations briefly at the start of class and before student work times. Mr. Carroll gave a lesson on using Spanish vocabulary related to travel, modeled with guided practice with a sample travel brochure, asking questions related to the travel to model the practice activity. Then Mr. Carroll gave specific directions for working in pairs to complete the practice activities related to the schoolwide expectations of "Be Respectful" and "Be Accountable," referring to the posted expectation matrix of classroom behaviors.

•**Step 3: Provide clear directions and checks for understanding.** From Miss Germer's observations, Mr. Carroll felt confident in the clarity of his directions, and so he refined his lesson to include time at the end of instruction to allow for clarification and questions before students began work. When giving directions, Mr. Carroll referred to the lesson, pointing out how this demonstrated the activity expected. He used two strategies to check for understanding. First, when students were going to work in groups, he gave students 1 minute to talk through the assignment with each other. At the end of the 1 minute, one member of each group asked any clarifying questions. Second, when independent work was expected, Mr. Carroll provided a checklist on the board for students to confirm completion (i.e., read travel brochure; answer the five questions that were written with my partner; proofread and confirm answers with the reading [brochure]). Mr. Carroll also emailed Artie a copy of the checklist to cross off each task as completed on his iPad. This individual list was also shared with other students at their request.

•**Step 4: Plan opportunities for practice and feedback.** Students needed opportunities to practice speaking and writing the newly learned travel-related vocabulary, and so Mr. Carroll planned activities with this in mind. Based on the feedback from Miss Germer and the selected strategy to increase students' engagement in practice activities, he planned to use active supervision to monitor students' engagement during practice and to offer instructional feedback to confirm, fine-tune, and clarify students' application of the new learning to avoid practicing errors, to increase engagement and work completion, and to improve learning.

•**Step 5: Implement active supervision and provide instructional feedback.** Next, the major change in Mr. Carroll's instruction was that, instead of catching up on email and grading, he was actively engaged with students during practice. Mr. Carroll used active supervision while students were working in pairs and independently. He monitored assignment progress and behavior and provided feedback to pairs as well as individual students. He provided feedback to students on process, for example, "Read your sentence aloud and check the verb conjugations" and "Use your dictionary to confirm your word choice for that sentence." He also commented on their level of engagement: "This group is really showing respect for each other by listening to everyone's ideas" and "I saw that you revised your response based on your group's feedback." In some instances, he distributed a PBIS ticket paired with this behavior-specific praise (BSP).

•**Step 6: Provide time and direction for students to review work or have additional opportunities to practice.** Mr. Carroll paid attention to and took notes on the vocabulary that students clearly understood and offered BSP to the class and individual students. He used the information from misunderstandings to develop the next day's bell work so that students had additional practice on key concepts that needed revisiting.

•**Step 7: Evaluate instructional practices.** Each day after class, Mr. Carroll used the information he gathered on student questions during the check for understanding to refine his directions. He and Miss Germer reflected on changes observed and measured in student performance. He also used observations to refine the types of practice assignments, length of assignments, and instruction to make certain that he was providing the information students needed to be successful in meeting the goals.

•**Step 8. Offer students an opportunity to give feedback on how instructional feedback is being offered.** Miss Germer and Mr. Carroll were interested in the students' opinions about having increased instructional feedback from Mr. Carroll during Spanish class assignments instead of only after assignments were completed. They created a five-item, Likert-type survey to assess students' initial perceptions of the plan for offering more immediate feedback prior to assessment during Spanish. These data were averaged across all students to gain a sense of the opinion of the class as a whole. However, they also looked at the opinions of students for whom instructional feedback was used as a targeted support (see Artie's opinions in Figure 5.3). Teachers also asked students for their opinions on the instructional feedback strategy after using the strategy for the travel vocabulary unit to see whether the strategy meet, exceeded, or fell short of their initial expectations.

Looking at How Well Instructional Feedback Worked

Miss Germer and Mr. Carroll decided to collect specific data on academic engagement (referred to as academic engaged time [AET]), work accuracy (percentage of correct answers), and attendance for the three students who were initially failing the class to see how they responded to this low-intensity support. Together they created an operational definition of AET that included a definition as well as examples and non-examples so that everyone could be certain they were observing the same behaviors.

- *Label*. Academic engaged time (AET).
- *Definition*. AET refers to engaging in teacher-assigned activities.
- *Examples*. Examples of academic engaged time included reading the Spanish textbook or supplemental readings, working on the assigned practice tasks, engaging in conversations with group members related to the instructional task, and using materials according to their intended purposes.
- *Non-examples*. Non-examples included engaging in tasks other than those assigned by the teacher, talking about topics not related to the instructional task, and using materials for other than their intended purpose.

AET was collected using a momentary time-sampling procedure in which Miss Germer wore an electronic device (a MotivAider®) preprogrammed to vibrate every 2 minutes over a 40-minute period during independent work time in Spanish class. Before collecting data, Miss Germer and Mr. Carroll practiced using this recording system together to make sure they collected academic engagement data reliably.

Specifically, they practiced observing the three target students using a self-constructed interval data collection form over 3 consecutive days.

In Figure 5.1, the three figures depict Artie's (Panel A), Paola's (Panel B), and Becca's (Panel C) AET as illustrations. Some of the data points in Artie's graph have an asterisk (*) above them indicating which sessions were observed by both Miss Germer and Mr. Carroll to make sure they were accurately recording the behavior. On these sessions (2, 5, 7, 10, 13, 16, and 19), they collected reliability on the AET data for each of the students.

In addition to collecting information on AET, Mr. Carroll also collected data on work accuracy (graphed in Figure 5.1). Work accuracy was evaluated using the assignment scores and grades. Scores ranged from 0 to 100% completion.

To make certain the intervention was used regularly and as planned, either Mr. Carroll or Miss Germer completed a daily treatment integrity form (see Figure 5.2 for treatment integrity data on during the instructional feedback intervention). Each day they recorded whether the intervention component was *not in place* (0), *partially in place* (1), or *fully in place* (2). Figure 5.2 shows the percentages of implementation for each session for 1 week (at the bottom of each column). These data were very important, as they help to interpret how students responded to instructional feedback. For example, in looking at panels A, B, and C in Figure 5.1, the AET data were much lower during baseline compared with the first introduction of instructional feedback intervention. Then, the levels of AET and assignment accuracy again declined when feedback was removed during the withdrawal phase and again increased when the intervention was reintroduced—with the exception of session 10. On this day, the level of integrity was lower than the other days (particularly for Artie and Paola), with only a partial check of understanding, practice, and feedback. In general, when the intervention was in place as planned, all three students were more engaged and had higher assignment accuracy.

Prior to beginning and at the end of the intervention, Miss Germer and Mr. Carroll decided to ask the students their opinions about the use of instructional feedback. They asked all students in the class to rate five short statements about their experience (see Figure 5.3). In brief, all students—including Artie (ratings shown in Figure 5.3)—liked having Mr. Carroll clarify directions and provide feedback during practice. They indicated they earned better grades when they received feedback from Mr. Carroll during practice. For Artie, the intervention actually exceeded his initial expectations (scores increase from 60 to 100%), and he believed that his grades improved because of the feedback he received.

After running this "test," Miss Germer and Mr. Carroll put the intervention back in place and continued to monitor student performance. They continued until each student had 5 consecutive weeks of daily academic engagement at 80% or better and assignment accuracy at 90% or better for in-class practice. Mr. Carroll also saw class quiz and test scores improve. After all students met these criteria, the teachers decided to continue using instructional feedback as part of regular instruction, as they saw benefits for all students and it was easy to incorporate into each lesson.

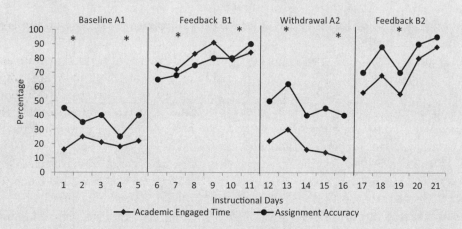

Panel A. Artie's Academic Engagement and Spanish Assignment Accuracy

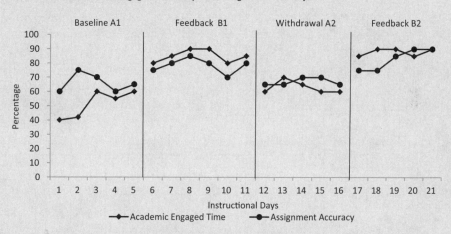

Panel B. Paola's Academic Engagement and Spanish Assignment Accuracy

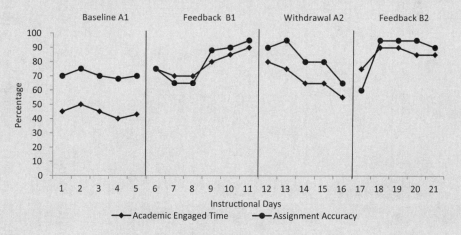

Panel C. Becca's Academic Engagement and Spanish Assignment Accuracy

FIGURE 5.1. Examining the effects: Percentage of students' academic engaged time (diamonds) and assignment accuracy (circles) during Spanish class.

Teacher: Mr. Carroll   ☒ Self-report   ☐ Observer   Scale: 0 = Not in place
1 = Partially in place
2 = Fully in place

Lesson: _Spoken and written interpersonal communication: The student understands a variety of vocabulary, including idiomatic and culturally appropriate expressions._

Component	Session 6 Tuesday 3/5/2016 Artie (0 1 2)	Paola (0 1 2)	Becca (0 1 2)	Session 7 Wednesday 3/6/2016 Artie (0 1 2)	Paola (0 1 2)	Becca (0 1 2)	Session 8 Thursday 3/7/2016 Artie (0 1 2)	Paola (0 1 2)	Becca (0 1 2)	Session 9 Friday 3/8/2016 Artie (0 1 2)	Paola (0 1 2)	Becca (0 1 2)	Session 10 Monday 3/21/2016 Artie (0 1 2)	Paola (0 1 2)	Becca (0 1 2)
I identified and shared learning goals.	2	2	2	2	2	2	2	2	2	2	2	2	2	2	2
I provided instruction to meet the established goals.	2	2	2	2	2	2	2	2	2	2	2	2	2	2	2
I provided clear directions and checked for understanding.	2	2	2	0	0	0	2	2	2	1	1	1	1	1	1
Students had opportunities to practice.	2	2	2	2	2	2	2	2	2	2	—	2	1	1	1
I used active supervision and provided instructional feedback.	2	2	2	0	2	2	1	2	2	1	—	2	1	1	2
I provided time, direction for students to review work or have additional opportunities to practice.	2	2	2	2	2	2	2	2	2	2	—	2	1	1	1
I evaluated instruction based on student response.	2	2	2	2	2	2	2	2	2	2	—	2	2	2	2
Percentage Session Integrity: (Total points earned/# points possible) × 100	100%	100%	100%	71%	86%	86%	93%	100%	100%	86%	—%	93%	64%	64%	79%

FIGURE 5.2. Making certain the strategy is in place: Treatment integrity checklist used by Ms. Germer and Mr. Carroll to monitor the extent to which each step was put in place as planned. For session 9, Paola had an early dismissal from Spanish class and, therefore, (–) was used to indicate that she was not present and did not receive the instructional feedback support for that day.

SOCIAL VALIDITY FORM: INSTRUCTIONAL FEEDBACK

I would like your opinion, Artie	0 No, not really	1 sometimes	2 Yes, definitely
I would like to have questions answered before beginning an assignment in Spanish.			✓
I would like my teacher to answer questions and provide clarification before we begin an assignment.			✓
I would feel more successful if my teacher let me know I was on the right track while I was working on the assignment in class.		✓	
It would be helpful for my teacher to give me more practice during bell work to clarify information that I am unsure of before I am asked to take a test or quiz.		✓	
I think that I would get better grades in Spanish if I received feedback during class practice assignments.	✓		
Percentage: (total number/total number possible) × 100 =	60%		

I would like your opinion again, Artie	0 No, not really	1 sometimes	2 Yes, definitely
I liked having questions answered before beginning my work.			✓
I liked that my teacher answered my questions and helped me when I was working.			✓
I felt more successful because my teacher let me know I was on the right track.			✓
It was helpful for my teacher to give me more practice during bell work to clarify information that I was unsure of before I took a test or quiz.			✓
I got better grades in Spanish because I received feedback during class practice assignments.			✓
Percentage: (total number/total number possible) × 100 =	100%		

FIGURE 5.3. Examining stakeholders' views: Social validity form developed by Ms. Germer and Mr. Carroll to examine students' views on the use of instructional feedback during Spanish class.

Summary

Instructional feedback is a highly effective strategy with strong evidence as supporting student learning (Hattie, 2009). It is a relatively easy-to-use strategy requiring minimal preparation that can be used to confirm and fine-tune understanding, clarify misinformation, and restructure current schemas (Butler & Winne, 1995). Instructional feedback is appropriate for use in PreK–12 classrooms across academic, behavioral, and social skill domains. Used with active supervision, instructional feedback offers benefits for teachers and students alike. Teachers access on-the-spot data regarding instructional choices, and students receive prompt feedback to correct errors and receive confirmation of progress. Another feature is that teachers develop a context for supporting all learners by providing prompt and individualized positive and specific feedback; in this way students who may not elicit positive teacher interactions—those with behavioral and learning challenges—benefit from this strategy (Alber et al., 1999). Ideally, all students gain skills in developing self-regulated learning. This strategy is designed to support that effort.

CHAPTER 6

A Look at High-Probability Request Sequences

Within schools that employ multi-tiered prevention models such as comprehensive, integrated, three-tiered (CI3T; Lane, Kalberg, & Menzies, 2009) models, positive behavior interventions and supports (PBIS; Sugai & Horner, 2002b), and response to intervention (RTI; D. Fuchs & Fuchs, 2006), educators utilize proactive, positive practices that focus on environmental conditions as the target of systemic change. The relation between individuals and their environment is central to these models. Over the past few decades, educators have moved away from previously used deficit models in which educators looked first to the individual to determine interventions to ameliorate academic deficits and then most often resorted to punitive practices to address problematic behaviors or social skill deficits. One way in which educators now respond to students' needs is through environmental changes of events that immediately precede academic and behavioral problems, known as antecedent-based intervention (Davis & Brady, 1993; Kern & Clemens, 2007). The focus of this chapter is on using one type of antecedent-based intervention called *high-probability (high-p) request sequences* (Mace et al., 1988). High-*p* requests are designed to increase the likelihood of students engaging in low-probability (low-*p*) behaviors. High-*p* behaviors are those that the student is most likely to comply with or demonstrate (e.g., touch your nose, write your name), and low-*p* behaviors are those the student is unlikely to comply with or demonstrate (e.g., transitioning between tasks, completing work).

Noncompliance in the school setting is one of the most prevalent concerns of teachers (Esch & Fryling, 2013) and often results in students being sent to time-out or the principal's office, effectively escaping the undesired task or behavior.

In contrast, when students follow teacher directions (i.e., comply), they are more likely to display reduced levels of disruption, increased academic engaged time (AET), and more practice with peer interactions (Lane, Smither, Huseman, Guffey, & Fox, 2007). Noncompliant behaviors may be sustained when a teacher unintentionally reinforces the student's behavior by providing the escape of the nonpreferred activity or task (Umbreit et al., 2007). For example, a student is asked to take out his writing journal and pencil, the student responds by putting his head down on his desk, the teacher repeats the request, the student yells or cries, and the teacher asks the student to leave the room or learning space. Other times the student may put his head down and, because no classroom disruption occurs, the teacher may not make the second request and continue instruction with the other students. In either case, the student does not comply with the request, resulting in the student escaping the writing task. Students who do not engage in learning activities have lower rates of academic and social success (Pianta, Hamre, & Allen, 2012). Utilizing fairly simple antecedent-based strategies such as high-p request sequences can increase the likelihood the student will follow teacher directions and engage in learning tasks. In this chapter we offer steps for using the high-p strategy to increase compliance and student engagement in classroom activities.

What Is the High-Probability Request Sequence Strategy?

The high-probability (high-p) request strategy is implemented by the teacher, who requests behaviors that the student is likely to respond to, provides reinforcement for appropriate responding, and then delivers a low-probability (low-p) request in close succession to the previous reinforcement (e.g., within 10 seconds; Davis & Brady, 1993). Compliance with the high-p requests, in effect, generalizes to the low-p requests, resulting in increased compliance for the low-p request (Mace et al., 1988). The use of this strategy can result in highly durable behavioral changes, as naturally occurring reinforcement (e.g., praise, successful completion of tasks, peer interactions) sustains the increased compliance with the low-p behavior (e.g., completing classroom assignments, engaging with peers; Stokes & Baer, 1977; Davis, Brady, Hamilton, McEvoy, & Williams, 1994).

Behavioral momentum was theorized by Nevin, Mandell, and Atak (1983), who likened the persistence of behavior to Newton's law of motion in terms of its resistance to change. Mass is represented by "the level of reinforcement associated with a specific stimulus condition" and velocity represented by the "rate of responding" (Lee, 2006, p. 313). Mace and colleagues (1988) applied this theory to the high-p request sequence strategy, by which the high-p request compliance and reinforcement for the high-p behavior serve to change the momentum of the behavior, thus increasing the student's response for a low-p behavior. For example, a student responds to three high-p requests, such as "touch your nose," "touch your ear," "touch the table," receiving reinforcement for each compliance; then the low-*p* "pick up your pencil" is delivered with a greater chance of compliance based on the increased levels of compliance and reinforcement for compliance immediately prior to the request. Much of the initial work with high-*p* request sequences targeted increasing compliance in young children (Davis, Brady, Williams, & Hamilton, 1992), compliance in adults with severe disabilities (Mace & Belfiore, 1990; Mace et al., 1988), and responding to social interactions in children with severe disabilities (Davis et al., 1994). All studies were conducted in specialized settings, such as the home, clinical environments, and self-contained special education settings. However, since these early experiments, high-*p* request sequences have been used successfully in general education contexts with school-age students. This chapter reviews the application of the theory of behavioral momentum through high-*p* request sequences to increase students' work completion, decrease the amount of time needed to engage in a task or transition between tasks/activities, and increase the use of social skills (Banda & Kubina, 2006; Lee, Belfiore, Scheeler, Hua, & Smith, 2004; Lee & Laspe, 2003; Wehby & Hollahan, 2000).

This strategy can be seen in regularly used compliance practices in many early childhood classrooms; for example, when teachers gather students at circle time on the carpet, they may use a simple song to prompt students to keep their hands to themselves: "Open, shut them. Open, shut them. Give a little clap. Open, shut them. Open, shut them. Put them in your lap." This rhyme is intended to increase compliance beyond what might be achieved through a request by the teacher to "please put your hands in your lap." Although this is a simplistic example, the principle holds true for other classroom and social activities. For academic work completion activities, the high-*p* request strategy can be used to reduce the amount of time to begin assignments by creating tasks that intersperse preferred tasks (high-*p*) with the new, desired activities or tasks (low-*p*). For example, students may be asked to spell three words that they are familiar with and can easily spell and write before beginning a low-*p* writing activity (Lee & Laspe, 2003).

Why Are High-Probability Request Sequences Effective?

Far too often noncompliance is met with punishment procedures that, in fact, may be serving to maintain the noncompliant behavior. As previously mentioned, if the punishment results in removal from the activity or environment, then an escape-motivated behavior will be reinforced, thereby increasing the probability that the behavior will occur again (Cooper et al., 2007). Within proactive prevention models such as CI3T, teacher practices serve to provide a context for appropriate responding and reinforcement for the desired response or behavior (Lane et al., 2013). Higher rates of appropriate behaviors allow students to fully engage in their academic and social programs and also solicit natural reinforcement that maintains the desired behaviors.

Supporting Research for High-Probability Request Sequences

Studies examining the use of high-*p* requests have targeted peer interactions, classroom transitions, math work completion, journal writing, compliance with parent requests, and feeding. Selected studies are described in this section as illustrations of the high-*p* request strategy's use in increasing desired student behaviors (low *p*). A summary of these and other applications of this strategy are provided in Table 6.1.

Increasing Compliance during Inclusive Elementary Classroom Transitions

Transitions in the classroom between tasks and settings can waste precious instructional time. Ysseldyke, Christenson, Thurlow, and Bakewell (1989) found that 14% of instructional time consisted of preparing and transitioning between tasks (e.g., taking out and putting away materials). Roth, Brooks-Gunn, Livner, and Hofferth (2003) found a similar rate of *maintenance* activities (e.g., bathroom breaks, cleaning up, announcements, unpacking), with 14.6% of the elementary school day spent on these tasks. Transitions occur frequently and may prompt noncompliance in students—for example, some students may not want to leave a preferred task—further adding to the time that transitions require.

Ardoin, Martens, and Wolfe (1999) worked with a second-grade teacher to examine the utility of the high-*p* request strategy on the noncompliance of three typically developing students. As part of the regular routine, the teacher provided one five-step direction for students transitioning to morning calendar time. The direction included actions such as "clear your desk" and "take out a pencil" and was delivered in the same order each day. These five steps were considered low-*p* requests, as the three students participating in the study did not often comply with the requested steps. The researchers worked with the teacher to generate a list of high-*p* requests of a similar topographical nature (e.g., "clap your hands," "touch your head") and subsequently tested the behaviors on the list. To test the identified high-*p* requests, the teacher gave the high-*p* requests on five different occasions, one at a time, at 15-second intervals. If the students complied in 100% of the sessions, these tested high-*p* requests were retained on the list and were used as the high-*p* requests.

The authors used a multielement design to test the intervention. Prior to implementing the intervention, the teacher delivered the five-step direction with a 20-second wait time for compliance between each step. Students were not praised for compliance. Compliance or noncompliance was recorded for each request, along with the time to respond (i.e., latency) up to the end of the 20-second wait time. Once the participating students' patterns of responding were measured (baseline), the intervention began. The teacher had a written script with the high-*p* requests, students' names for delivering praise, and low-*p* requests. The script supported the teacher in randomizing the high-*p* requests and allowed all participating students to receive praise. To implement the strategy, the teacher gave three consecutive high-*p* requests 5 seconds apart before each of the low-*p* transition requests. The teacher provided praise to students according to the names listed on the script. Once high levels of student compliance with the low-*p* transition requests was observed, the teacher faded the support by reducing the high-*p* requests from three to two prior to each transition direction. Following the same pattern, the high-*p* requests were further reduced to one per transition request. The intervention lasted, with fading, for approximately 20 sessions. Follow-up data were collected 2–3 weeks after the high-*p* one-request phase ended (so, through all three phases). During each phase the low-*p* requests were independently tested to see whether the effects of the high-*p* responding had transferred to the low-*p* requests, thus increasing the compliance to the low *p*.

Using the high-*p* requests to increase compliance for the transition requests (low *p*) increased compliance in all three students; however, the results for two students were inconsistent. Authors suggested that lower levels of praise provided (treatment integrity concern) may have affected the responding for one student. Another finding was that students with lower levels of low-*p* compliance were also observed to have lower levels of high-*p* compliance. These findings illustrate two important points. First, monitoring treatment integrity is critical, and, second, for this strategy to be effective, the high-*p* requests must elicit compliance, or the desired behaviors. Without the compliance to high-*p* requests, the behavioral momentum is not established (Lee, 2006).

Treatment integrity data for the sequence of the strategy was 100%, although there were lower levels of praise for compliance. In fact, praise for the student with the highest level of response to the low *p* was at 100%; meanwhile, praise was delivered only 56% of the time for the student with the lowest response. This highlights the critical nature of assessing treatment integrity for all prevention and intervention programs and strategies (Gresham, 1989). Without these data we might assume that the student with the lower response was not responsive to the intervention, when in fact the intervention was not delivered with sufficient fidelity.

Social validity data from the teacher's perspective showed that she found the intervention procedures appropriate and effective for the given problem. Social validity was high, with a score of 5.7 out of 6. Teacher acceptability and student outcomes indicated that the high-*p* strategy was feasible and effective when used by the classroom teacher in a general education setting, specifically when supporting students in transitioning between activities.

TABLE 6.1. Supporting Research: High-Probability Requests

Authors and journal	Students	Intervention setting	Intervention	Measures	Design
Davis, Brady, Hamilton, McEvoy, & Williams (1994). Effects of high-probability requests on the social interactions of young children with severe disabilities (JABA)*	N = 3 male children (Max, age 5; Tim, age 6; Alan, age 6), all diagnosed with severe autism, mental retardation, speech handicap	Play settings with invited peers (n = 8 typically developing boys and girls) Regular school campus and afterschool day care Self-contained classroom and playground	Peer play activities with high p used to increase social interactions. 1. Preferred toys selected 2. A pool of low-p social requests generated by adults 3. 10 trials of low p conducted to make sure child could perform request (< 50% = low p) 4. Same procedure for high p (> 80% = high p) 5. Typical peers trained to recognize students' initiations and responses 6. 3–5 high-p requests given in rapid succession (10 seconds), praise upon compliance, low p delivered within 5 seconds of third consecutive compliance	*Dependent variables:* Direct observation of prompted and unprompted behaviors: initiations, responses, duration of interactions, low-p and high-p responses *Treatment integrity:* Procedural integrity of low-p and high-p responses recorded and percentages reported by student; range M = 92–97% *Social validity:* Not measured	Multiple baseline across participants
Belfiore, Lee, Vargas, & Skinner (1997). Effects of high-preference single-digit mathematics problem completion on multiple-digit mathematics problem performance. (JABA)*	N = 2 female students (Allison, age 14, and Roberta, age 15)	Classroom in a community-based alternative education school	1. Preference assessment (both girls referred single-digit problems) 2. Baseline: low-preference packets (five three-digit problems) 3. Intervention: high-preference packets included interspersal of single-digit problems with multiple-digit problems (see text p. 129).	*Dependent variables:* 1. Worksheet selection (during preference assessment phase) 2. Latency (during baseline and intervention) *Treatment integrity:* procedural components were collected during 40% of sessions, with 100% agreement *Social validity:* Not measured	ABAB reversal design

Study	Participants	Setting	Procedure	Dependent variables	Design
Ardoin, Martens, & Wolfe (1999) Using high-probability instruction sequences with fading to increase student compliance during transitions (JABA)*	$N = 3$ students, nominated for general noncompliance	Second-grade general education classroom; 20 students, 1 teacher	High-p requests paired with 5-step daily transition sequence 1. A list of high-p requests generated and tested 2. Three high-p requests provided prior to the low-p transition steps 3. Teacher prompted to praise target students by name and other students randomly contingent on compliance 4. Once students responded with high levels of low-p compliance, high-p prompts were faded from 3 to 2 to 1	*Dependent variables:* Percent compliance with low-p requests; mean observation session latency for compliance within 20 seconds *Treatment integrity:* Monitored daily by observer. Integrity of the high-p sequence use was 100%; teacher use of praise was monitored 44% of session with 100%, 83%, and 56% (low use of praise was used to explain limited response for that student) *Social validity:* Teacher-completed Likert-type scale, Intervention Rating Profile (IRP-15; Martens, Witt, Elliott, & Darveaux, 1985)	Multielemental design
Wehby & Hollahan (2000) Effects of high-probability requests on the latency to initiate academic tasks (JABA)*	13-year-old female with a learning disability in written language and math, typical intellect	General education classroom (grade not reported)	High-p requests for math assignment completion compliance. 1. Instruction and modeling by teacher 2. Teacher used proximity with student to provide request sequences 3. High-p request given by teacher if compliance within 10 seconds, praise provided and next high p given (3 consecutive compliances) 4. Low p given 5. Teacher walked away	*Dependent variables:* 1. Occurrences of low-p requests, high-p requests, and praise 2. Latency of engagement of the low p 3. Compliance with high p 4. Disengagement with low p > 10 seconds Direct observation recorded with MOOSES (Tapp, Wehby, & Ellis, 1995) 30-minute daily sessions, IOA on 33% of sessions *Treatment integrity:* Measured and reported (95% adherence) *Social validity:* Not measured	Single-case design ABABACB

123

(continued)

TABLE 6.1. (continued)

Authors and journal	Students	Intervention setting	Intervention	Measures	Design
Dawson et al. (2003) Use of the high-probability instructional sequence and escape extinction in a child with food refusal (JABA)	3-year-old female with developmental delays and gastrostomy (G) tube dependence	Day treatment program	Four conditions of the interventions: 1: Escape + No High *p* 2: Escape + High *p* 3: Escape Extinction + No High *p* 4: Escape Extinction + High *p* 1. Defined and tested low-*p* behaviors 2. Generated list of high-*p* behaviors 3. Presented food at 30-second intervals 4. During high *p*, compliance with three high-*p* requests preceded low-*p* accepting and swallowing spoonful of food) 5. Verbal praise for low *p* within 5 seconds	*Dependent variables:* 1. Compliance with low *p* within 5 seconds 2. Low-*p* request at 30-second intervals 3. Measured until 12 low-*p* compliances *Treatment integrity:* Not measured *Social validity:* Not measured	Multielement and reversal designs
Lee & Laspe (2003) Using high-probability request sequences to increase journal writing (JBE)	*N* = 4 students, ages 10 and 11, one student with a learning disability and emotional disturbance, two students with traumatic brain injury, and one student with an unspecified neurological impairment	Public elementary school, self-contained special education class for students with multiple disabilities. One teacher and two instructional assistants, language arts period	1. High-*p* and low-*p* tasks were identified. High-*p* words were selected from the classroom word wall. 2. To test the high-*p* selected words, the teacher asked students to write 10 words per day from the wall for 5 days; if request was complied with in 3 seconds, then it was retained as a high-*p* word. 3. Story starters were selected as the low-*p* requests and assessed. The teacher presented the starter and student selected a happy, sad, or neutral face to indicate preference. 4. Four conditions were tested:	*Dependent variable:* Number of words written in 20 minutes *Independent variable:* Intervention efficiency measured by the number of high-*p* requests and verbal prompts given *Treatment integrity:* Checklist of procedures completed by a second teacher for 15% of sessions Reported at 100% *Social validity:* Not measured	Alternating-treatments design with reversal components

Study	Participants	Setting	Conditions/Procedures	Measures	Design
			Condition 1: When off task for 1 minute, teacher prompted students to write three high-*p* words, then continue on story prompt. Condition 2: Same as condition 1 except teacher provided verbal praise for compliance with high *p*. Condition 3: Same as condition 1 except in place of the high *p*, student was prompted. to continue writing. Condition 4: Same as condition 3 with the addition of verbal praise.	*Dependent variables:* Percent compliance with the low *p* within 5 seconds and completion of the low *p* (e.g., "turn off the TV") and the high *p* *Treatment integrity:* Second observer of 33% sessions for adherence to correct instructions; reported at 100% (IOA not collected) *Social validity:* Not measured	Concurrent multiple-baseline design across low-*p* tasks and an alternating-treatment design comparing two conditions
Esch & Fryling (2013) A comparison of two variations of the high-probability instructional sequence with a child with autism (ETC)	6-year-old male child diagnosed with autism; behaviors of concern were tantrums and physical aggression	Student's home, living room and dining room	1. Preferred toys for high-*p* leisure instructions and high-*p* behaviors for maintenance instructions were identified by adults and through observation (90% compliance on two 10-trial blocks). 2. Low-*p* behaviors were determined by parents. 3. Condition 1: High-*p* maintenance instructions provided and child complied within 5 seconds: general praise given and the next high *p*; after compliance with three high-*p* requests within 5 seconds the low *p* was given. All noncompliance and maladaptive behaviors were ignored. 4. Condition 2: Same procedures for the high-*p* leisure instructions.		

Note. IOA, interobserver agreement; ETC, *Education and Treatment of Children*; JABA, *Journal of Applied Behavior Analysis*; JBE, *Journal of Behavioral Education*; *indicates full text is available through Google Scholar.

Increasing Compliance of Young Children with Disabilities with Parent Requests at Home

As we discussed, compliance is considered a key school readiness behavior (Webster-Stratton, Reid, & Stoolmiller, 2008). The use of high-*p* request sequences in the home setting to increase young children's compliance may also have benefits for a child's school experience. Esch and Fryling (2013) worked with parents of a 6-year-old male child with autism to increase compliance in the home setting. The student, Daniel, exhibited tantrums and aggression at home and school. Parents participated in a high-*p* intervention with researchers to increase Daniel's compliance with three home requests: cleaning up trucks by putting them in a basket, turning off a movie, and doing a puzzle. Specifically, they tested two types of high-*p* requests: (1) maintenance requests such as "clap your hands" and "touch your tummy" and (2) leisure requests, which were behaviors related to preferred toys, such as "fly your plane" and "turn on the movie." For the interested researchers or graduate students, we mention that the authors used a multiple-baseline design across the three low-*p* tasks and an alternating treatment design comparing two conditions (i.e., maintenance and leisure).

First, parents and researchers worked together to identify high-*p* maintenance requests and preferred leisure items (e.g., monster trucks, model airplanes, toy trains), which were presented in multiple pairs to Daniel to assess preference. Once the most preferred items and requests (high *p*) were selected, they were tested. High-*p* requests were operationally defined as initiating the requested task independently within 5 seconds and completing the task. Those requests that Daniel complied with for at least 90% of trials during two 10-trial blocks were retained as high-*p* requests. Next, the low-*p* requests were tested. The parents defined the three previously mentioned low-*p* requests for which an increase in Daniel's compliance was desired. The three behaviors were presented to Daniel 10 times during a session with the percentage of compliance calculated.

After testing the requests, the researchers established current rates of low-*p* compliance (i.e., baseline performance). The request was applied to each low-*p* behavior on a delayed time schedule. That is, the low-*p* requests were provided in 10 consecutive trials at each session, with percentage of compliance within 5 seconds calculated and graphed for each low *p* and time to complete the task measured. The time it took for Daniel to complete the low-*p* tasks ranged from 30 seconds to 2 minutes. The high-*p* strategy was then introduced one behavior at a time using a multiple-baseline and alternating-treatment (i.e., two types of high-*p* requests) design. The sessions alternated between the high-*p* maintenance requests and leisure requests. All six of the high-*p* requests were used during each session. Each of three high-*p* requests was given consecutively within 30 seconds to 2 minutes of compliance with the previous request. Generic praise ("good job") was given after each compliant response. Noncompliance or other maladaptive behaviors were ignored. If Daniel did not comply with all three high-*p* requests or delayed compliance for more than 5 seconds, then the low-*p* request was not given and the trial not included.

Using the high-*p* maintenance requests increased compliance for the three low-*p* behaviors overall, but some compliance percentages were similar to those prior to the intervention. However, the high-*p* leisure requests did increase overall compliance with the tasks Daniel had previously refused to complete. The study showed that another explanation (in addition to treatment integrity concerns) for varied results with the strategy may be the type of high-*p* selected. Often, maintenance high-*p* requests—that is, actions that elicit compliance—are used. For young children, however, it may be that incorporating preferred leisure items results in higher levels of compliance. Further, it may be the leisure requests "turn on the movie" and "drive the monster truck down the ramp" were more similar in topography to the low-*p* requests of "turn off the movie" and "put all of your trucks in the basket." This study provided additional evidence for the recommendation of selecting high-*p* requests that are of similar topography, instead of any high-*p* behaviors.

Treatment integrity was monitored for the implementation of the request sequences and was reported at 100%. The use of associated praise was not monitored. Social validity was also not assessed but is always recommended. As a result, the information learned from this study must be considered preliminary. Treatment integrity data on the use of the reinforcement procedure would allow us to determine whether differential levels of reinforcement were used for the different high-*p* conditions, contributing to the differences in Daniel's response. Further, it is critical that the perspectives of stakeholders (e.g., parents, teachers, other caregivers) be assessed so that socially desirable behaviors are targeted for intervention and socially meaningful changes occur as a result of the intervention (Lane & Beebe-Frankenberger, 2003).

Increasing Math Work Engagement in an Inclusive Elementary Classroom

One expected behavior in academic settings is that students complete assigned work (Lynass, Tsai, Richman, & Cheney, 2012). For students with academic and behavioral difficulties, starting and completing work may present challenges. In fact, students' problem classroom behaviors may serve as a way to escape too-difficult tasks (Umbreit et al., 2007). The high-*p* request strategy may be used to increase work completion for students.

Wehby and Hollahan (2000) worked with an elementary teacher to support Meg, a 13-year-old student with a learning disability in math and writing, in beginning and completing math assignments using the high-*p* strategy. The researchers worked with the teacher to identify high-*p* requests—those with 85% or higher compliance. The high-*p* requests were related to assignments (e.g., "put your name on the paper") and were confirmed as high-*p* during direct observation of the student in the classroom. The low-*p* requests were to begin the math assignment and engage until the math work was completed. Meg's time to begin the work (latency) and time engaged in the work were measured through direct observation.

Authors used an ABABACB design to test the intervention. Before the intervention began, the teacher explained and modeled the activity for the day. Once students started the assignment, the teacher walked within close proximity of Meg's desk and asked her to begin. If she complied with the low-*p* request to begin work within 10 seconds, she was praised by the teacher. If not, the teacher walked away (baseline, A phase).

During the intervention (B phase), the procedures for instruction were the same. When the teacher walked within close proximity of Meg's desk, however, he delivered a high-*p* request, "Get out a sheet of paper." If Meg complied within 10 seconds, the teacher praised her and then delivered the next high-*p* request. This process was repeated until Meg complied with three consecutive high-*p* requests. Then the teacher delivered the low-*p* request "begin independent seat work" and walked away. The use of the high-*p* requests decreased the amount of time it took Meg to begin her work from an average of 11 minutes to under 1 minute (or an average 21 seconds). The effect of the intervention on engagement (first 10 minutes of the work time) showed increased engagement, although there was variability between days and the differences were not as pronounced as with the decreases in the time to begin the activity. Authors also measured the effect of neutral social comments (C phase) that replaced the high-*p* requests. In that phase, the teacher walked within close proximity of the student and made a comment such as "It is hot today." These types of comments were counterproductive, as they resulted in the longest time to begin the assignments and lowest levels of engagement (Wehby & Hollahan, 2000).

Treatment integrity was monitored by researchers for the delivery of the high-*p*, low-*p*, and neutral social comments. The teacher was able to implement the strategy with high levels of fidelity (95%; Wehby & Hollahan, 2000). The use of praise was not monitored, nor was social validity assessed. As noted in other work on this strategy, both are important considerations.

The findings of this study are important for teachers to consider. First, teachers may use neutral social comments with students who are slow to begin and to complete tasks as a means of connecting with the student and trying to engage him or her in classroom activities. The study suggests this may serve to reduce engagement for some children, so teachers could consider using only task-related high-*p* requests at the time that work engagement is expected. This study is an example of using the high-*p* request strategy in an elementary classroom for work engagement, and the high rate of treatment integrity serves as a marker for the feasibility of the strategy.

Increasing Math Work Engagement in an Alternative School

Belfiore, Lee, Vargas, and Skinner (1997) also addressed math work engagement. In this study, the two students, Allison and Roberta (ages 14 and 15), were attending an alternative school because they had been expelled from the regular school setting for noncompliant behaviors. Researchers used the high-*p* strategy to increase compliance with starting math assignments using a reversal (ABAB) design.

First, a preferences assessment was done to determine the high-*p* math problems. This application of the strategy differs from those previously presented in that the high-*p* requests were a type of math problem to be completed on paper and not a verbal request related to the task. In determining low-*p* and high-*p* problems, worksheets were created and tested. Math worksheets with either single-digit or multiple-digit multiplication problems requiring 90 total digits for completion were presented to students. Students were given one of each type of work sheet and asked to select one and complete it. Ten trials were conducted to establish the high-*p* problems. Both students preferred the single-digit problems. To prepare for the intervention, two types of packets of problems were prepared. Packets included five low-*p* math problems with multiple-digit multiplication presented on cards with one problem per card. For the high-*p* packets, the high-*p* problems (one-digit multiplication) were interspersed among the low-*p* problems so that there were three high-*p* cards preceding each of the five low-*p* problem cards. Prior to the intervention, the low-*p* packets were completed by students, and the time it took them to begin the problems (latency) was measured. During the intervention, the high-*p* packets were completed and measured the same way. No feedback or praise was offered to students as part of the intervention.

The high-*p* strategy was successful in reducing the amount of time it took students to begin work on the math problems. Treatment integrity data were collected on the procedural components for 40% of the sessions, with 100% agreement. Social validity data were not reported. This study offers teachers one way to use behavioral momentum and the high-*p* strategy for older students to improve academic behavior. This presents a feasible approach for increasing work completion of nonpreferred or challenging problems by interspersing preferred or high-*p* problems. Given the design of this intervention, it could be used for multiple students in one class and aligns with the principles for differentiated instruction (Tomlinson, 2005).

Summary

These studies illustrate the use of a relatively low-intensity, proactive, and positive intervention for addressing noncompliance in the classroom and home settings. Although much of this research has addressed the needs of students with disabilities, more recent applications were conducted in general education settings with students with and without identified disabilities (Table 6.1 offers a summary of additional studies). Within three-tiered models of prevention, following directions (compliance) and completing and turning in work are among the most common schoolwide expectations (Lynass et al., 2012). Further, student engagement in school learning environments is one of the most targeted replacement behaviors of behavioral interventions (Liaupsin, Umbreit, Ferro, Urso, & Upreti, 2006).

Increased engagement results in decreases in off-task, disruptive, and noncompliant behaviors (Lane et al., 2007).Therefore, using a short-term intervention such as high-p request sequences will support students in accessing schoolwide reinforcement systems.

Benefits and Challenges

The high-p request sequences strategy is easy to use with purposeful planning. There are a few considerations to think about in order to use it effectively.

Benefits

The use of high-p request sequences to increase compliance fits within the proactive response of a CI3T model of prevention and within the PBIS framework. The high-p request sequence strategy allows students to encounter success through the teacher's careful choice of requests that are most likely to elicit compliance or engagement and then providing behavior-specific praise (BSP) for meeting that request (Lee & Laspe, 2003). Behavioral momentum theory indicates that quick successes and praise encourage the student to continue the behavior—compliance or engagement (Lee, 2006). Therefore, this approach is considered a positive and respectful way to support students with noncompliance and difficulties with engaging in class assignments. The strategy can be applied in any school setting in which there are specific behaviors to target (e.g., transitioning from the playground, following a cafeteria routine, arrival to school).

Challenges

Critical to the success of this strategy is the selection of the high-p requests. High-p requests are those requests that elicit a response at least 80% of the time (see Davis & Reichle, 1996), and in some cases researchers have selected behaviors with 100% compliance on tested trials. Lower rates of responding on the high p make it difficult to establish enough behavioral momentum to transfer to the low-p desired behaviors (Austin & Agar, 2005). This strategy should be considered at the first sign of concern, before natural reinforcement allows the maladaptive behavior to become too effective. This recommendation applies to both home and school settings. At home and at school, noncompliance may be intermittently reinforced—sometimes holding firm and other times giving in to the students' behavior—establishing the persistence of the behavior and potentially leading to antisocial patterns of behavior for the student (Walker et al., 2004). In either setting, if noncompliance allows the student to escape a nonpreferred or too-difficult activity, then over time escaping the task supports the persistent use of the behavior (Dawson et al., 2003).

Essential to the use of this strategy are careful planning and preparation for the sequence of activities/requests, attention to reinforcing the requested behavior, and removing reinforcement from the noncompliant behaviors. In the next section, a step-by-step process for successfully implementing high-p request sequences in the classroom is explained in more detail.

Implementing High-Probability Request Sequences in Your Classroom: Checklist for Success

In the following sections, we offer a step-by-step approach for implementing high-p request sequences in your classroom. The steps are also available in Table 6.2 as an implementation checklist. A hypothetical illustration of how these steps can be used in a CI3T model at the upper elementary school level is provided in Box 6.1.

- **Step 1: Identify and operationally define the targeted low-probability (low-p) behavior.** High-p requests require specific procedures when addressing the needs of individual students (Davis, 1995; Davis et al., 1994). First, identify the target behavior (i.e., low-p behavior), such as increased work completion, peer initiations, task engagement, or transitions within or between locations or activities. Operationally define the behavior to include a label, definition, and examples and nonexamples so the behavior can be reliably observed by any adult in the classroom (Umbreit et al., 2007).

- **Step 2: Generate a list of several high-probability (high-p) behaviors that are similar to the desired low-p behavior.** Consult with those who best know the student (remember to consider the student's ideas) to generate a list of high-p behaviors that require a topographically similar response (Lee, 2006). For example, if

---

TABLE 6.2. Implementation Checklist for Success: High-Probability Request Sequences

- Step 1: Identify and operationally define the targeted low-probability (low-p) behavior.
- Step 2: Generate a list of several high-probability (high-p) behaviors that are similar to the desired low-p behavior.
- Step 3: Test the behaviors by giving the requests 10 times each.
- Step 4: Administer three to five high-p requests in succession, followed by praise for demonstrating the target behavior.
- Step 5: Deliver the low-p request within 10 seconds of the last high-p response.
- Step 6: Praise the low-p behavior upon compliance or demonstration.
- Step 7: Offer stakeholders an opportunity to give feedback on the use of the high-p strategy.

Note. Based on high-p request strategy steps discussed by Ardoin et al. (1999); Davis et al., (1994); and Wehby and Hollahan (2000).

the low p for a fourth-grade student is completing a multiple-digit multiplication math problem, then a similar high-p behavior for this student might be a single multiplication math fact (Lee & Laspe, 2003; see Box 6.1). When selecting high-p requests, select ones that require active responding, such as completing a task: "touch your nose" or "write the word *happy* at the top of your paper." Rates of low-p may be higher when the high p requires action by the student as opposed to simply engaging with the adult or peer.

• **Step 3: Test the behaviors by giving the requests 10 times each.** High-p request behaviors can be briefly tested to ensure they are actually high-probability behaviors. This can be done by providing the requests 10 times for each behavior. If the high-p behavior occurs in less than 50% of the trials, it is considered low p. If the high-p behaviors occur more than 80% of the time, they are considered high p. This step is essential, because if the student does not comply with the high-p request during the test sequence, there will be also be a low response to the low-p request (Ardoin et al., 1999). For some students, particularly older ones, the high-p list can be generated with their participation. As an example, the teacher may have two sets of math cards, two math worksheets, or problems presented electronically—one with single-digit math facts and the other with multiple-digit multiplication problems. The student may be provided with these two sheets and asked to complete the one he or she prefers. After several presentations of different types of math problems, the preferred type of math problems or high-p problems is determined (see Wehby & Hollahan, 2000). Once the lists of high-p behaviors are confirmed, proceed with the fourth step.

• **Step 4: Administer three to five high-p requests in succession, followed by praise for demonstrating the target behavior.** Next, the teacher provides three to five high-p prompts—for example, math facts in close succession (approximately 10 seconds apart)—while providing praise for compliance within the determined guideline. In the illustration in Box 6.1, students were expected to begin the independent math practice problems within 30 seconds of receiving the prompt "please begin work." Three successful high-p responses are achieved prior to delivering the low-p request. These may be delivered verbally, in writing (such as in the independent math practice illustrated in the box), or electronically in a program designed for that student.

• **Step 5: Deliver the low-p request within 10 seconds of the last high-p response.** After the high-p prompts, the low-p request is delivered in the same succession, and praise is delivered for compliance if the task is completed verbally. To continue the example of using this with written tasks, the teacher creates a worksheet with three single-digit math facts, followed by one multiple-digit math problem, with the pattern continuing for the entirety of the math worksheet.

• **Step 6: Praise the low-p behavior upon compliance or demonstration.** After the student responds as expected, the teacher provides BSP (a topic addressed in Chapter 3) for the student's compliance or completion: "You gave your best effort today by getting started on your math practice quickly," or "You are being responsible by completing all of your math assignment today!" For schools with established schoolwide expectations (e.g., "Give Best Effort," "Be Responsible"), being specific about the schoolwide behavior used will serve to reinforce those expectations and will allow students to access the school reinforcement system (e.g., "bear bucks" or "tribal tokens"; see Lane, Kalberg, & Menzies, 2009).

- **Step 7: Offer stakeholders an opportunity to give feedback on the use of the high-*p* strategy.** Finally, as with any intervention, we encourage an opportunity for all stakeholders—teachers, parents, students, and support staff—to provide their opinions on the goals, procedures, and outcomes (social validity, a point developed in the next section). It is important to learn what stakeholders felt were strengths and weaknesses of the intervention or of elements of the intervention in order to continually refine practices that support instruction and parenting supports. Practices that are feasible are more likely to be implemented (Spear, Strickland-Cohen, Romer, & Albin, 2013). Further, feedback supports the refinement of practices for current and future students.

The steps for implementing this strategy for specific students are linear and meant to be followed in the recommended order. However, as the published research (presented in Table 6.1 and discussed in the studies shared in the text) shows, there is some flexibility in the way that the high-*p* requests are tested (Step 3). In some cases the high-*p* requests are tested in multiple trials, with a student's response recorded (e.g., Esch & Fryling, 2013). In others, the student is presented with two tasks and asked to evaluate his or her preference (e.g., story starters, as in Lee & Laspe, 2003).

Reinforcement in the form of praise is used in some studies and not in others. In terms of reinforcement, we recommend using BSP (see Chapter 3), reinforcement consistent with the school's schoolwide PBIS plan, and extinction procedures (i.e., removal of previously maintaining reinforcement such as escaping the task requested; Janney, Umbreit, Ferro, Liaupsin, & Lane, 2013), as these practices are well established in the behavioral literature.

Examining the Effects: How Well Is It Working?

Testing the Strategy: Design Considerations

When implementing high-*p* request sequences, it is important to collect data on student performance to know how well this strategy is working. In many of the studies featured in this book, researchers have used single-case methodology to "test" the intervention effects. This is a particularly useful design approach for teachers, as it is highly flexible and very practical. It can be used with any of the strategies introduced in each chapter.

It is important to use an experimental design such as an ABAB or multiple baseline across settings, tasks, or students to establish a functional relation between the introduction of the intervention and changes in student performance (Gast &

Ledford, 2014). In other words, this design helps determine whether or not the intervention worked. This information is helpful to both general education and special education teachers for a variety of reasons. The first, of course, is that it allows you to evaluate the effectiveness of your instruction. With this information, you can decide how to adjust your instructional practices so they work better for your students. Second, members of the CI3T team or members of professional learning communities (PLCs) can use these data to determine how students are responding to these low-intensity supports. Before moving on to student-focused Tier 2 (e.g., Check-In/Check-Out, behavior contracts, or self-monitoring strategies) or Tier 3 (e.g., functional assessment-based interventions; Umbreit et al., 2007) supports, we want to be certain we have examined the extent to which teacher-driven strategies (e.g., high-p request sequences) have been effective in addressing students' needs (academically, behaviorally, and/or socially). Using an experimental design is one way to show whether or not this has occurred. We recommend that these teams (e.g., CI3T and PLC) be composed of a range of individuals, including general and special education teachers, as they each bring unique talents. For example, special education teachers are a critical resource for implementing and delivering specialized intervention; they can assist general educators with evaluating strategy implementation, as well as carefully measuring the effects of any given intervention for a particular student, as is demonstrated in Box 6.1. This is especially critical when focused on more intensive supports, such as functional assessment-based interventions that require careful monitoring of students' performance (e.g., academic engagement, disruption). The ability to use single-case methodology is a critical skill in assessing the effectiveness of Tier 2 and 3 supports.

These designs begin with a baseline phase during which data on student performance are collected (referred to as the A phase), then the intervention is introduced for the first time (B), while still collecting data on student performance using the same data collection method used during the baseline phase (see Figure 6.1 in Box 6.1). Although it is tempting at this point to say the intervention was effective, two more replications are needed to be certain the intervention was responsible for the change and not something else. One demonstration (e.g., the change from A to B phases) along with two other replications can provide evidence that the introduction of the strategy produced the changes (the shift from B to A and then A to B; Gast & Ledford, 2014).

Although some designs, such as the ABAB design, require removal and then reintroduction of the intervention, it is also possible to explore a functional relation using multiple baseline across settings designs. This means the strategy is used in different settings such as a different instructional period (math instead of reading) or a different physical location (playground instead of the lunchroom).

Making Certain the Strategy Is in Place: Treatment Integrity

In addition to using an experimental design to test the intervention, collecting treatment integrity data helps determine the extent to which the intervention is being implemented as planned. Figure 6.2, Panel A, is an example of a completed treatment integrity checklist for using high-*p* request sequences. (Figure 6.2, Panel B, for a more general treatment integrity form for use.) Although there are many different ways to collect treatment integrity data, one way is to have the teacher collect these data each day by indicating the degree to which each intervention component was implemented as planned for each student. For example, in Figure 6.2 in Box 6.1, Panels A and B, each item is a completed using a 3-point Likert-type scale as follows: 0 = *not in place*, 1 = *partially in place*, or 2 = *completely in place*. Each day the items are summed, divided by the total number of points possible, and divided by 100 to obtain a percentage of implementation for each student. These data can be used to interpret intervention outcomes (see Box 6.1). In addition, behavior component checklists not only determine the level of implementation but also serve as a prompt or reminder to implement each step.

Using an outside observer to collect treatment integrity data for approximately 25% of the sessions in each phase is recommended. An additional observer is important for establishing the accuracy of the data collected.

Examining Stakeholders' Views: Social Validity

Finally, in addition to collecting information on student performance and implementation (treatment integrity), it is important to understand how stakeholders felt about the intervention goals, procedures, and intended outcomes. Figure 6.3 in Box 6.1 is an example of a measure examining one elementary student's perceptions of the social validity of high-*p* request sequence.

It is important to obtain all stakeholders' views —the teacher, the student, and the parent—ideally before the intervention begins and again at the conclusion of the first "test." If social validity is low at the onset of the intervention, then it is wise to provide additional training to increase people's knowledge of the strategies, as well as their confidence in using the strategy prior to implementation. In theory (and in some instances in actuality; see Lane, Kalberg, Bruhn, et al., 2009), the opinions of those implementing and participating in the intervention may predict the extent to which the interventions are implemented as planned. In essence, a socially valid intervention is likely to be put in place with a high degree of integrity, leading to improvements in student performance that maintain over time and in new settings and with new people.

BOX 6.1. A Hypothetical Illustration of High-*p* Request Sequences in a CI3T Model

Ms. Bounds is a special education teacher who works at Tyler Elementary School, where they implement a comprehensive, integrated, three-tiered (CI3T) model of prevention. The CI3T plan addresses academic programming, behavioral expectations, and social skills instruction. As part of their academic program, students in Ms. Bound's class are learning math concepts aligned with the Common Core State Standards (CCSS; National Governors Association Center for Best Practices & the Council of Chief State School Officers, 2011) during a 60-minute instructional block Monday through Friday; they participate in a positive behavior intervention and support (PBIS) plan with instruction, modeling, and reinforcement for expected behaviors; and they engage in developing social skills using the Social Skills Improvement System—Classwide Intervention (Elliott & Gresham, 2007) curriculum (teaching one skill per month, 10 lessons total). Ms. Bounds supports the CI3T plan through inclusive educational programming for students with special needs in partnership with general education teachers. During one of her monthly professional learning community meetings with the fourth-grade team, Ms. Bounds and Mr. Henry (a fourth-grade teacher) reviewed the students' performance data and found that three students were struggling in their behavioral performance, each scoring in the moderate risk range on the Student Risk Screening Scale (SRSS; Drummond, 1994) on the winter screening time point, and were also having trouble with work completion and independent work habits in math, as noted on their semester report cards with "unsatisfactory" and also reflected in their math grades of C on the same report cards. Despite evidence of grade-level skills on state assessment scores and AIMSweb fall and winter benchmarking data (see *https://aimsweb.pearson.com/*) and having fewer than two absences during the first semester, Pamela, Abby, and Richie struggled to begin independent math practice assignments during their math instructional block. Mr. Henry indicated the students were often getting out of their seats to ask unrelated questions or were unprepared to begin work (e.g., not having a sharpened pencil during independent work time).

Support	Description	Entry criteria	Data to monitor progress	Exit criteria
High-*p* request sequence	Interspersing preferred math problems (high *p*) with new learning practice problems (low *p*) during math, independent practice assignments	SRSS Moderate risk and report card: Work completion and independent work habits (unsatisfactory) and math grade C or below	*Student performance:* • Time to begin assignment after directions given and a check for understanding • Percentage of work completed *Treatment integrity:* Component checklist *Social validity:* Student- and teacher-completed surveys	6 consecutive weeks of average latency at less than 30 seconds and work completion at 90% or better

Ms. Bounds suggested the possibility of using a high-*p* request sequence strategy for the three students. Mr. Henry felt that the high-*p* strategy had two potential benefits for Pamela, Abby, and Richie. It could facilitate successful completion of the high-*p* problems, for which he could provide higher rates of praise, and the behavioral momentum could support students' attempts at the more difficult problems (low-*p* problems). Collecting data would give Mr. Henry and Ms. Bounds information on how the three students responded to this low-intensity support. Ms. Bounds and Mr. Henry thought this strategy could be beneficial not only for Pamela, Abby, and Richie but also for other students in the class as well because it could provide them an opportunity to choose which type of assignments to complete (see Chapter 8 on instructional choice).

Ms. Bounds worked through the seven-step process with Mr. Henry as follows. These steps can also be found in Table 6.2.

Preparing for and Delivering High-Probability Request Sequences: The Intervention

• **Step 1: Identify and operationally define the targeted low-probability (low-*p*) behavior.** Together the teachers identified and operationally defined the low-*p* behaviors for the three students, including the label, a definition, and examples and nonexamples, so that everyone would be certain they were targeting the same low-*p* behavior. Because the behaviors for all students were identified as beginning assigned work and work completion, one definition was written for all students for the two target behaviors.

Target Behavior 1
- **Label.** Low-probability behavior: Beginning assigned work
- **Definitions.** Beginning work referred to engaging in the assigned instructional task as directed by the teachers.
- **Examples.** Examples included beginning the teacher-assigned task within 30 seconds of teacher directions, raising a hand to be called on, asking a related question, talking with a peer on the task topic, working problems on paper, computing with the calculator.
- **Non-examples.** Non-examples included getting out of seat after independent math work time began, lacking materials to complete the assignment (e.g., paper, pencil, eraser), talking with a peer or teacher about an unrelated topic, putting head down on desk, sitting quietly but not working.

Target Behavior 2
- **Label.** Low-probability behavior: Work completion
- **Definitions.** "Work completion" refers to completing the teacher-assigned task within the given time period with at least 90% of the assignment completed.
- **Examples.** Completing assigned math problems (90% or more).
- **Non-examples.** Completing some of the practice problems (fewer than 90%).

• **Step 2: Generate a list of several high-probability (high-*p*) behaviors that are similar to the desired low-*p* behavior.** The teachers generated a list of high-*p* problems by examining Pamela, Abby, and Richie's AIMSweb benchmark data, specifically the type of problems that the students consistently answered correctly and also previous math assignments completed. Once types of problems were identified, Ms. Bounds entered them into a computer survey tool (such as a Google Form, Qualtrics, or Survey Monkey) to generate a list of high-*p* problems that students were asked to respond to with a "yes" or "no" to the question, "Do you like this type of problem?" They were not asked to complete the problems during this step. In this way, Ms. Bounds generated a list of problems the students preferred. Now she was ready to test these out.

• **Step 3: Test the behaviors by giving the requests 10 times each.** To test the selected high-*p* math problems, Ms. Bounds prepared 10 short math worksheets of five problems each using the problems from Step 2 to make the randomly generated worksheets. The sheets were prepared for each of the three students based on their preferred problems. At the start of each math period, when all students were doing warm-up problems, Mr. Henry gave Pamela, Abby, and Richie the worksheets that were created to test the high-*p* problems. Ms. Bounds observed each student to see whether they began within the 30 seconds and whether they completed all of the problems within the given warm-up time. Praise was not given by either teacher. Problems were retained on the high-*p* list if they were started within 30 seconds and if 80% were completed within the allotted time. (*Note.* The 80% criteria is used to determine whether a high-*p* behavior is truly a high-*p* behavior as described in the text. This is different from the expected percentage of problems finished for the assignment to be considered complete. See target behavior 2, work completion, in Step 1.)

• **Step 4: Administer three to five high-*p* requests in succession, followed by praise for demonstrating the target behavior.** Ms. Bounds then created specialized independent practice worksheets for the three students. On these worksheets three high-*p* problems preceded each low-*p* problem. The addition of the high-*p* problems increased the number of problems to 40, so students were asked to complete 10 of the new learning problems (low *p*). For example, Pamela's sheet gave her 3 one-digit multiplication facts (2's, 5's, and 6's) preceding each multidigit problem, with 10 multidigit problems in all. Mr. Henry provided the individualized practice sheets to the three students and the regular 10-problem sheets to the rest of the students in the class. All were given the same amount of time to complete the work. Students were praised for beginning the assignment within 30 seconds and again for completion of the assignment.

• **Step 5: Deliver the low-*p* request within 10 seconds of the last high-*p* response.** Because this use of the high-*p* strategy included written requests, the timeliness of the delivery of each request was designed to be part of the assignment. So the problems were successive, with the praise offered initially for beginning the task and afterward for expected completion. If students fell below the expected performance in beginning the assignment or in completion of it on any day, Ms. Bounds and Mr. Henry examined the completion and accuracy of the high-*p* request to make certain that the high-*p* problems were, in fact, completed a high percentage of time (> 80%). If not, then those types of problems were discarded as high-*p*, and new ones were selected from the original list.

• **Step 6: Praise the low-*p* behavior upon compliance or demonstration.** Again because of the design (written high *p* instead of verbally delivered), praise was planned to address both of the expected behaviors—beginning within 30 seconds and completing at least 90% of the assignment. As Ms. Bounds collected data on the same two variables as in Step 4—time to begin work and percentage of low-*p* problems completed—if students began work within the expected 30 seconds, Ms. Bounds signaled Mr. Henry, who walked by the working students and praised them for giving their best effort and beginning their work quickly. "Best effort" is a Tyler Elementary schoolwide PBIS expectation, and so the praise for beginning work was connected to the school's expectations for all students in all areas, as well as the specific example of what the students did in math class to earn the recognition, thus increasing the chance that they would repeat the desired behavior (see Chapter 3 for details on behavior-specific praise [BSP]). When the papers were collected, Mr. Henry provided praise for students "being responsible" (another schoolwide expectation) by completing their math practice (90% or higher).

• **Step 7: Offer stakeholders an opportunity to give feedback on the use of the high-*p* strategy.** Prior to beginning and at the end of the intervention, Ms. Bounds and Mr. Henry decided to ask the students what they thought about the newly designed and specialized independent math practice. They asked all three students in the class to rate five short statements about their experience (see Figure 6.3). They felt that getting the students' opinions was particularly important because the students were completing more problems than their classmates overall (the extra high-*p* problems).

Looking at How Well High-*p* Requests Worked

Ms. Bounds and Mr. Henry decided to collect specific data on the time it took students to begin the independent math work (referred to as *latency*) and work completion (percentage of problems completed in the given time) for Pamela, Abby, and Richie to see how they responded to this low-intensity support. Operational definitions (one for each behavior) were developed in step 1.

Latency was collected using a stopwatch to measure total seconds to begin the independent math practice. Once Mr. Henry completed the instruction, directions, and check for understanding, he gave the key phase "please begin the practice" as the agreed-upon signal to start measuring latency. Ms. Bounds began the stopwatch at that moment and observed each of the three students. She observed each student begin and marked the time the student began work according to the definition. Before collecting data, Ms. Bounds and Mr. Henry practiced using this recording system together to make sure they collected latency data in a reliable manner.

GARY PUBLIC LIBRARY

Specifically, they practiced observing the three students using a data collection form for recording the seconds to begin a task over 3 consecutive days. Next, baseline data were collected on each target behavior. Praise was not given to students during this phase by either teacher. These data were graphed by Ms. Bounds and reviewed daily with Mr. Henry (see Figure 6.1 for student outcomes) to see whether the number of seconds for each student to begin was stable or whether the trend was countertherapeutic (i.e., changing in the undesired direction by taking increasingly longer times to begin).

Figure 6.1 presents three figures showing Pamela's (Panel A), Abby's (Panel B), and Richie's (Panel C) latency in seconds. Notice that some of the data points in Pamela's graph are marked with an asterisk (*), indicating which sessions were observed by both Ms. Bounds and Mr. Henry to make sure they were seeing the same behavior. On these sessions, they collected reliability data on the latency for each of the students. Typically, Mr. Henry observed one time per week, when he placed his stopwatch and data collection sheet on his podium and supervised students from there until all three students began work.

In addition to collecting information on latency, Ms. Bounds also collected data on work completion (not graphed in Figure 6.1). Work completion was evaluated using a daily report card in which Ms. Bounds or Mr. Henry evaluated the assigned instruction task, with scores ranging from 0 to 100% completion.

To make certain the intervention was happening as planned, either Ms. Bounds or Mr. Henry completed a daily treatment integrity form (see Figure 6.2, Panel A, for treatment integrity data on the first introduction of the high-*p* strategy use). Each day they recorded whether the intervention component was *not in place* (0), *partially in place* (1), or *fully in place* (2). Figure 6.2, Panel A, shows a percentage of implementation for each session (at the end of each column). These data were very important, as they helped the teachers to interpret how students responded to the high-*p* problems within the independent practice. For example, Panels A, B, and C in Figure 6.1 show that time to begin assignments was much higher during baseline compared with the first introduction of the high-*p* strategy. Then, the time to begin increased (and work completion declined, although that is not shown in this graph) when the high-*p* problems were removed during the withdrawal phase, and again time to begin decreased when the intervention was reintroduced—with the exception of Session 7 for Richie and Session 8 for Pamela. On these days, the level of integrity was quite low for Richie (33%) and Pamela (50%), and, as expected, there was a slight increase in the time to begin (latency) and a slight decrease in percentage of completion. In general, when the intervention was in place as planned, all three students began work in less time and completed more work. (See Figure 6.2, Panel B, for a more general treatment integrity form for use).

Together, Ms. Bounds and Mr. Henry reviewed the students' social validity surveys to evaluate the intervention design. In brief, all students (Pamela's ratings are shown in Figure 6.3) agreed that having more problems they found to be easier helped them get started faster, and they liked having these extra problems even though it meant more work for them. For Pamela, the intervention actually

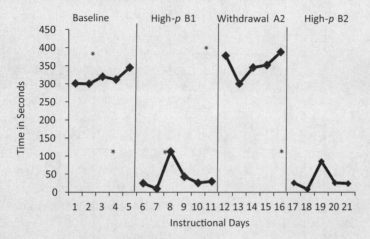

Panel A. Pamela's Independent Math Practice Latency

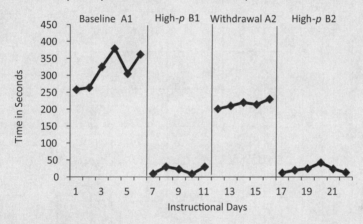

Panel B. Abby's Independent Math Practice Latency

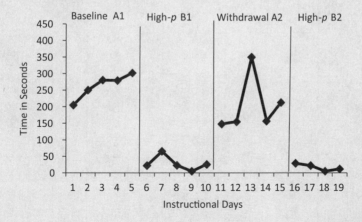

Panel C. Richie's Independent Math Practice Latency

FIGURE 6.1. Examining the effects: Students' latency (time in seconds) to begin independent math practice.

TREATMENT INTEGRITY CHECKLIST: HIGH-PROBABILITY REQUEST SEQUENCES

Panel A

Teacher: <u>Mr. Henry</u>

Lesson: <u>CCSS.MATH.CONTENT.4NBT.B.5</u>

Multiply a whole number of up to 4 digits by a one digit whole number.

☒ Self-report ☐ Observer Scale: 0 = Not in place; 1 = Partially in place; 2 = Fully in place

(Each student column below shows the scale 0 1 2 with the recorded value indicated.)

Component	Session 6 Monday 3/23/2015			Session 7 Tuesday 3/24/2015			Session 8 Wednesday 3/25/2015			Session 9 Thursday 3/26/2015			Session 10 Friday 3/27/2015		
	Pamela	Abby	Richie	Pamela	Abby	Richie	Pamela	Abby	Richie	Pamela	Abby	Richie	Pamela	Abby	Richie
The individual worksheets were prepared.	2	—	2	2	2	2	2	2	2	2	2	2	2	2	2
I modeled and checked for understanding.	2	—	2	2	2	2	2	2	2	2	2	2	2	2	2
I provided the phrase to begin work "please begin work."	2	—	2	0	0	0	2	2	2	2	2	2	2	2	2
I provided praise when student began work ≤ 30 seconds.	2	—	2	2	2	0	0	2	2	1	2	2	2	2	2
I checked student's paper for completion.	2	—	2	2	2	0	0	2	2	2	2	2	2	2	2
I praised student's completion if ≥ 90%.	2	—	2	2	2	0	0	2	2	0	2	2	2	2	2
Percentage Session Integrity: (Total points earned/ # points possible) × 100	100%	Baseline	100%	83%	83%	33%	50%	100%	100%	75%	100%	100%	100%	100%	100%

FIGURE 6.2. Making certain the strategy is in place: Treatment integrity form used by Ms. Bounds and Mr. Henry to monitor the extent to which each step was put in place as planned. Panel A depicts a completed checklist specific to the elements of daily use in the hypothetical illustration (Box 6.1). Panel B depicts a blank form including the planning steps. The darker gray cells indicate steps that are not applicable for the column—either intervention planning or daily implementation.

From *Supporting Behavior for School Success: A Step-by-Step Guide to Key Strategies* by Kathleen Lynne Lane, Holly Mariah Menzies, Robin Parks Ennis, and Wendy Peia Oakes. Copyright 2015 by The Guilford Press. Permission to photocopy this figure is granted to purchasers of this book for personal use only (see copyright page for details). Purchasers can download a larger version of this figure from *www.guilford.com/lane4-forms*.

Panel B

Teacher: _____

Lesson: _____

☐ Self-report ☐ Observer

Scale: 0 = Not in place
1 = Partially in place
2 = Fully in place

Procedural Step	Intervention Planning			Session			Session			Session			Session			Session		
	0	1	2	0	1	2	0	1	2	0	1	2	0	1	2	0	1	2
Identified and operationally defined low-*p* behavior																		
Generated a list of high-*p* behaviors that are similar to the desired low-*p* behavior																		
Tested the behaviors by giving the requests (10 times each)																		
Administered 3 to 5 high-*p* requests																		
Praised expected response																		
Delivered low-*p* request within 10 seconds of the last high-*p* response																		
Praised expected low-*p* behavior upon compliance or demonstration																		
Assessed social validity from stakeholders																		

Percentage Session Integrity:
(Total points earned/# points possible) × 100

(continued)

FIGURE 6.2. *(continued)*

From *Supporting Behavior for School Success: A Step-by-Step Guide to Key Strategies* by Kathleen Lynne Lane, Holly Mariah Menzies, Robin Parks Ennis, and Wendy Peia Oakes. Copyright 2015 by The Guilford Press. Permission to photocopy this figure is granted to purchasers of this book for personal use only (see copyright page for details). Purchasers can download a larger version of this figure from *www.guilford.com/lane4-forms*.

SOCIAL VALIDITY FORM: HIGH-PROBABILITY REQUEST SEQUENCES

Before we get started . . . What do you think, Pamela?	☹ 0 No, not really	1 sometimes	☺ 2 Yes, definitely
I would like to have some easier math problems to get started on during the independent math practice each day.		✓	
Having easier problems would help me get started faster.		✓	
I could get more of my work done if I had some more problems that I liked to do.			✓
Other students in my class would enjoy having specially made practice sheets too.		✓	
I would like having the special practice sheets even though I will be doing more practice problems than other students in my class.		✓	
Percentage: (total number/total number possible) × 100		*60%*	

Now that you have tried it . . . What do you think, Pamela?	☹ 0 No, not really	1 sometimes	☺ 2 Yes, definitely
I like having some easier math problems to get started on during the independent math practice each day.			✓
Having easier problems helps me get started faster.			✓
I get more of my work done because I have more problems that I like to do.			✓
Other students in my class would enjoy having specially made practice sheets too.			✓
I like having the special practice sheets even though I am doing more practice problems than other students in my class.			✓
Percentage: (total number/total number possible) × 100		*100%*	

FIGURE 6.3. Examining stakeholders' views: Pamela's views on the high-probability request sequences prior to beginning and after completing the intervention.

exceeded her initial expectations (scores increase from 60 to 100%), and she thought other students would also like this strategy. After the first attempt to use this strategy, Ms. Bounds and Mr. Henry decided to put the intervention back in place and continued to monitor student performance. They continued this process until each student had 6 consecutive weeks of beginning independent math practice within 30 seconds and work completion at 90% or better. After all three students met these criteria, the teachers decided to leave the intervention in place for the three students and discussed ways to include the strategy as part of regular instruction, as they saw benefits for other students as well, especially as it was such a simple strategy to add to their daily instruction. The partnership of the special education and general education teacher working together made this strategy easy to implement, with little additional preparation required of either of the teachers.

Summary

The high-*p* request sequences strategy is effective, efficient, and relatively simple to use in both the school and home settings. It can be used to increase students' compliance with adult requests, including work completion. High-*p* requests should be used in conjunction with BSP and is similar to offering instructional choice (see Chapter 8) when used in the classroom, particularly to increase work completion. Noncompliance is challenging for teachers to address in the classroom setting and is one of the most prevalent misbehaviors noted for young children (Esch & Fryling, 2013). This strategy offers teachers a starting place for students with challenging behaviors. By beginning with requests with which students are more likely to comply, a teacher can build behavioral momentum that will generalize to desired behaviors that improve a student's behavioral and academic success (Nevin et al., 1983).

CHAPTER 7

A Look at Precorrection

Many times the everyday problems faced in schools can be solved with a little proactive planning. Anticipating activities, areas of the classroom/school, or times of day that are likely to occasion problem behaviors and then addressing them with preventative strategies can be very effective and easily incorporated into class/school routines. One proactive strategy that addresses this need is *precorrection*. Precorrection is an antecedent-based strategy, which means that it involves making changes to the environment before behavior occurs.

School-based research in the area of precorrection can be traced back to the early 1990s. Using precorrection strategies has been shown to reduce problem behaviors in a variety of settings, both instructional, such as the classroom (e.g., Colvin, Sugai, & Patching, 1993; DePry & Sugai, 2002; Stormont, Smith, & Lewis, 2007), and noninstructional, such as morning gym (e.g., Haydon & Scott, 2008), recess (e.g., Lewis, Colvin, & Sugai, 2000), and transitions (e.g., Colvin et al., 1997; Haydon et al., 2012). The variety of settings represented in this body of research is a testament to the flexibility of precorrection, as it can be used in virtually any setting and is easily adaptable given the activity and problem behavior that it aims to prevent occurring.

Precorrection is a simple strategy that many effective teachers use almost subconsciously. For example, teachers often make on-the-spot decisions about using one instructional practice versus another based on anticipated behavior problems. One of the most common examples of this is teachers' decisions about which students to partner together based on knowledge about problem behaviors that may occur if certain students are paired to work together. This chapter discusses ways to implement precorrection strategies more explicitly, so that the potential benefits from precorrection can be maximized. In addition, this chapter highlights relevant research to demonstrate how precorrection can be used in instructional and noninstructional settings to both prevent and decrease problem behaviors. As we discussed in Chapter 4 on active supervision, behavior in noninstructional settings (e.g., playground, transitions) often affects behavior in instructional settings and can either detract from or promote learning in the classroom. If teachers use precorrection strategies to anticipate problem behaviors before they occur and modify the environment to promote student success, student performance can be improved throughout the school day.

What Is Precorrection?

Precorrection is a preventative behavioral strategy that involves identifying predictable contexts that often result in problem behavior and providing students with supports, prompts, and reinforcement for engaging in appropriate behavior. Using precorrective strategies is a shift from controlling behavior with consequences alone (i.e., reinforcement and punishment of behavior) to also incorporating the use of antecedent (i.e., what comes before behavior) strategies (Crosby, Jolivette, & Patterson, 2006). Historically, however, we have instead relied on punishment procedures (e.g., office discipline referrals, raised voices, or the withholding of recess) when problems do occur or reinforcing a student for engaging in a more appropriate behavior.

One of the limitations of managing behavior with consequences alone (e.g., creating an action plan for three alternatives to yelling at a peer) is that it requires waiting until the behavior occurs to respond. Precorrection allows us to anticipate what activities may cause inappropriate behaviors to occur and make adjustments in advance. Rather than waiting for a problem to occur and then responding, precorrection allows us a respectful way of "getting in front" of a challenge behavior by intervening before it happens. Once we have determined when precorrection is needed, then we can decide what form that precorrection will take. Precorrection may consist solely of a gentle reminder to students of what behavior is expected of them prior to an activity. For example, a teacher who knows that her students often get noisy in the hallway on the way to lunch can review the expectations for hallway behavior before dismissing the class for lunch (e.g., while pointing to a positive behavior intervention and support [PBIS] matrix posted by the door in a classroom, the teacher might point to the poster and say, "Remember on the way to lunch we walk with closed mouths and hands at our sides on the right side of the hallway"). This also may involve having students answer questions about and be engaged in the review of expectations (e.g., "Janice, can you tell us on which side of the hallway we walk? . . . . That is right! Please stand up, push in your chair, and line up at the door"). This may also involve a review of the desirable consequences of appropriate hallway behavior (e.g., "The lunch group that shows me the best hallway behavior will be dismissed first tomorrow"). Depending on the need of the students and the severity of the behavior, precorrection may involve a multistep plan for preventing problem behavior and supporting appropriate behavior.

Colvin and colleagues (1993) developed a seven-step precorrection strategy for preventing problem behaviors based on a plan for minimizing academic errors. The seven steps are as follows: (1) identify the context and predictably challenging behaviors, (2) define the expected behavior, (3) modify the context (i.e., teacher behavior, environmental changes) to promote student success, (4) provide students with an opportunity to practice the expected behavior, (5) provide students with strong reinforcement for completing the expected behavior, (6) create a prompting plan to remind students to engage in the expected behavior, and (7) develop a monitoring plan to determine the effectiveness of the precorrection plan. These seven steps are more comprehensive and involve the manipulation of both antecedents and consequences to prevent problem behaviors and promote appropriate behaviors.

This seven-step plan was developed in an effort to take an instructional approach to the management of problem behaviors. For example, if a student missed a math problem, we would take steps to analyze what errors he or she was making, then try to reteach or put in place supports to prevent the student from making the same error pattern in the future. These same procedures, the seven steps just detailed, can and should be used to help improve students' social behaviors.

Precorrection plans can be developed to address the needs of one student who is likely to engage in problem behaviors, but it is more often used to change the behavior of a group of students. Even if a precorrection plan is designed with one or a small group of students in mind, it can have a positive impact on the behavior of many.

Why Is Precorrection Effective?

Many teachers have used precorrection, but all teachers have used correction or instructional feedback (see Chapter 5). Correction involves notifying a student (or group of students) that an error has occurred, providing corrective statements that detail how to perform a correct response, giving opportunities to perform the task, and providing reinforcement for correct performance (Colvin et al., 1993). Precorrection is different from correction in several ways, the first and most prominent being that precorrection is proactive and involves anticipating activities, settings, or times of day that could potentially result in behavior problems rather than waiting for them to occur and implementing the correction steps afterward. Second, precorrection involves the manipulation of both antecedents and consequences, whereas correction involves the manipulation of consequences only. By manipulating antecedents (e.g., how we set up our classrooms, what we do or say during certain activities/settings, what visual cues we set up in the classroom/school), we can often prevent problem behaviors or errors from ever occurring. Third, correction involves a focus on the inappropriate behavior students have committed. By using precorrective strategies, we focus on what students should do instead of what it is that they have done inappropriately. Fourth, correction can often lead to negative interactions between teachers and students. Many students, in particular those with and at risk for emotional and behavioral disorders (EBD), can be particularly sensitive to criticism of their behavior. For this reason, correction from adults can often result in the escalation of or worsening of inappropriate behavior. Precorrection is designed to intervene before problem behavior occurs, which in turn serves as a reminder of appropriate behavior rather than correction for inappropriate behavior, thus preventing the potential for escalating behavior patterns. Likewise, because precorrection seeks to prevent problem behaviors from occurring, it can often prevent negative student–teacher interactions, thus allowing more time for positive student–teacher interactions (Colvin et al., 1993).

Precorrection is also effective because it fits seamlessly with a schoolwide positive behavior framework (such as those present in PBIS and comprehensive, integrated, three-tiered [CI3T] models of prevention). Schools across the country have adopted such models, as they are proactive and focus on preventing problem behaviors from occurring by clarifying expectations and then developing procedures for teaching, monitoring, and reinforcing those expectations. In this respect, precorrection is also a proactive strategy that seeks to teach, monitor, and reinforce appropriate behavior. For example, step 2, defining the expected behavior, may have already been completed when the schoolwide expectation matrix was composed, with input from all faculty and staff to make certain it was clear enough for students to be successful in each setting (see Ennis, Schwab, & Jolivette, 2012; Lane, Oakes, Jenkins, Menzies, & Kalberg, 2014). Further, the schoolwide methods for teaching behavioral expectations could include precorrection plans for common areas of the school building where problem behaviors occur. For example, your school's CI3T team could develop precorrection plans for the lunchroom behavior or after-school transitions and teach them at the beginning of the school year, when schoolwide behavior expectations are taught. Because precorrection can be used with a targeted group of students, it could also be used as a Tier 2 (targeted) intervention within a three-tiered model of prevention.

Supporting Research for Precorrection

Research highlighting the effectiveness of precorrection has been conducted in a variety of settings at the prekindergarten, elementary, and middle school levels. Much of the research highlighted in Chapter 4 on active supervision involved a combination of both active supervision *and* precorrection, as one of the components of creating a precorrection plan, modifying the context, often involves increasing the active supervision of students. As you begin using precorrection in the classroom or school, consider revisiting the literature discussed in Chapter 4. This research is also described in Table 7.1.

Decreasing Problem Behaviors in Head Start Classrooms

Stormont and colleagues (2007) worked with two female teachers and one female teaching assistant working in two Head Start centers to increase their use of pre-corrective and behavior-specific praise (BSP) statements and to decrease their use of reprimands. The Head Start centers had been trained to implement program-wide PBIS through a 2-day team training, and two 2-hour inservices for all teach-ers and staff. As a part of the PBIS program, teachers were observed for their rates of BSP and reprimands. Teachers with low levels of BSP and high levels of reprimands were invited to participate in a study to help reduce problem behaviors. Student participants were 25 (14 boys, 11 girls) students ages 3–5 participating in small groups of 7 or 8 students each. Data collection and intervention took place during daily teacher-directed small-group activities.

The researchers used a teacher behavior observation form to track event-recording data on teacher's use of BSP, precorrective statements, and reprimand statements. Researchers also collected data on students' problem behavior. A mul-tiple baseline across teacher participants was used to evaluate the effectiveness of the intervention, in which baseline or "business as usual" data were collected on all participants and then the intervention was introduced in a staggered fashion. At the conclusion of baseline data collection, teachers were taught to (1) use pre-corrective statements during a review of expectations with students prior to the small-group lesson and (2) increase use of BSP for students meeting behavioral expectations. The training consisted of a 30-minute meeting with each teacher individually. During the training, researchers used examples of potential precor-rective and BSP statements that they saw the teacher using during small-group baseline observations. Also during training, teachers were given the opportu-nity to practice using these statements with the researchers. During intervention, researchers provided teachers with feedback at the end of each small-group ses-sion on whether or not they had used the precorrection strategy and their fre-quency of praise statements.

Two of the three teachers increased their use of the precorrection strategy, using precorrection for 100% of intervention sessions. The third teacher par-ticipant maintained a high rate of precorrection use (baseline 78%, intervention 75%). All three teachers decreased their use of reprimands and increased their use of BSP statements. In turn, student problem behavior decreased in all three small groups. Following the intervention, all three teachers rated the intervention positively using a 7-item social validity questionnaire, with two teachers strongly agreeing with statements such as "I will use the intervention in other settings" and "The intervention proved to be an effective and efficient method for reducing problem behaviors."

TABLE 7.1. Supporting Research: Precorrection

Authors and journal	Students	Intervention setting	Intervention	Measures	Design
Colvin, Sugai, Good, & Lee (1997) Using active supervision and precorrection to improve transition behaviors in an elementary school (SPQ)	N = 475 students, 42 staff members (24 certified, 18 classified, and 1 principal); 44% free and reduced-price lunches; elementary (grades K–5)	Entering the school building, moving from the classroom to the cafeteria, and leaving the school building	Precorrection and active supervision strategies: 1. Defined expected behaviors: walk, keep hands and feet to self, and use a quiet voice 2. Schoolwide discipline team taught strategies (15 minutes) 3. Active supervision: Move around, look around, interact with students 4. Precorrection: Remind students of expected behaviors just before entering the transition area	*Dependent variables:* 1. Setting characteristics (number of supervisors, number of students) 2. Supervisor behavior (escorting, scanning, and interacting) 3. Student behavior (frequency of problem behavior: running, pushing, shouting, sliding, throwing, or other rule violations) *Treatment integrity:* Not measured (addressed as a limitation) *Social validity:* Not measured	Multiple-baseline design across the three settings
Lewis, Colvin, & Sugai (2000) The effects of precorrection and active supervision on the recess behavior of elementary students (ETC)	N = 475 students, 42 staff members (24 certified, 18 classified, and 1 principal); 44% free and reduced-price lunches; elementary (grades K–5)	Recess on an elementary school playground	Precorrection: 1. Identified problem behaviors exhibited by students at recess 2. Identified expected or replacement responses for problem behaviors 3. Printed rules and expectations for recess were reviewed with students 4. Students were precorrected regarding rules and expectations prior to being released to the playground for recess Active supervision (15-minute meeting): 1. Move around 2. Look around 3. Interact with students	*Dependent variables:* 1. Students' problem behavior 2. Playground monitor supervision behavior *Treatment integrity:* Programmed for, but not measured *Social validity:* Not measured	Multiple-baseline design across groups

(continued)

151

TABLE 7.1. (continued)

Authors and journal	Students	Intervention setting	Intervention	Measures	Design
De Pry & Sugai (2002) The effect of active supervision and precorrection on minor behavioral incidents in a sixth-grade general education classroom (JBE)*	N = 26 sixth-grade students, 1 teacher with 20+ years of experience; elementary (grades 4–6)	Elementary general education social studies class	Package–instructionally based intervention: 1. Active supervision: circulate while teaching, scan to attend to all areas, interact with students verbally and nonverbally, and reinforce demonstrations of expected academic and social behavior as part of instruction 2. Precorrection: instructional prompt before students entered a context in which a problem behavior was likely to occur 3. Daily data reviews between teacher and researcher each morning (5–10 minutes)	*Dependent variable:* Minor behavioral incidents (partial interval recording; IOA 85%) *Treatment integrity:* Assessed by an outside observer *Social validity:* Assessed using a Likert-type scale	ABAB withdrawal design
Stormont, Smith, & Lewis (2007) Teacher implementation of precorrection and praise statements in Head Start classrooms as a component of a program-wide system of positive behavior support (JBE)*	N = 23 students ages 3–5; 3 teachers	Head Start program; teacher-directed small groups	30-minute meeting with teachers during which examples of potential precorrection statements were given and practiced; feedback following each observation session	*Dependent variables:* 1. Teacher precorrection statements 2. Teacher praise 3. Teacher reprimands 4. Student problem behaviors *Treatment integrity:* Not assessed *Social validity:* Teacher-completed Likert-type scale	Multiple baseline across teachers

152

Citation	Sample	Setting	Intervention	Measures	Design
Haydon & Scott (2008) Using common sense in common settings: Active supervision and precorrection in the morning gym (ISC)	N = 400; 50% free and reduced-price lunches; school level: elementary (grades 3–5)	Morning gym in an elementary school	Active supervision and precorrection: 1. Identify contexts 2. Determine expected behaviors 3. Adjust environment 4. Practice expected behaviors 5. Acknowledge expected behaviors 6. Remind students of expected behaviors (gestural, verbal, environmental, manual prompts) 7. Observe effects	*Dependent variable:* Office referrals during morning gym *Treatment integrity:* Not measured *Social validity:* Not measured	Pre/post
Haydon, DeGreg, Maheady, & Hunter (2012) Using active supervision and precorrection to improve transition behaviors in a middle school classroom (JEBPS)	N = 534 students; 90% free or reduced-price lunches; high transiency; urban district, middle school (grades 6–7)	Seventh-grade health class in middle school; transitioning in from lunch in the cafeteria	Precorrection Active supervision Explicit timing procedure B: Active supervision + precorrection C: Active supervision + precorrection + timing procedure	*Dependent variables:* 1. Teachers' redirections 2. The number of minutes during transition *Treatment integrity:* Checklist completed by outside observer *Social validity:* Teacher-completed Likert-type scale	ABCBC + maintenance phase

Note. ETC, *Education and Treatment of Children*; ISC, *Intervention in School and Clinic*; JEBPS, *Journal of Evidence-Based Practices for Schools*; JBE, *Journal of Behavioral Education*; SPQ, *School Psychology Quarterly*; *indicates full text is available through Google Scholar.

Decreasing Problem Behavior on an Elementary School Playground

Lewis and colleagues (2000) explored the utility of a precorrection strategy paired with active supervision to improve student outcomes on the playground. Participants included 42 staff members (24 certified teachers, 18 classified staff) and 475 students in kindergarten through fifth grades, 44% of whom were receiving free and reduced-price lunches. Researchers collected data on playground monitors' behaviors, classifying monitoring behavior as either active (movement beyond 15 feet from a previous point, interactions with students) or nonactive (interaction with other adults, gestures to students more than 10 feet away, or blowing a whistle in response to behavior). Researchers also collected data on student problem behavior, which was classified as putting their hands on others, misuse of equipment, inappropriate language/name calling, threats, interference with games, and arguing.

The intervention consisted of two main components: precorrection and active supervision. The precorrection component involved (1) identifying problem behaviors displayed during recess, (2) identifying expected appropriate behaviors, (3) printing expectations and reviewing them with students, and (4) providing precorrective statements to students prior to their release for recess. The active supervision component of the intervention involved a 15-minute meeting and a 10-minute follow-up session, during which playground supervisors were instructed to move around, look around/scan all areas, and interact with students. A multiple-baseline design across recess periods was used, in which the intervention was introduced in a staggered fashion.

Following the precorrection and active supervision training sessions, there was little to no change in playground monitor behavior. However, there was a significant decrease in student problem behavior during both structured and unstructured activities as a result of the precorrection strategy. Prior to the intervention, there were significantly more problem behaviors during unstructured activities. After the intervention, however, there was no meaningful difference in the rate of problem behavior based on activity type, which is notable given that problem behavior is often higher during unstructured activities. Also, notable from the findings is that student behavior changed dramatically following the posting of rules and reminders of playground behavioral expectations, even though playground monitor behavior did not change to a marked degree. This suggests that precorrection can be effective even if the environmental changes only occur prior to the targeted activity.

Decreasing Problem Behaviors during Morning Gym

Haydon and Scott (2008) used the seven-step precorrection strategy developed by Colvin et al. (1993) to decrease problem behaviors in a noninstructional setting—the morning gym where students waited prior to the school day to be released to class. Participants were 3 gym supervisors and 400 elementary students in grades 3–5, 50% of whom received free and reduced-price lunches.

After a year of 77 office referrals generated from this setting alone, the gym supervisors developed a seven-step precorrection plan. First, the gym supervisors identified the predictable behaviors and contexts in which problem behavior occurred; the behaviors were talking, yelling, and being out of line, in particular during the last 20 minutes of morning gym. Second, they identified the four behaviors they expected to see during morning gym (i.e., walk, talk to students nearest you, be quiet when you hear the whistle blow, raise hand for assistance), which they later narrowed to two: use inside voices and use self-control. Third, they adjusted the environment by posting a sign with the morning gym rules and positioning a supervisor near the door to greet students and remind them of the expectations. Fourth, supervisors gave students opportunities to rehearse the behavioral expectations by randomly asking students to state the expectations or answer questions about expected gym behavior. Fifth, supervisors used high rates of praise for students engaging in expectations and implemented an interdependent group contingency that involved rewarding the best behaved grade level with outside recess time during morning gym the following day. Sixth, the gym supervisors developed a series of prompting strategies (gestural, verbal, environmental, and manual) to remind students of the expectations. Seventh, the supervisors sent names of students not following expectations to the cafeteria supervisors for follow-up, and office discipline referrals (ODR) were noted.

Prior to implementation, 77 ODR were recorded for the school year during morning gym. During the first year of implementation only 12 ODR were reported. This rate was maintained for a second year of implementation. Considering that ODR require a minimum of 20 minutes of administrator attention, approximately 21 hours (or 2.5 days) of administrator time was saved over the course of each school year by implementing this simple plan during morning gym.

Summary

This research illustrates how one simple strategy added to routines in both the classroom and nonclassroom settings can result in significant improvements in student behavior. It is also important to note that precorrection is a strategy that works seamlessly with other strategies, such as active supervision, prompting, praise, and group contingencies. The three studies outlined all used unique approaches to implement precorrection in the classroom, gym, and playground. Illustrations detailed in Chapter 4 also used precorrection during transitions throughout the school building in an elementary school (Colvin et al., 1997), an elementary social studies class (DePry & Sugai, 2002), and a middle school health class (Haydon et al., 2012). Table 7.1 contains a list of additional studies that illustrate the relationship between the use of precorrection strategies and improved student responding in variety of settings, some of which are also highlighted in Chapter 4.

Benefits and Challenges

Precorrection is an effective and efficient strategy to prevent problem behaviors from occurring; however, there are a few considerations to think about in order to use it effectively.

Benefits

Precorrection is an effective strategy for preventing problem behaviors from occurring by making contextual changes to activities/settings that traditionally occasion problem behaviors. Many teachers report that responding to inappropriate behaviors can be overwhelming and stressful, a feeling that may lead to teacher burnout (Ingersoll & Smith, 2003). That is the beauty of precorrection, as it seeks to prevent problem behaviors from ever occurring by taking a proactive approach to addressing problem behavior rather than relying on strategies that are reactive (Colvin et al., 1993). It is important to note that there are varying levels of intensity with which precorrection can be implemented. A simple precorrect may consist solely of a gentle reminder to engage in appropriate behavior before beginning an activity or entering an area of the school. However, in an effort to be more comprehensive, researchers have developed and several teachers have implemented a seven-step precorrection plan in an effort to strategically prevent and respond to inappropriate, as well as acknowledge appropriate, behavior (Colvin et al., 1993). Whereas a simple precorrective statement involves only manipulating antecedents, or what comes before a behavior, the more involved seven-step precorrection plan involves manipulating both antecedent and consequences of behavior.

Challenges

It is important to note that focusing on precorrection or preventative approaches may constitute a shift in thinking from traditional, consequence-based-only approaches to school discipline. With the widespread use of PBIS and CI3T, there is evidence to suggest that many teachers and schools are shifting to a proactive and preventative approach to schoolwide discipline (e.g., Lane, Oakes, et al., 2013). However, if you do not work in a school with this type of model, it may be necessary to help those around you understand the benefits of proactive approaches such as precorrection.

Further, in order to know for which contexts to develop precorrection plans (i.e., which contexts occasion problem behaviors and what types of behaviors are likely to result), you must have some experience with or knowledge of a given setting. However, even for new teachers or for teachers working in new settings, precorrection can be used if teachers or teams of teachers are willing to carefully consider or reflect upon their daily schedules and routines in order to anticipate what problems are likely to arise. The level of intensity of precorrection (e.g., simple precorrective statements or seven-step precorrection) and exact components can always be adjusted as needed based on the needs of students. If you are working in a tiered system of support that includes PBIS, this caveat can be avoided, as the expectations for each setting will already be defined (Lane, Oakes, Jenkins, et al., 2014).

Implementing Precorrection Strategies in Your Classroom: Checklist for Success

Table 7.2 includes a summary of the seven-step approach to implementing precorrection developed by Colvin et al. (1993). These steps are designed to assist you in taking an instructional approach to remediating behavior problems. Box 7.1 illustrates an example of how precorrection can be used within the context of a school implementing at CI3T model.

• **Step 1: Identify contexts and anticipated behaviors.** Step 1 consists of identifying a context in which problem behavior predictably occurs. This involves anticipating what times of day or activities during the school day occasion inappropriate behaviors. Precorrection plans can be developed independently by one teacher or by an entire team (e.g., content area, grade level, after-school care) of teachers and school faculty. If you are working in a school with a PBIS or CI3T model, your school's leadership team (e.g., CI3T team) may want to look at data from your school to determine what times of day, locations in the building, and/or groups of students are generating the highest percentage of ODR and develop a precorrection plan for that setting and/or group (Ennis et al., 2012).

As a part of this step, teachers also identify predictable problem behaviors that are likely to occur. This includes providing descriptions of anticipated problem behaviors that are operationally defined. Operationally defining a behavior involves describing behaviors with a level of detail so that anyone observing the student or group of students could identify the behavior when it occurred. For example, rather than just stating that students were horseplaying in the hallways, we may specify that students were jumping up to touch the doorframe, playfully shoving one another, high-fiving across other students, and shouting to one another

---

TABLE 7.2. Implementation Checklist for Success: Precorrection

- Step 1: Identify contexts and anticipated behaviors.
- Step 2: Determine the expected behaviors.
- Step 3: Adjust the environment.
- Step 4: Provide opportunities for behavioral rehearsal.
- Step 5: Provide strong reinforcement to students engaging in expected behavior.
- Step 6: Develop a prompting plan to remind students about the expected behavior.
- Step 7: Develop a monitoring plan to determine the effectiveness of the precorrection plan.
- Step 8: Offer students an opportunity to give feedback on this strategy.

Note. Based on Colvin, Sugai, and Patching (1993).

from distances greater than 5 feet. This description clearly articulates what kinds of behavior predictably occur and is then used to develop step 2, which is identifying and defining the expected behaviors.

• **Step 2: Determine the expected behaviors.** This step requires the teacher or other school staff members to clearly define what behaviors they expect a student behaving appropriately to display during the given activity and/or in the given context. Oftentimes this can be done by clearly defining the opposite of the anticipated inappropriate behaviors. Once the expectations have been clearly defined, the teacher or team developing the precorrection plan can more thoroughly develop the other components of the precorrection plan. Again, if you are working in a school with a PBIS or CI3T model in place, many of these expected behaviors have already been defined and are included in the schoolwide expectations matrix.

• **Step 3: Adjust the environment.** Step 3 is to modify the context to promote student success. Altering the context can involve a variety of components, including alterations to the classroom/school environment, alterations to teacher behaviors, and alterations to school/classroom schedules. Many of the strategies discussed in other chapters can be used to adjust the environment, including proximity control and active supervision (Chapter 4) and providing instructional choice (Chapter 8).

• **Step 4: Provide opportunities for behavioral rehearsal.** Step 4 involves giving students time to rehearse the expected behaviors. This often involves a minilesson in which the expected behaviors are discussed and even modeled for students. Depending on the needs of the students, this may involve activities such as role-playing correct behavior. If the behavior in question does not occur in the classroom, behavioral rehearsal may need to take place within the given context in which problem behaviors are likely to occur (e.g., in the hallway, on the playground). During this time, teachers may want to strategically invite students who have a history of problem behaviors in this setting to be a part of the discussion and/or model to support them with extra practice. This will provide the teacher with evidence that the target students understand the expectations for the identified context.

Depending on the context and how many times the expectations have been taught/modeled for the students, behavior rehearsal can take place immediately before the activity or at greater intervals (e.g., the day before the manipulative activity). It is important to note that behavior rehearsal is most effective when it takes place immediately before the activity, but variations may be necessary given the class or school schedule.

• **Step 5: Provide strong reinforcement to students engaging in expected behaviors.** Step 5 is to provide reinforcement for the expected behavior. As with modifying the context, there are several different ways to provide reinforcement. As discussed in Chapter 3 (Behavior-Specific Praise), reinforcement is a great tool for teaching new behaviors. It is important when teaching any behavior that we follow steps to tell, show, and do. *Tell* and *show* are covered during behavior rehearsal in Step 4, when students discuss and practice the expectations. Step 5 involves students engaging in the expected behavior (*do*) and then receiving acknowledgment and BSP for engaging in the expected behavior accurately (again, reinforcing effort, not ability). In this context, praise can be used to acknowledge students who are behaving appropriately, as well as to prompt students who are behaving inappropriately to modify their behavior.

Colvin et al. (1993) suggest that in step 5 we provide a strong reinforcement (i.e., a higher rate and/or higher quality of reinforcer than previously available in the context) for appropriate behavior. If we consider that the activity or setting we are targeting for the precorrection plan is one that has historically occasioned inappropriate behavior, it may be necessary to increase the rate of reinforcement typically provided (e.g., PBIS tickets). However, we strongly recommend staying with the schoolwide reinforcement system and not introducing a new reinforcement system. We want to help students recognize the multiple ways they can access reinforcement (programming for generalization) by using the same system. Over time, these tickets are continually paired with naturally occurring reinforcers (e.g., smiles, desirable outcomes such as good grades and enjoyable recess times). If a school does not include a schoolwide PBIS framework, it may be necessary to establish a classwide group contingency plan to promote students' success. However, again, we caution not to develop an independent classwide system if a schoolwide approach is in place.

There are three types of group contingencies: independent, interdependent, and dependent (Hulac & Benson, 2010). Independent group contingencies involve each student working independently to earn a reward, such as a token economy system in which each student earns, saves, and spends his or her own tokens, and the behavior of his or her peers does not influence his or her earning potential. Interdependent group contingencies involve groups of students working together to earn a reward for the group. In this model, all students work together to earn the reward, and the behavior of the entire group affects the outcome—all are rewarded or all are not. Dependent group contingencies involve one student or group of students being responsible for earning a reward for the entire group. In dependent group contingencies the identity of the person(s) responsible for earning the reward may be known or unknown (i.e., a mystery hero). Any one of these models can be used to provide strong reinforcement for meeting the expected behavior. However, it is important to monitor the use of group contingencies and make sure that students are engaging in positive peer pressure rather than scapegoating or bullying behaviors. Dependent group contingencies, in particular, can result in one student or group of students being mistreated by peers if a reinforcer is not earned, which is the reason a mystery-hero technique or using independent or independent options may be more effective (Coogan, Kehle, Bray, & Chafouleas, 2007).

- **Step 6: Develop a prompting plan to remind students about the expected behavior.** Step 6 is to develop a plan for how to respond to students who do not automatically engage in the expected appropriate behaviors. Again, this could take several forms, including gestural (e.g., pointing, holding up the "quiet" sign), verbal (e.g., restating expectations, counting down from 10), environmental (e.g., posting signs, sectioning off areas of the room with tape or dividers), and manual (e.g., facing students, using proximity control) prompts (Haydon & Scott, 2008).

This could also involve a system of least-to-most prompting. Least-to-most prompting is a strategy that employs prompts on a graduated continuum from least to most intensive (Spriggs, Gast, & Ayres, 2007). For example, the teacher may: (1) move to the location in the classroom where students are misbehaving, (2) point to the sign of expectations posted in the front of the classroom, (3) verbally remind students of expected behaviors, (4) model or assist students with correct behavior. As you can see, these examples increase in intensity with each prompt. These steps could also be repeated, focusing on an individual student rather than a group of students. Developing a prompting plan ahead of time can help teachers respond more systematically to inappropriate behaviors as they arise.

• **Step 7: Develop a monitoring plan to determine the effectiveness of the pre-correction plan.** With any classroom-based intervention, you want to have a plan for monitoring student progress. Specific considerations for step 7 are discussed in the following section.

• **Step 8: Offer students an opportunity to give feedback on this strategy.** Finally, we recommend offering students an opportunity to give feedback on the strategy used. In addition, you will want to solicit feedback from other stakeholders involved in the intervention or working with students in the identified context (e.g., other teachers, paraprofessionals, parents). It is important for all stakeholders to have a voice in determining future classroom practices. In particular, soliciting the feedback of students can help identify more effective strategies and/or reinforcers. We discuss this further in the next section.

Examining the Effects: How Well Is It Working?

Testing the Strategy: Design Considerations

When implementing precorrection, it is important to collect data on student performance to know how well this strategy is working. In many of the studies featured in this book, researchers have used single-case methodology to "test" the intervention effects. This is a particularly useful design approach for teachers, as it is highly flexible and very practical. It can be used with any of the strategies introduced in each chapter.

It is important to use an experimental design such as an ABAB or multiple baseline across settings, tasks, or students to establish a functional relation between the introduction of the intervention and changes in student performance (Gast & Ledford, 2014). In other words, this design helps determine whether or not the intervention worked. This information is helpful to both general education and special education teachers for a variety of reasons. The first, of course, is that it allows you to evaluate the effectiveness of your instruction. With this information, you can decide how to adjust your instructional practices so they work better for your students. Second, members of the CI3T team or members of professional learning communities (PLCs) can use these data to determine how students are responding to these low-intensity supports. Before moving on to student-focused Tier 2 (e.g., Check-In/Check-Out, behavior contracts, or self-monitoring strategies) or Tier 3 (e.g., functional assessment-based interventions; Umbreit et al., 2007) supports, we want to be certain we have examined the extent to which teacher-driven strategies (e.g., precorrection) have been effective in addressing students' needs (academically, behaviorally, and/or socially). Using an experimental design is one way to show whether or not this has occurred. We recommend these teams (e.g., CI3T and PLC) be composed of a range of individuals, including general and special education teachers, as they each bring unique talents. For example, special education teachers are a critical resource for implementing and delivering specialized intervention; they can assist general educators with evaluating strategy implementation, as well as carefully measuring the effects of any given intervention for a particular student, as is demonstrated in Box 7.1. This is especially critical when focused on more intensive supports, such as functional assessment-based interventions, that require careful monitoring of students' performance (e.g., academic engagement, disruption). The ability to use single-case methodology is a critical skill in assessing the effectiveness of Tier 2 and 3 supports.

These designs begin with a baseline phase during which data on student performance are collected (referred to as the A phase), then the intervention is introduced for the first time (B) while still collecting data on student performance using the same data collection method used during the baseline phase (see Figure 7.1 in Box 7.1). Although it is tempting at this point to say the intervention was effective, two more replications are needed to be certain the intervention was responsible for the change and not something else. One demonstration (e.g., the change from A to B phases) along with two other replications can provide evidence that the introduction of the strategy produced the changes (the shift from B to A and then A to B or shifts from A to B for multiple students; Gast & Ledford, 2014).

Although some designs, such as the ABAB design, require removal and then reintroduction of the intervention, it is also possible to explore a functional relation using multiple baseline across settings designs, as illustrated in Figure 7.1. This means the strategy is used in different settings, such as a different instructional period (math instead of reading) or a different physical location (playground instead of the lunchroom).

Making Certain the Strategy Is in Place: Treatment Integrity

In addition to using an experimental design to test the intervention, collecting treatment integrity data helps determine the extent to which the intervention is being implemented as planned. Figure 7.2 in Box 7.1 is an example of a treatment integrity checklist for precorrection, with Panel A showing a completed checklist and Panel B showing a blank template for your use. Although there are many different ways to collect treatment integrity data, one way is to have the teacher collect these data each day by indicating the degree to which each intervention component was implemented as planned for each student. For example, in Figure 7.2, Panels A and B, each item is completed using a 3-point Likert-type scale as follows: 0 = *not in place*, 1 = *partially in place*, or 2 = *completely in place*. Each day the items are summed, divided by the total number of points possible, and divided by 100 to obtain a percentage of implementation for each student. These data can be used to interpret intervention outcomes (see Box 7.1). In addition, behavior component checklists not only determine the level of implementation but also serve as a prompt or reminder to implement each step.

Using an outside observer to collect treatment integrity data for approximately 25% of the sessions in each phase is recommended. An additional observer is important for establishing the accuracy of the data collected.

Examining Stakeholders' Views: Social Validity

Finally, in addition to collecting information on student performance and implementation (treatment integrity), it is important to understand how stakeholders felt about the intervention goals, procedures, and intended outcomes. Figure 7.3 in Box 7.1 is an example of a measure examining one student's perceptions of the social validity of precorrection. Again, Panel A shows a completed form, and Panel B shows a blank template for your use.

It is important to obtain all stakeholders' views—the teacher, the student, and the parent—ideally before the intervention begins and again at the conclusion of the first "test." If social validity is low at the onset of the intervention, then it is wise to provide additional training to increase people's knowledge of the strategies, as well as their confidence in using the strategy prior to implementation. In theory (and in some instances in actuality; see Lane, Kalberg, Bruhn, et al., 2009), the opinions of those implementing and participating in the intervention may predict the extent to which the interventions are implemented as planned. In essence, a socially valid intervention is likely to be put in place with a high degree of integrity, leading to improvements in student performance that maintain over time and in new settings and with new people.

BOX 7.1. A Hypothetical Illustration of Precorrection in a CI3T Model

Ms. Johnson is a general education teacher at Hillwood High School, an urban high school currently implementing a comprehensive, integrated, three-tiered (CI3T) model of prevention. As part of their CI3T plan, they use Common Core State Standards to teach academics, a positive behavior intervention and support (PBIS) framework, and weekly problem-solving lessons using the Building Decisions Skills

(Institute for Global Ethics, 2008; Leming, 2001) to teach social skills to all students. Ms. Johnson teaches ninth-grade algebra five periods a day. Three of those classes are cotaught classes, for which Mrs. Edwards, a special education teacher, joins her to support the needs of all students in the classroom. During those periods both general education students and students receiving special education services (e.g., for learning disabilities, autism spectrum disorder, emotional and behavioral disorders) according to the Individuals with Disabilities Education Improvement Act (IDEA, 2004) are in the class. As a part of their weekly planning time together, Ms. Johnson and Mrs. Edwards noted that during activities using manipulatives (e.g., algebra tiles, dry-erase boards) they had difficulty maintaining the students' attention and that students often misused the manipulatives. They evaluated their discipline referral data and noted that on days when they used manipulatives, there were more than three discipline referrals per day from each class. In particular, they noted that there were two to three students in each class who were responsible for generating 50% or more of the discipline referrals because of their disruptive and distractible behavior. Ms. Johnson and Mrs. Edwards saw the benefit of using manipulatives on their students' math reasoning, so they devised a plan to make these activities run more smoothly in their classroom.

Support	Description	Entry criteria	Data to monitor progress	Exit criteria
Precorrection	Plan to modify teacher behavior and environmental contexts to support appropriate behavior and prevent problem behaviors from occurring	Class with more than three discipline referrals per day during manipulative use; students who are moderate risk as measured by the Student Risk Screening Scale (Drummond, 1994)	*Student performance:* • Student discipline referrals • Number of manipulatives returned • Accuracy of work completion *Treatment integrity:* Component checklist *Social validity:* Student-completed survey	2 consecutive weeks of < 1 discipline referral per day during manipulative use

Mrs. Edwards suggested the possibility of developing a precorrection plan, a low-intensity support easily implemented in the classroom, to potentially benefit all students in their classes, with special focus on improving the behavior of students with high levels of discipline referrals. Mrs. Edwards and Ms. Johnson agreed that this was something they could try in all their classes, but that they would try it out in only one period initially to see whether it was helpful. They decided to start with first period, in which there were three students who were generating the majority of the discipline referrals: Morgan, a girl receiving special education services for other health impairment because of her diagnosis of attention-deficit/hyperactivity disorder, and two boys, David and DJ, who were not identified as having disabilities but who had recently been identified by the school's systematic screening process as at moderate risk for antisocial behavior according to the Student Risk Screening Scale (SRSS; Drummond, 1994). All three students earned a C average during the first 9 weeks of school.

Mrs. Edwards worked through the eight-step process with Ms. Johnson as follows. These steps can also be found in Table 7.2.

Preparing for and Delivering Precorrection: The Intervention

• **Step 1: Identify contexts and anticipated behaviors.** The teachers had already identified the activity during which problem behaviors were occurring: manipulative use in the classroom. Together, they identified and clearly defined the ways in which the students were using the manipulatives incorrectly: horseplaying, stacking, using independent manipulatives in conjunction with a peer, using the manipulatives in a way other than their intended use, talking during manipulative instruction, breaking or losing manipulatives, talking or horseplaying while walking to pick up or return manipulatives, and failure to return manipulatives to the designated area.

• **Step 2: Determine the expected behaviors.** Mrs. Edwards and Ms. Johnson then listed what behaviors they expect students to display instead. They defined these as appropriate manipulative use.

   ○ **Label.** Appropriate manipulative use.
   ○ **Definition.** *Appropriate manipulative use* refers to using the manipulative as requested by the teacher, for the intended instructional purposes.
   ○ **Examples.** Examples include following teacher directions when picking up and returning manipulatives, using manipulatives only as directed, using only the manipulatives assigned to you, listening to teacher directions and instructions with still hands, and handling manipulatives with care.
   ○ **Nonexamples.** Nonexamples include the behaviors identified in step 1: horseplaying, stacking, using independent manipulatives in conjunction with a peer, using the manipulatives in a way other than their intended use, talking during manipulative instruction, breaking or losing manipulatives, talking or horseplaying while walking to pick up or return manipulatives, and failure to return manipulatives to the designated area.

• **Step 3: Adjust the environment.** When developing a plan for the next manipulative day, they decided that Mrs. Edwards would stand by the manipulatives table to oversee and provide feedback and behavior-specific praise (BSP) as students picked up and returned manipulatives. In an effort to minimize confusion during this time, they also decided to assign one person from each row to pick up and return the manipulatives for the other students in their row. If the activity was independent, they made sure students' desks were arranged in rows so that they would be less likely to try to work together. If the activity was partnered, they instructed students to push their desks together in twos so they had enough room to work and could talk in a low voice while working together. Finally, they decided that both teachers would actively supervise and remain in close proximity to all students during manipulative activities.

• **Step 4: Provide opportunities for behavioral rehearsal.** On the day before a manipulative activity, Ms. Johnson and Mrs. Edwards reviewed the expectations for using manipulatives. They also had students model how to pick up, use, and return manipulatives. Both the review and the modeling took just a few minutes to demonstrate. They made sure to involve Morgan, David, and DJ in these discussions and demonstrations so the students could have the extra practice and the teachers could be confident that each of them understood the expectations. They decided doing this the day before was best, so that students could pay attention without the added distraction of already having the manipulatives in their hands.

• **Step 5: Provide strong reinforcement to students engaging in expected behaviors.** To reinforce students who used manipulatives correctly, the teachers decided to provide BSP to students they observed using the manipulatives correctly while supervising them with close proximity and intermittently handing out PBIS tickets, also paired with BSP. In addition, for every manipulative day that the entire class went without a discipline referral, the teachers would place a PBIS ticket on the board, taping out the word "MATH." Once the class spelled out MATH, they earned 20 minutes of free time. This plan was explained to students during behavior rehearsal, so they knew up front what they could earn for appropriate responding during manipulative lessons.

• **Step 6: Develop a prompting plan to remind students about the expected behavior.** To prompt students to engage in appropriate behaviors, they decided to verbally remind students of expectations for using manipulatives (focusing on what was expected of them, rather than reprimanding them). For example, while circulating around the room, Ms. Johnson would model how to use the algebra tiles if she noted a student or pair of students using them incorrectly. Both teachers also reminded the students that they were working for free time if they noticed students start to horseplay or talk during the lesson.

• **Step 7: Develop a monitoring plan to determine the effectiveness of the precorrection plan.** Ms. Johnson's and Mrs. Edwards's plan for evaluating effectiveness is detailed in the next section.

• **Step 8: Offer students an opportunity to give feedback on this strategy.** Ms. Johnson and Mrs. Edwards developed a questionnaire to gain students' opinions of the intervention, including questions about the students' perceptions of the effectiveness of the intervention for them and for other students. They planned to have students complete the questionnaire both before and after the intervention.

Looking at How Well Precorrection Worked

While Ms. Johnson and Mrs. Edwards used discipline referrals and SRSS scores to identify classrooms and students to target, they chose to monitor data on the replacement behaviors they identified to determine whether the intervention was effective. Since this was a problem in all of their cotaught classes, they decided to collect baseline data on the percentage of time students were engaged in appropriate manipulative use. These data were collected using a momentary time-sampling procedure, in which Mrs. Edwards used an interval timer app to prompt her to observe students' behavior every minute. In order to get a snapshot of the entire class, Mrs. Edwards would rotate between each of the four work groups (observing group 1 for the first interval, group 2 for the second, etc.). Before collecting data, Mrs. Edwards and Ms. Johnson practiced using this recording system together to make sure they collected academic engagement data reliably. Specifically, they observed each class together with high reliability for three consecutive sessions to ensure they were interpreting the definition of appropriate manipulative use correctly.

Figure 7.1 contains the results of each class's percentage of intervals with appropriate manipulative use per day. Once Ms. Johnson and Mrs. Edwards observed a marked increase in appropriate manipulative use in the first period, they implemented their precorrection plan with the fifth period. Once a marked increase was observed in the fifth period, they introduced it to their third-period class as well. By trying it out in one class at a time, they were able to determine that it was the precorrection plan that improved the students' behavior on manipulative days rather than other factors (e.g., the chapter being taught, changes to the schoolwide discipline plan, seasonal changes in student behavior). When you compare percentage of intervals with appropriate manipulative use in each class prior to the implementation of the precorrection plan, you will see a marked increase for each class. For example, if you look at the data for the first period, you will notice that students were displaying appropriate manipulative use from 40 to 60% of the time. Once the plan was put into place, students in the first period, including targeted students, were engaging in appropriate manipulative use from 80 to 100% of the time.

In addition, Ms. Johnson and Mrs. Edwards also collected data on the number of manipulatives returned correctly at the end of the period, as this was a type of permanent product data that they did not have to collect while they were teaching. Each day, Ms. Johnson would count all materials that were correctly returned to the table before the next class entered. By recording these data, she was able to determine that students were using the materials appropriately.

Finally, they also decided to grade students' in-class math assignments for accuracy to see whether appropriate manipulative use was helping to improve the math performance of their target students (not graphed in Figure 7.1). Accuracy was evaluated by dividing the number of problems completed accurately (if a problem was not attempted, it was marked as incorrect) by the number of problems assigned and multiplying by 100 to obtain a percentage. Morgan, David, and DJ, as well as target students from the third and fifth periods, all made improvements in accuracy as a result of the precorrection plan and improvements in their behavior.

To make certain the intervention was happening as planned, either Ms. Johnson or Mrs. Edwards completed a daily treatment integrity form (see Figure 7.2, Panel A, for a sample completed treatment integrity form). Each day they recorded whether the intervention component was *not in place* (0), *partially in place* (1), or *fully in place* (2). During baseline (prior to precorrection plan implementation), Ms. Johnson and Mrs. Edwards did not implement any of the components of the

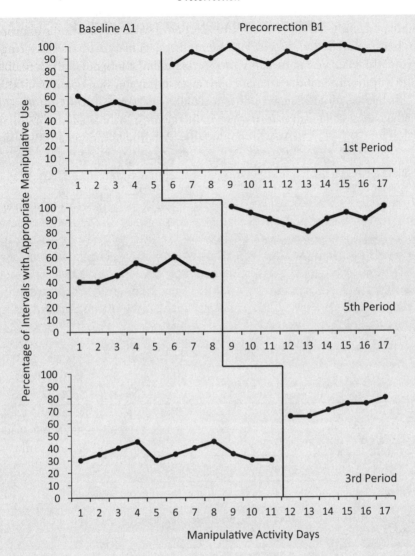

FIGURE 7.1. Examining the effects: High school student outcomes (percentage of appropriate manipulative use).

precorrection plan. Once they began implementing the precorrection plan, they were consistently implementing 90–100% of the essential elements, as measured by the treatment integrity form. Figure 7.2, Panel A, shows that the average implementation that day was 91.67% because one item was only partially implemented.

In addition, Mrs. Edwards and Ms. Johnson also sought out feedback from students to get their overall impressions of the intervention. Figure 7.3 shows David's social validity ratings. When the intervention was initially explained to him, he had a favorable opinion (rating all items but one as "agree" or "strongly agree"). Following the intervention, however, he had an even more favorable rating of the intervention, rating all items as "strongly agree" except one (rated "agree").

TREATMENT INTEGRITY CHECKLIST: PRECORRECTION

Panel A

Setting: ☒ Classroom: _Algebra_   Observer: ☐ Primary: _Mrs. Edwards_

         ☐ Hallway: _____   ☐ Secondary: _Ms. Johnson_

         ☐ Recess: _____

Predictable challenging behaviors: _horseplaying, stacking, using independent manipulatives in_ _conjunction with a peer, using the manipulatives in a way other than their intended use, talking during_ _manipulative instruction, breaking or losing manipulatives, talking or horseplaying while walking to pick_ _up or return manipulatives, and failure to return manipulatives to the designated area._

Expected behaviors: _follow teacher directions when picking up and returning manipulatives, only use_ _manipulatives as directed, only -use manipulatives assigned to you, listen to teacher directions and -_ _instructions with still hands, and handle manipulatives with care_

Date: _10/03/16_   Start time: _10:15_   End time: _10:55_   Total time: _40 min_

Notes: _algebra tiles for solving equations_

0 = *not in place*, 1 = *partially in place*, or 2 = *completely in place*.

Item	Rating
1. Did I identify the context and determine the expected behavior?	0 1 ②
2. Did I modify the environment to promote student success?	0 1 ②
3. Did I provide students with an opportunity to practice the expected behavior?	0 ① 2
4. Did I provide students with strong reinforcement for completing the expected behavior?	0 1 ②
5. Did I prompt students to remind them to engage in the expected behavior?	0 1 ②
6. Did I monitor student behavior?	0 1 ②
TOTAL	11
$(N \div [12]) \times 100 =$	91.67%

(continued)

FIGURE 7.2. Making certain the strategy is in place: Treatment integrity checklist used to monitor the extent to which each step of the precorrection plan was put in place as planned. Panel A shows the completed checklist, and Panel B shows a blank checklist for 1 day.

TREATMENT INTEGRITY CHECKLIST: PRECORRECTION

Panel B

Setting: ☐ Classroom: _____   Observer: ☐ Primary: _____

☐ Hallway: _____   ☐ Secondary: _____

☐ Recess: _____

Predictable challenging behaviors: _____

_____

_____

_____

Expected behaviors: _____

_____

_____

_____

Date: _____   Start time: _____   End time: _____   Total time: _____

Notes: _____

_____

0 = not in place, 1 = partially in place, or 2 = completely in place.

Item	Rating		
1. Did I identify the context and determine the expected behavior?	0	1	2
2. Did I modify the environment to promote student success?	0	1	2
3. Did I provide students with an opportunity to practice the expected behavior?	0	1	2
4. Did I provide students with strong reinforcement for completing the expected behavior?	0	1	2
5. Did I prompt students to remind them to engage in the expected behavior?	0	1	2
6. Did I monitor student behavior?	0	1	2
TOTAL			
$(N \div [12]) \times 100 =$			

FIGURE 7.2. *(continued)*

From *Supporting Behavior for School Success: A Step-by-Step Guide to Key Strategies* by Kathleen Lynne Lane, Holly Mariah Menzies, Robin Parks Ennis, and Wendy Peia Oakes. Copyright 2015 by The Guilford Press. Permission to photocopy this figure is granted to purchasers of this book for personal use only (see copyright page for details). Purchasers can download a larger version of this figure from *www.guilford.com/lane4-forms*.

SOCIAL VALIDITY FORM: PRECORRECTION

Panel A

Preassessment: David	Strongly disagree	Disagree	Agree	Strongly agree
I would like to have a precorrection plan in my classroom (reminders of what is expected, rewards).	1	2	(3)	4
Having a precorrection plan would help improve my behavior in class.	1	2	(3)	4
Having a precorrection plan would help other students.	1	2	3	(4)
Having a precorrection plan would help me do better in school.	1	2	(3)	4
Having a precorrection plan would help me getting along better with my teacher.	1	(2)	3	4
Percentage: (total number/total number possible [20]) × 100 =	75%			

Postassessment: David	Strongly disagree	Disagree	Agree	Strongly agree
I liked having a precorrection plan in my classroom (reminders of what is expected, rewards).	1	2	3	(4)
Having a precorrection plan helped improve my behavior in class.	1	2	3	(4)
Having a precorrection plan would help other students.	1	2	3	(4)
Having a precorrection plan helped me do better in school.	1	2	3	(4)
Having a precorrection plan helped me get along better with my teacher.	1	2	(3)	4
Percentage: (total number/total number possible [20]) × 100 =	95%			

(continued)

FIGURE 7.3. Examining stakeholders' views: Social validity form developed to examine students' views on the use of precorrection. The form has two parts: one to be completed before the strategy is used and a second to be completed after the strategy has been implemented. Panel A shows David's ratings. Panel B is a blank version of the form. This form is based on the Children's Intervention Rating Profile developed by Witt and Elliott (1985).

SOCIAL VALIDITY FORM: PRECORRECTION

Panel B

Preassessment:	Strongly disagree	Disagree	Agree	Strongly agree
I would like to have a precorrection plan in my classroom (reminders of what is expected, rewards).	1	2	3	4
Having a precorrection plan would help improve my behavior in class.	1	2	3	4
Having a precorrection plan would help other students.	1	2	3	4
Having a precorrection plan would help me do better in school.	1	2	3	4
Having a precorrection plan would help me getting along better with my teacher.	1	2	3	4
Percentage: (total number/total number possible [20]) × 100 =				

Postassessment:	Strongly disagree	Disagree	Agree	Strongly agree
I liked having a precorrection plan in my classroom (reminders of what is expected, rewards).	1	2	3	4
Having a precorrection plan helped improve my behavior in class.	1	2	3	4
Having a precorrection plan would help other students.	1	2	3	4
Having a precorrection plan helped me do better in school.	1	2	3	4
Having a precorrection plan helped me get along better with my teacher.	1	2	3	4
Percentage: (total number/total number possible [20]) × 100 =				

FIGURE 7.3. *(continued)*

From *Supporting Behavior for School Success: A Step-by-Step Guide to Key Strategies* by Kathleen Lynne Lane, Holly Mariah Menzies, Robin Parks Ennis, and Wendy Peia Oakes. Copyright 2015 by The Guilford Press. Permission to photocopy this figure is granted to purchasers of this book for personal use only (see copyright page for details). Purchasers can download a larger version of this figure from *www.guilford.com/lane4-forms*.

Ms. Johnson and Mrs. Edwards were so pleased with their findings from their cotaught classes that they shared them with their principal, who was the leader of the school's CI3T team, and the full faculty during a regularly scheduled faculty meeting. The principal decided to look at schoolwide data to identify activities and times of day that precorrection plans could be developed for common areas of the school (e.g., lunchroom, dismissal).

Summary

Precorrection is an antecedent-based strategy that can be implemented quite simply in any classroom or school setting. The beauty of precorrection is that it is designed to prevent problem behaviors from ever occurring. This strategy can facilitate classrooms and schools that are positive and smoothly run. Anticipating times in the school day when problem behaviors are likely to occur and taking steps to prevent them from occurring is something that many educators do without even realizing it. Using a comprehensive precorrection plan, such as the seven-step plan detailed here, will help teachers and other school staff think through all components of how to precorrect students effectively (e.g., context modifications, behavior rehearsal). In addition, this seven-step plan includes procedures for responding to students who continue to engage in inappropriate behavior (e.g., prompts), as well as procedures for monitoring and reinforcing student behavior. Precorrection is a versatile and simple strategy that can have tremendous effects on the behavior of students.

CHAPTER 8

A Look at Instructional Choice

As educators have become more focused on better understanding the relation between instruction and student behavior, the role of positive behavior interventions and supports (PBIS) has become increasingly more important. For example, researchers and practitioners studying applications of PBIS have demonstrated how relatively simple shifts in environmental variables can make problem behaviors "irrelevant, inefficient, and ineffective" for students (Horner, 2000, p. 182). Rather than focusing exclusively on a student's behavior, adjusting the environment—which can be done before challenging behaviors occur (antecedent-based interventions)—can reduce the likelihood of undesirable behaviors occurring and will support students to engage more fully in the tasks at hand (Shogren, Faggella-Luby, Bae, & Wehmeyer, 2004). Many would argue that choice (the focus of this chapter) is directly related to quality of life for all individuals—including those with disabilities (Felce & Perry, 1995; Shogren et al., 2004).

Some examples of PBIS that emphasize the environment include increasing students' opportunities to respond (see Chapter 2), using active supervision (see Chapter 4), and incorporating choice and preferred activities (Kern & State, 2009). Research on choice has focused on three main areas: (1) assessing student preferences, (2) increasing students' opportunities to make choices, and (3) using choice as an intervention (Kern et al., 1998). In this chapter we focus on the latter application of choice: examining the impact of choice on various student outcomes such as academic engagement, task completion, and disruptive behavior. More specifically, we look at instructional choice.

What Is Instructional Choice?

Instructional choice is an antecedent-based, positive behavior support that can be easily implemented by practitioners as part of their instructional repertoire to decrease problem behaviors as well as increase students' academic engagement and work completion. Although there are many different definitions of instructional choice, we look to the definition offered by Jolivette, Stichter, and McCormick (2002): "opportunities to make choices means that the student is provided with two or more options, is allowed to independently select an option, and is provided with the selected option" (p. 28).

Instructional choices can include a range of options. For example, teachers might offer students the choice of a task or activity by giving each student the option to either write a brief report or create a YouTube video lecture on the causes of the Civil War. A choice of task sequence could be offered that allows a student to select the order in which tasks are completed or to choose which task to work on first. Another option would be to provide the choice of which materials to use to complete an assignment, such as using colored markers or crayons to complete the illustration. Choosing to work with a partner or choosing which person to work with (e.g., peers, teachers, paraprofessional) are also possibilities. Teachers might also allow students to choose where they complete their assignments, such as working at their desks, in the writing center, or in the library, keeping in mind that adult supervision is required for any setting offered. Flexibility with time is another way to incorporate choice. Students can give input on how long they think it should take to complete a task or when to take a short break. Finally, even where work is done can be a way to provide students with choices. For example, students may opt to complete some assignments at home rather than at school or in a special seat in the classroom, such as at a standing work station (see Kern & State, 2009; Skerbetz & Kostewicz, 2013).

Rispoli and colleagues (2013) suggested instructional choices can be broadly grouped in two main types: across-activities choices and within-activities choices. Across-activities choices allow students to choose between different tasks, meaning that within the same time period students could be completing different tasks or activities, or at least completing tasks in the sequence of their choice. Within-activities choices keep the instructional task or activity fixed but allow students to make a choice in terms of instructional materials or environmental arrangements.

Why Is Instructional Choice Effective?

Instructional choice is effective for a number of reasons. This antecedent-based intervention is easy to incorporate into teachers' instructional repertoire of skills, requires very little time, money, or material resources, and is a highly effective strategy for decreasing disruptive behavior (Kern & State, 2009). In addition, focusing on choice-making skills and providing opportunities is an often used and highly effective intervention for promoting self-determination skills for students with disabilities (Algozzine, Browder, Karvonen, Test, & Wood, 2001; Kern & State, 2009).

There are different theories as to why choice is effective. One explanation is that offering students the opportunity to make choices allows them to access activities they enjoy, and because they are engaging in preferred activities and tasks, they behave better. But reinforcement alone does not fully explain the way choice works to improve behavior, particularly given that behavior improves even when students are given only the choice of selecting nonpreferred or moderately preferred tasks (e.g., Bambara, Ager, & Koger, 1994; Vaughn & Horner, 1997). In addition, other studies offering choice of sequence (e.g., "Which task would you like to do first?") of nonpreferred activities also resulted in reduced rates of problem behaviors (Kern, Mantegna, Vorndran, Bailin, & Hilt, 2001). Thus it appears that more than just reinforcement is playing a role in the effectiveness of choice.

Another theory suggests there is "something innate in all of us that makes us like to have choices, and liking choices has helped us to survive" (Kern & State, 2009, p. 4). Kern and State (2009) offer an illustration in which they describe how animals that lived in places with a variety of food sources were more likely to survive if one of the food sources became scarce. Having the choice of something else to eat may have facilitated survival (see Kern & State, 2009, for a more detailed discussion of how the desire for choice may rest within us).

Yet another theory as to why choice is an effective intervention may stem from the fact that when we have choices we can get what we want and avoid what we do not want *at the time*. Given that preferences change over time (from pumpkin spice lattes to green tea, from crayons to sparkly markers), we may value choice because it prevents us from being restricted to our original interests or preferences (Kern & State, 2009).

Too often in schools students have very few choices, so much so that some adolescent students may say things like *this place feels like a prison*. Statements like this indicate the opportunities for choice are too few. This is particularly true for students with emotional and behavioral disorders (EBD), whose teachers often remove preferred tasks and the option for choice making in an effort to gain control. It is not surprising that several studies of choice have focused on incorporating choice to support students with and at risk for EBD, as discussed in the next section (e.g., Dunlap et al., 1994).

Supporting Research for Instructional Choice

Studies examining instructional choice document how this intervention increases academic engagement and decreases challenging behaviors for a range of students, including those with developmental disabilities, EBD, and autism, as well as typically developing students (Kern & State, 2009; Rispoli et al., 2013). In addition, instructional choice-making activities have been used across the PreK through high school continuum and in a range of instructional settings, from residential treatment facilities to self-contained classrooms on public school campuses to inclusive contexts (see Table 8.1). The following studies illustrate how instructional choice has been applied in a range of settings to support students with and at risk for EBD.

Increasing Engagement and Decreasing Disruption in Elementary Self-Contained Classrooms

Dunlap and colleagues (1994) examined the effect of choice-making activities to enhance adaptive behavior on elementary school-age students who had emotional and behavioral challenges. In the first study they worked with two 11-year-old boys, Wendall and Sven, during independent seat work time in their self-contained classroom. Wendall's intervention took place during English and Sven's during spelling. There were nine students in the classroom staffed by a teacher, a full-time paraprofessional, and two to three behavioral consultants. The behavioral consultants were responsible for data collection.

Dunlap et al. (1994) used a reversal design in which two behaviors were monitored—task engagement and disruption—using direct observations (15-minute sessions, 15-second continuous interval system) during the 20- to 30-minute sessions. After collecting baseline data (Phase A, no choice) and determining the data were stable, the intervention (Phase B, choice) was introduced. Then the intervention was withdrawn (Phase A, no choice) and again reintroduced (Phase B, choice).

During the no-choice conditions, daily assignments were selected by the teacher, listed on the blackboard, and instructions provided. Students were expected to complete the assignments after the instructions were given and then take their finished assignment to the paraprofessional, who scored them (ranging from 1 to 10 points). As part of the intervention phase, students were allowed to choose from a menu of academic tasks related to their educational objectives. Each boy was given an individualized menu of tasks for his respective content area on a notebook-sized piece of paper. The menu content was developed by the teacher in partnership with the consultant and included the assignments presented in the no-choice phase (e.g., worksheets in English; writing spelling words three times each)—none of which were viewed favorably by students, as evidenced by frequent complaining when assigned these tasks in the no-choice condition. Teachers informed students they could complete any assignment from their menu and that they could also change their selection during any session (which rarely happened). Results showed that during both choice phases, the students had increased levels of task engagement and decreased levels of disruption compared with no-choice conditions.

TABLE 8.1. Supporting Research: Instructional Choice

Authors and journal	Students	Intervention setting	Intervention	Measures	Design
Dunlap et al., (1994) Choice making to promote adaptive behavior for students with emotional and behavioral challenges (JABA)	$N = 3$ students with EBD, ages 5–11 (2 in Study 1 and 1 in Study 2)	In a public elementary school's self-contained classroom for students with emotional disabilities, during English, spelling, or story telling	Choice of assignments	*Dependent variables:* 1. Task engagement 2. Disruptive behavior *Treatment integrity:* Not mentioned *Social validity:* Not mentioned	Reversal
Jolivette, Wehby, Canale, & Massey (2001) Effects of choice-making opportunities on the behavior of students with emotional and behavioral disorders (BD)	$N = 3$ students with EBD, ages 6–10 years	Self-contained special education classroom for students with EBD who exhibited internalizing disorders, during math led by the special education classroom teacher	Instruction choice (which task to complete first of three options)	*Dependent variables:* 1. Task engagement 2. Off-task behavior 3. Disruption 4. Attempted task problems 5. Problems correct *Treatment integrity:* Direct observations of videos by outside observers (100%) *Social validity:* Teachers completed TARF-R	Multiple baseline across participants
Kern, Mantegna, Vorndran, Bailin, & Hilt (2001) Choice of task sequence to reduce problem behaviors (JPBI)	$N = 3$ students; Danny: 7-year-old, ADHD; Kelly: 15-year-old, intellectual disability; Shannon: 11-year-old, mild intellectual disability, ADHD	Danny and Shannon: in patient facility (temporary placement); Kelly: private school for those with EBD	Choice of sequence of task completion	*Dependent variables:* 1. Danny: Direct observation of problem behavior and engagement 2. Kelly: engagement 3. Shannon: problem behavior *Treatment integrity:* Not mentioned *Social validity:* Not mentioned	Reversal

(continued)

TABLE 8.1. (continued)

Authors and journal	Students	Intervention setting	Intervention	Measures	Design
Kern, Bambara, & Fogt (2002) Class-wide curricular modification to improve the behavior of students with emotional or behavioral disorders (BD)	$N = 6$ male students ages 13–14 with labels of severe emotional disturbances	Self-contained science class in a university-affiliated private school for students with behavioral challenges	Classwide curricular modification 1. Choice making 2. High-interest activities	*Dependent variables:* Engagement and destructive behavior *Treatment integrity:* Assessed by data collectors (100%) and teacher-completed logs *Social validity:* Students complete a class evaluation sheet daily, teachers completed the TARF-R at the end	ABAB withdrawal design
Ramsey, Jolivette, Patterson, & Kennedy (2010) Using choice to increase time on-task, task completion, and accuracy for students with emotional/ behavioral disorders in a residential facility (ETC)	$N = 5$ adolescent students with EBD, ages 13–16	Residential setting, conducted by the three special education classroom teachers during independent academic task time in math and language arts classes	Choice of task sequence	*Dependent variables:* 1. Time on task 2. Task completion 3. Accuracy *Treatment integrity:* Assessed via direct observations of 30% of the sessions ($M = 99.33\%$) *Social validity:* Structured interviews with the teachers; student survey	ABAB withdrawal design and maintenance A = no choice B = choice
DiCarlo, Baumgartner, Stephens, & Pierce (2013) Using structured choice to increase child engagement in low-preference centres (ECDC)	$N = 6$ children ages 3–4	Inclusive, 4-day-a-week, half-day program; led by a teacher with a master's in early childhood education and two graduate assistants	Structured choice intervention (choice between two low-preference centers)	*Dependent variables:* 1. Time spent in low-preference interest centers 2. Time spent engaged with materials *Treatment integrity:* Not mentioned *Social validity:* Not mentioned	Multiple baseline

178

Citation	N	Setting	Choice type	Dependent variables/measures	Design
Rispoli et al. (2013) A comparison of within- and across-activity choices for reducing challenging behavior in children with autism spectrum disorders (JoBE)	N = 4 students ages 5–11 with ASD	Alex's (11 years) sessions in a resource room during language arts; Dylan's (5 years) sessions in a self-contained classroom for students with autism in a public school; Kelly's (11 years) sessions in a university-based autism clinic; Eddie's (7 years) sessions after school in Eddie's home	Within- and across-activity choices	*Dependent variable:* Challenging behavior *Treatment integrity:* Direct observations using procedural task analysis (96%) *Social validity:* Not mentioned	Alternating treatment design embedded in intervention phase of an ABAB design A = no choice B = choice (within and across)
Skerbetz & Kostewicz (2013) Academic choice for included students with emotional and behavioral disorders (PSF)	N = 5 adolescent students at risk for EBD, age 13	Inclusive setting in a public charter school in a large, urban city	Assignment choice	*Dependent variables:* 1. Task engagement 2. Academic performance: task accuracy and amount of time to complete *Treatment integrity:* Assessed using videotapes (100%) *Social validity:* Teacher and student surveys	ABAB withdrawal design A = no choice B = choice

Note. JABA, *Journal of Applied Behavior Analysis;* BD, *Behavioral Disorders;* JPBI, *Journal of Positive Behavior Interventions;* ETC, *Education and Treatment of Children;* ECDC, *Early Child Development and Care;* JoBE, *Journal of Behavioral Education;* PSF, *Preventing School Failure;* TARF-R, Teacher Acceptability Rating Form—Revised (Reimers & Wacker, 1988); *indicates full text is available through Google Scholar.

A similar study was conducted with a 5-year-old kindergarten boy named Ahmad. The procedures were the same, except that the second no-choice phase was yoked to the first choice phase. This means that in the second no-choice condition, the teacher used the same sequence of tasks Ahmad had selected when he could choose the order of the tasks. It was very interesting to note that even though the activities were presented in the same order Ahmad had previously selected, his level of engagement was higher in the choice phases and lower in the no-choice phases and his level of disruption was lower in the choice condition and higher in the no-choice condition.

Findings suggest there is a functional relation between the introduction of choice and changes in task engagement and disruption for these three students, meaning students were more engaged and less disruptive when offered instructional choices. This study also raises the point that choice may have unique benefits as a positive behavior support over and above preference. The intervention supported Ahmad in completing the activities, and it was the *choice* that was associated with improved behavioral performance.

Increasing Time on Task, Task Completion, and Accuracy in Residential Facilities

Ramsey, Jolivette, Patterson, and Kennedy (2010) looked at how instructional choice improved the behavior of the most challenged students, adolescents (3 females, 2 males) with EBD in a residential treatment facility. The intervention was led by three teachers. Each of them had a bachelor's degree, prior experience as behavior specialists, and experience in the facility, and all were pursuing special education certification. The intervention took place in three classrooms during reading and math instruction between 2:10 and 3:10 P.M., with the special education teacher and two behavior specialists present to support the 8–10 students present.

Ramsey and colleagues (2010) used an ABAB withdrawal design, with a maintenance probe to assess generalizability (to see whether the changes occurred beyond the settings in which the intervention was first implemented). In this study three behaviors were monitored: being on task (percentage of engagement), task completion (percentage completed), and accuracy (percentage accurate), with data collected during 15-minute sessions. The materials for independent work time were taken from the existing math and language arts curricula with supplemental worksheets.

During all phases of the study, the teacher prompted the class to begin their independent work time, offered individual assistance as needed, praised students for their effort, and allocated points for students who met schoolwide behavioral expectations. If a student became disruptive, the behavior specialists removed the student from the classroom for a brief break to "cool down" in the hallway.

During the no-choice phase, the teacher let the students know they had two tasks to complete and presented these tasks in random order. The teacher placed the first assignment on each student's desk and told him or her to complete the delivered assignment first. The teacher asked whether there were questions and responded to any questions posed.

In the choice condition, the teachers did the following: (1) presented two independent tasks by putting them on the students' desks and explained how to do them; (2) asked whether there were any questions about the assignment and offered clarifications if there were; (3) asked which task the student would like to do first, marking a #1 on that assignment before handing it back; and (4) prompted the student to make a choice if a selection was not made. This process was completed individually for each of the five students.

Treatment integrity data were collected using a 9-item "choice" and a 5-item "no choice" checklist. Teachers implemented the intervention with a very high level of fidelity (average of 99%). Overall, results indicated that when students were allowed to choose the order in which tasks were completed, they were more engaged and completed more work. However, it did not affect the accuracy of their work. Social validity data from teacher and student perspectives were quite favorable. Teachers noted that sometimes it was difficult to plan for independent tasks that took the full 15-minute session; however, teachers reported that the intervention was easy to use and that they would likely use it in the future. Teachers also indicated they felt this intervention was empowering to students, who they believe could help them advocate for themselves in other areas of their lives. Students all reported enjoying having a choice and that they would like to have similar choices in other classes.

Increasing Task Engagement and Improving Academic Performance in an Inclusive Setting

Skerbetz and Kostewicz (2013) conducted a study looking at using academic choice with five 13-year-old eighth-grade students with EBD in an inclusive setting. All sessions took place in a general education classroom during a brief vocabulary development section of language arts. During the sessions, these 5 students, another 20 students, a classroom teacher, and a trained data collector were present. Sessions were videotaped, focusing on the 5 students in this study.

Again an ABAB withdrawal design was used to examine the impact of choice on task engagement (percentage of intervals engaged), task accuracy (percentage correct), and completion time (time to complete a task) during a daily 7-minute session. Materials included units from the Word Up Project, Level Blue (Flocabulary, 2007), with the authors dividing each 15-word list unit into four groups containing three words, distributed Monday through Thursday.

The teacher started the lesson with vocabulary instruction. She asked students to take out their vocabulary workbooks and turn to the page for the day as they entered the room. Next, students followed along with an audiotaped song pertaining to the daily vocabulary assignment. When the song concluded, the teacher passed out the daily assignment with instructions to begin working and have the assignment completed within 7 minutes (monitored by a timer).

During the no-choice condition (A), students received predetermined, randomized vocabulary assignments developed by the experimenter. Assignments included one of the following: (1) cloze sentences and multiple-choice items, (2) sentence writing, (3) fill-in-the-blank and yes/no items, and (4) word maps.

During the choice condition, students were given a packet of these assignments and were asked to select one of the four options to complete. They focused on the three words chosen for the given day when completing their selected activity.

Treatment integrity was checked by viewing the videotapes and coding each session using a component checklist. Skerbetz and Kostewicz (2013) reported 100% integrity and indicated that for 4 of the 5 students, a functional relation was established. Namely, when choice was offered, students were more engaged, completed more work, and were more accurate in their work than when choices were not offered. Social validity surveys completed by the teacher and students were positive. Students reported they liked having a choice and the teacher indicated she would use this intervention again.

Summary

These studies represent but a few demonstrations of how to incorporate instructional choice for students with challenging behavior in a range of settings: a self-contained classroom, a residential treatment facility, and an inclusive classroom (see Royer, Lane, Swogger, & Messenger, 2014). In Table 8.1, other illustrations are offered in elementary (Rispoli et al., 2013) and preschool (DiCarlo, Baumgartner, Stephens, & Pierce, 2013) settings. The next section discusses some of the benefits and challenges associated with instructional choice.

Benefits and Challenges

Choice is a simple and easy-to-use strategy; however, there are a few considerations to think about in order to use it effectively.

Benefits

Incorporating choice into instructional activities is feasible, does not require excessive preparation, is easy to implement, and supports content instruction (Kern & State, 2009; Morgan, 2006; Ramsey et al., 2010). In general, the preplanning activities do take some time. However, once the options for choice are established, it becomes quite simple to incorporate a range of options within and across choice tasks into lesson plans. Also, this intervention is a useful support that can be applied in inclusive settings (Rispoli et al., 2013; Skerbetz & Kostewicz, 2013).

Providing students (including those with disabilities and emotional and behavioral challenges) with opportunities to make choices teaches them self-determined behaviors, which has the potential to support positive academic and behavioral performance. More specifically, using instructional choice as an antecedent-based intervention results in positive teacher–student interactions, decreased levels of inappropriate behavior, and increased levels of engagement (Barth et al., 2007; Jolivette, Wehby, Canale, & Massey, 2001; Kern et al., 1998; Shogren et al., 2004). In addition, incorporating choice into instruction has the potential to support students with decision-making skills and offer them a sense of control that can improve the immediate and long-term quality of their lives (Jolivette et al., 2001). Offering instructional choice opportunities—especially for students with and at risk for EBD and more severe disabilities—may assist educators in managing student behavior in the general education classroom (Powell & Nelson, 1997).

Challenges

From a practitioner perspective, there are some challenges that warrant consideration. For example, it is important to note that in some of the studies, teachers reported challenges in preparing independent tasks for the time provided. However, these same teachers indicated they planned to use instructional choice in the future (Ramsey et al., 2010). This is encouraging, as use is a behavioral marker for social validity, meaning that teachers are likely to use interventions they find acceptable (Gresham & Lopez, 1996).

In addition, we recognize that it does take time to incorporate choice into instructional tasks. Teachers are more than capable of embedding choices into various lesson plans that involve a range of activities (e.g., cooperative learning activities, independent tasks, think–pair–share discussions); but we note that, as with all new practices, initially it will be important to allow for a little additional planning time to build instructional choices into lesson plans. However, once a teacher builds fluency with these procedures, providing choices can be quickly and seamlessly incorporated into a variety of activities.

Another noteworthy point is that it will be important to think about procedures for collecting and evaluating different types of assignments. For example, if someone develops a video, another person makes a diorama, and another person submits a written paper, the teacher needs to be clear on how each will be collected and evaluated. In thinking about how to collect a range of products, a teacher might require that all types of products be turned in on the same day (perhaps allowing some assignments, such as large posters, to be turned in before school so students do not have to store them in their lockers) or staggered according to the type of product submitted (e.g., all videos due on Tuesday). In thinking about grading such diverse options, it will be important for the teacher to consider the learning objective for the task and develop a grading plan (e.g., rubric), which should be shared with the students so they can make good choices in how they complete the selected task. In essence, we recommend expectations be established and clearly communicated to avoid potential challenges associated with grading the range of products (or activities) completed (remember the case of the video on making crème brulée! See *www.youtube.com/watch?v=Hy5LOxhGDJg*).

Overall, managing more variability in a classroom can be challenging without prior planning, as a teacher already has so many other things to address within the course of the normal school day. Many instructional choices, such as choosing which assignment to complete first or completing a writing assignment in pen or pencil, will not yield these challenges. However, with some preplanning, these challenges can easily be anticipated and avoided.

For the reader interested in the science behind instructional choice, we mention that Morgan (2006) discussed several behavioral and methodological factors that may have an impact on the effectiveness of preference or choice making as classroom interventions. Some of the questions he posed include the following: Has preference or choice making consistently influenced the rate of academic engagement for students with behavior challenges? Are these patterns the same for students performing in a range of ability levels? Do these interventions work in classroom rather than lab settings? Is there really a difference between preference and choice-making interventions? Or are the outcomes associated with choice-making interventions really the result of giving students the opportunity to access their preferences (e.g., preferred tasks, preferred materials, preferred work space)?

At this time the evidence for the answers to these questions remains mixed, which is the reason it is important for researchers and practitioners to continue the inquiry needed to answer these questions. For example, it may be we need to consider underlying behavioral mechanisms when attempting to answer some of these questions (Morgan, 2006). Although preference and choice making are intended to influence student behavior, it may be that these interventions result in different rates or types of reinforcement or more immediate (rather than delayed) reinforcement, which may impact results (Romaniuk & Miltenberger, 2001). In his systematic review of the literature of 15 studies of preference and choice-making interventions, Morgan (2006) concluded that these interventions may improve behavioral and academic performance. However, he cautioned that studies that "most rigorously controlled for preference yielded only modest and limited effects for choice-making" (p. 185). Yet, as pointed out by Kern and State (2008), there have been studies showing that choice results in decreased problem behaviors even when students have to choose nonpreferred or moderately preferred activities (e.g., Vaughn & Horner, 1997). These improvements in student behavior when completing nonpreferred activities indicate that the preference of the activities students select in and of itself is not the only reason why choice is an effective intervention.

Given the several benefits and relatively few challenges associated with instructional choice, we recommend this easy-to-use strategy in a range of settings to support students with challenging behaviors to engage more fully in academic tasks. The following section details a step-by-step process for successfully implementing instructional choice in your classroom.

Implementing Instructional Choice in Your Classroom: Checklist for Success

In the following sections, we offer a step-by-step approach for implementing instructional choice in your classroom. The following steps are also available in Table 8.2 as an implementation checklist. A hypothetical illustration of how these steps can be used in a CI3T model at the elementary school level is provided in Box 8.1.

- **Step 1: Determine which type of choices you would feel comfortable offering and create a menu of choices.** We encourage teachers to begin by making a list of the various types of within- and across-task choices they would feel comfortable offering to students in their classes (Kern & State, 2009; Rispoli et al., 2013). For example, as part of an independent reading block some teachers may feel comfortable allowing students the option to sit on a beanbag chair in a writing center, on an inflatable ball at their desks, or in a traditional chair during an independent reading activity but would not feel comfortable allowing students to select their own reading materials. In contrast, other teachers may feel comfortable with students selecting one of two short stories to read but would prefer students remain in their traditional desk chairs. As part of a culminating activity, some may feel comfortable offering a range of options for final products. For example, students could "show what they know" (or in more professional language, demonstrate what they have learned) about an assigned novel (e.g., *Brave New World*) in a variety of ways: a group-made YouTube video, a traditional written report, a readers' theater presentation, or an exam. Yet others may allow students to pick from a list of approved books on utopias but require all students to participate in a class debate, with one group of students taking the affirmative and another the negative

---

TABLE 8.2. Implementation Checklist for Success: Instructional Choice

- Step 1: Determine which type of choices you would feel comfortable offering to students in your classroom and create a menu of choices.
- Step 2: Use the menu to determine which type of choice to add to a particular lesson.
- Step 3: After choice is built into the lesson, offer the established choices.
- Step 4: Ask the student to make his or her choice.
- Step 5: Provide wait time for the student to select his or her choice.
- Step 6: Listen to (or observe) student's responses.
- Step 7: Prompt the student to choose from one of the available options if he or she has not made a choice within the time allotted.
- Step 8: Reinforce the student's choice, providing him or her with the option selected.
- Step 9: Offer students an opportunity to give feedback on the choice they selected.

Note. Based on instructional choice steps discussed by Jolivette, Alter, Scott, Josephs, and Swoszowski (2013); Kern and State (2009); and Sigafoos, Roberts, Couzens, and Kerr (1993).

on the position statement: People would enjoy more independence in a utopia. In each scenario, some element of choice is offered to students while still remaining manageable for the teacher. This step is very important, as we would never want to offer a student a choice we are not willing to honor.

As we mentioned, it is important for teachers to decide which options they feel comfortable with, as these will be the basis for developing lesson plans that incorporate choice. One approach is to make a menu or table of various within and across choices to serve as a reference sheet when incorporating choice into daily lesson plans (Kern & State, 2009). Some teachers may initially feel comfortable offering all students the same choices, whereas others may want to begin by individualizing choice options for specific students according to their particular needs.

• **Step 2: Use the menu to determine which type of choice to add to a particular lesson.** After developing a menu of choices and considering the possibility of individual choices, the next step is to use them in lesson planning. When developing lesson plans, refer to the menu of choices and determine which types of choices are most appropriate for a particular topic, as well as where these choices could be incorporated in the lesson.

Ideally, instructional choices would occur frequently and throughout the curriculum. For example, during independent reading, students choose which book to read, and during math they choose the sequence in which they complete their assignments.

On other days, it may be that choice is incorporated into the entry activity to increase behavioral momentum (Nevin, 1996). For example, many teachers start a lesson with a writing prompt, to which students respond in their journals. In this case the teacher could offer students a choice of prompts rather than requiring them to answer a given prompt. Similarly, there could be a choice of starter activities. Students could have the option of reviewing the previous day's notes and completing a quick check for understanding instead of completing a journal response.

Eventually, teachers may even be able to incorporate choices into assessments. For example, on the day of an exam, the teacher may determine that all students need to complete a particular assessment that includes 25 multiple-choice questions and two short-answer responses. The choice for this particular assessment may be that students select which section to complete first. In this case, both will be done—but the sequence of activities is the choice.

The key here is to incorporate a range of choices in a range of contexts to enhance motivation and increase academic engagement (Shogren et al., 2004). Planning ahead is important in creating a variety of options. This will ensure that students have sufficient opportunities for choice making.

• **Step 3: After choice is built into the lesson, offer the established choices.** In step 3, students are offered the predetermined choices (at least two or more options), which may be offered to an individual student (e.g., "Katie, would you like to complete your reading first or start by making your flash cards?") or the whole class (e.g., "Thank you all for doing such a thorough job in completing your journal activity. You may now either read the chapter on photosynthesis or make flash cards of the vocabulary words").

One important reminder: make certain the choice is made explicit and students are clear as to the choices they have been given. This may be done using verbal, physical, or gestural prompts. For example, a teacher might hold up three writing utensils—a mechanical pencil, a wooden pencil, or an ink pen—and then ask a student: "Which one of these three would you like to use to complete the worksheet? You are welcome to use any one of these." The goal is to make it crystal clear what the options are and that there is not one correct choice.

Another important consideration is that if the choice is offered to the whole class, each individual student should get to pick his or her personal option. For example, if the teacher conducted a class vote on which task to do first and the whole class had to abide by the classwide choice, this means some students would not have had their choice. Although this strategy can be fine in some contexts, it is not consistent with principles of instructional choice in which students self-select their preference.

• **Step 4: Ask each student to make his or her choice.** After the choices have been offered, explained, and clarified, the next step is to ask students to make their decisions. For example, if the teacher decided students could choose where in the library to study for their physics exam (e.g., cubicle, small-group table, on the floor), students would need to be prompted to make their choice (e.g., "Okay, Nathan, where would you like to sit while you review your notes? Do you want to work at your desk, sit in the rocking chair, or work in the library?"). Or a teacher might say "You can write in pencil or pen on this assignment." Then the students would need to be prompted to make a choice (e.g., "Class, go ahead and take out either a pencil or a pen").

In some instances you might help guide their decision by directing them to a novel experience: "I have seen some really great illustrations from you in the last couple of weeks. I would really love to see some of your writing skills. For this week, will you please make a choice between a traditional essay and a commercial script on global warming?"

• **Step 5: Provide wait time for the student to select his or her choice.** After the options are made explicit and students are asked to make their choices, they will need to be given sufficient wait time to make their selections. For low-cost decisions, such as "Do you want to color with colored markers or sparkly markers?" (which can be an important decision when you are 6 years of age, Grace!), 10–15 seconds may be sufficient. However, other choice-making opportunities, such as "Would you like to take the AP statistics exam instead of the course final exam?" will likely require some additional thought. In some cases you might precorrect students by saying, "By the end of this week, I will need a firm decision as to whether or not you will be committing to taking the AP exam or the final exam."

Using instructional choice can assist students in developing self-determined behaviors such as choice making and goal setting.

Also, plan ahead regarding issues such as: Can students change their minds after making a choice? How many times can they change their minds? How will you handle the situation in which a student wants to make a late change that may impede his or her ability to complete the assignment within the allotted time?

• **Step 6: Listen to (or observe) the student's response.** In Step 6, teachers need to know which choice the student selected. Sometimes this can just be observed (e.g., the student picks up the sparkly markers), read (e.g., an email from the student saying, "Ms. Rivera, I have decided to commit to the AP statistics exam and will not be taking the course final. I appreciate your giving me this option"), or heard (e.g., "I would prefer to read in the beanbag, is that okay?"). One source of frustration often noted by students (or for that matter spouses!) is that they do not feel heard (e.g., "I told you . . . "). An important component of instructional choice is understanding (and remembering!) the choices that have been made.

Teachers participate in literally hundreds of teacher–student interactions in a day, and an important aspect of keeping these interactions positive is clear communication. In this case, communication is knowing and remembering the choice a student has selected. One strategy is to refer back to the lesson plans before grading an assignment to make certain you recall the choices offered. Another option is to create a rubric for grading assignments or activities that also notes the instructions and choices given and selected. Either of these strategies would facilitate teachers' understanding of which choices have been made so students are not accidentally punished for their choices (e.g., "Why did you write this essay in pen?").

• **Step 7: Prompt the student to make a choice from one of the available options if the student has not made a choice within the time allotted.** The choice-making process can be challenging for some students—particularly if they are not used to making choices or if they are concerned about making the wrong choice. Yet exercising choice is an important component of developing students' intrinsic motivation; moreover, it helps them to understand they can make choices that influence their school (and life) experiences in very positive ways and that school is not a series of events over which they have no control (Jolivette, Alter, Scott, Josephs, & Swoszowski, 2013). In the beginning, it may be best to start with relatively simple two- or three-choice formats (e.g., "Pick any one of these three new vocabulary words to learn this week") and then progress to more challenging choices (e.g., "Which college essay would you like to write first?"). When students are struggling to make the requested choices within the allotted time frame, it may be necessary to prompt them in an encouraging way (e.g., "Katie, it is time to make a choice. Do you want to make your presentation in a PowerPoint format or as a Prezi? I am sure either one will be great.")

• **Step 8: Reinforce the student's choice, providing him or her with the option selected.** Once the students have made their choices—either before or after your prompting—the next step is to reinforce the choices they made and then deliver the options. It would not be appropriate to say, "Oh, I really wish you would have decided to draw a map rather than make the travel brochure for this geography project. You know what, I am sorry —but you have to make the map." This would be highly counterproductive, as it does not facilitate the development of self-determined behaviors, and it is certainly less than motivating to make a choice that is not subsequently honored.

When offering praise, it is important to remember that not all students view public statements to be reinforcing. Be sure to praise students in a way that holds meaning for them: a behavior-specific praise (BSP) statement offered with the schoolwide PBIS ticket; or a pat on the upper back; or a smile and a BSP statement (see Chapter 3 on BSP).

• **Step 9: Offer students an opportunity to give feedback on the choice they selected.** Finally, as with any support, we encourage involving all stakeholders— teachers, support staff, related service providers, parents, *and* students—to offer their input on the goals, procedures, and outcomes to see what they thought (a point we develop in the next section). It is important to find out what students like or do not like about their instructional choices so we can continually improve instruction. Specifically, this information can be used to shape future strategy efforts for these and other students. Although it may not be practical to ask students at the end of each lesson what they thought about the choices offered, it would be helpful to ask for input at the end of some lessons or at the end of several days of using instructional choice.

Examining the Effects: How Well Is It Working?

Testing the Strategy: Design Considerations

When implementing instructional choice, it is important to collect data on student performance to know how well this strategy is working. In many of the studies featured in this book, researchers have used single-case methodology to "test" the intervention effects. This is a particularly useful design approach for teachers, as it is highly flexible and very practical. It can be used with any of the strategies introduced in each chapter.

It is important to use an experimental design such as an ABAB or multiple baseline across settings, tasks, or students to establish a functional relation between the introduction of the intervention and changes in student performance. In other words, this design helps determine whether or not the intervention worked. This information is helpful to both general education and special education teachers for a variety of reasons. The first, of course, is it allows you to evaluate the effectiveness of your instruction. With this information, you can decide how to adjust your instructional practices so they work better for your students. Second, members of the CI3T team or members of professional learning communities (PLCs) can use these data to determine how students are responding to these low-intensity supports. Before moving on to student-focused Tier 2 (e.g., Check-In/Check-Out, behavior contracts, or self-monitoring strategies) or Tier 3 (e.g., functional assessment-based interventions; Umbreit et al., 2007) supports, we want to be certain we have examined the extent to which teacher-driven strategies (e.g., instructional choice) have been effective in addressing students' needs (academically, behaviorally, and/or socially). Using an experimental design is one way to show whether or not this has occurred. We recommend these teams (e.g., CI3T and PLC) be composed of a range of individuals, including general and special education teachers, as they each bring unique talents. For example, special education teachers are a critical resource for implementing and delivering specialized intervention; they can assist general educators with evaluating strategy implementation, as well as carefully measuring the effects of any given intervention for a particular student, as is demonstrated in Box 8.1. This is especially critical when focused on more intensive supports, such as functional assessment-based interventions, that require careful monitoring of students' performance (e.g., academic engagement, disruption). The ability to use single-case methodology is a critical skill in assessing the effectiveness of Tier 2 and 3 supports.

These designs begin with a baseline phase during which data on student performance are collected (referred to as the A phase), then the intervention is introduced for the first time (B) while still collecting data on student performance using the same data collection method used during the baseline phase (see Figure 8.1 in Box 8.1). Although it is tempting at this point to say the intervention was effective, two more replications are needed to be certain the intervention was responsible for the change and not something else. One demonstration (e.g., the change from A to B phases) along with two other replications can provide evidence that the introduction of the strategy produced the changes (the shift from B to A and then A to B; Gast & Ledford, 2014).

Although some designs, such as the ABAB design, require removal and then reintroduction of the intervention, it is also possible to explore a functional relation using a multiple baseline across settings design, as illustrated in Figure 8.1. This means the strategy is used in different settings, such as a different instructional period (math instead of reading) or a different physical location (playground instead of the lunchroom).

Making Certain the Strategy Is in Place: Treatment Integrity

In addition to using an experimental design to test the intervention, collecting treatment integrity data helps determine the extent to which the intervention is being implemented as planned and is also critical for determining whether changes in performance are due to the intervention. Figure 8.2 in Box 8.1 is an example of a treatment integrity checklist for instructional choice. Although there are many different ways to collect treatment integrity data, one way is to have the teacher collect these data each day by indicating the degree to which each intervention component was implemented as planned for each student. For example, in Figure 8.2, each item is completed using a 3-point Likert-type scale as follows: 0 = *not in place*, 1 = *partially in place*, or 2 = *completely in place*. Each day the items are summed, divided by the total number of points possible, and divided by 100 to obtain a percentage of implementation for each student. These data can be used to interpret intervention outcomes (see Box 8.1). In addition, behavior component checklists not only determine the level of implementation but also serve as a prompt or reminder to implement each step.

Using an outside observer to collect treatment integrity data for approximately 25% of the sessions in each phase is recommended. An additional observer is important for establishing the accuracy of the data collected.

Examining Stakeholders' Views: Social Validity

Finally, in addition to collecting information on student performance and implementation (treatment integrity), it is important to understand how stakeholders felt about the intervention goals, procedures, and intended outcomes. Figure 8.3 in Box 8.1 is an example of a measure examining one elementary student's perceptions of the social validity of instructional choice.

It is important to obtain all stakeholders' views —the teacher, the student, and the parent—ideally before the intervention begins and again at the conclusion of the first "test." If social validity is low at the onset of the intervention, then it is wise to provide additional training to increase people's knowledge of the strategies, as well as their confidence in using the strategy prior to implementation. In theory (and in some instances in actuality; see Lane, Kalberg, Bruhn, et al., 2009), the opinions of those implementing and participating in the intervention may predict the extent to which the interventions are implemented as planned. In essence, a socially valid intervention is likely to be put in place with a high degree of integrity, leading to improvements in student performance that maintain over time and in new settings and with new people.

BOX 8.1. A Hypothetical Illustration of Instructional Choice in a CI3T Model

Miss Messenger is a special education teacher who works at Edison Elementary School, where they implement a comprehensive, integrated, three-tiered (CI3T) model of prevention. As part of their CI3T plan, they teach using the Scott Foresman reading program 5 days a week (90-minute instructional block Monday through Friday; *Scott Foresman Reading Street*, 2004), follow a positive behavior intervention and support (PBIS) plan, and address character development using the Positive Action (2008; *www.positiveaction.net*) curriculum (teaching one lesson each week). Miss Messenger supports inclusive educational experiences for students with special needs in partnership with the general education teachers. During one of the first-grade team's professional learning community meetings, Miss Messenger and Mrs. Brayfield noticed there were two first-grade students who were struggling in their behavioral performance, scoring in the moderate-risk range on the Student Risk Screening Scale (SRSS; Drummond, 1994) and who were also having trouble with work completion, noted on their first trimester report cards by a work completion grade of "Needs Improvement." Despite reading at grade level according to AIMSweb fall benchmarking data (2013; www.aimsweb.com) and having no absences during the first trimester, both Gus and Dan struggled to finish their language arts assignment during their reading block. Mrs. Brayfield indicated that they were often chatting with each other and disrupting other students during independent work time.

Support	Description	Entry criteria	Data to monitor progress	Exit criteria
Instructional choice	Within- and across-task choices offered during reading instruction (language arts assignments)	SRSS moderate risk and report card: Work completion and independent work habits (needs improvement)	*Student performance:* • Academic engaged time • Percentage of work completed *Treatment integrity:* Component checklist *Social validity:* Student-completed survey	5 consecutive weeks of daily academic engagement 80% or better and work completion at 90% or better

Miss Messenger suggested the possibility of using instructional choice for all students during Mrs. Brayfield's class and seeing how Gus and Dan responded to this low-intensity support. Miss Messenger thought this could benefit not only Gus and Dan but also another student, Steve, who was receiving special education services under the category of emotional disturbance (ED) according to the Individuals with Disabilities Education Improvement Act (IDEA, 2004) and who was fully included in Mrs. Brayfield's class.

Miss Messenger worked through the seven-step process with Mrs. Brayfield as follows. These steps can also be found in Table 8.2.

Preparing for and Delivering Instructional Choice: The Intervention

• **Step 1: Determine which type of choices you would feel comfortable offering and create a menu of choices.** Together the teachers made a menu of choices they felt comfortable offering to students in this class. The menu had approximately 12 options for choice, including within- and across-task choices such as:

  ○ Choice of where to read independently within the classroom (e.g., beanbag chair, carpet, desk, rocking chair)
  ○ Choice of whether to begin with writing their sentence about their favorite scene or drawing their illustration of their favorite scene first

- o Choice of which book to read during free reading time
- o Choice of reading silently or into a tape recorder
- o Choice of completing even or odds on a vocabulary development worksheet

• **Step 2: Use the menu to determine which type of choice to add to a particular lesson.** When developing weekly lesson plans for the reading block, they referred back to the menu of choices, decided which types of choices were most appropriate for a given lesson, and determined where to build in these choices. On some days there were two sets of options (e.g., which starter activity to complete, as well as which book to peruse during sustained silent reading).

• **Step 3: After choice is built into the lesson, offer the established choices.** After building various instructional choices into the lesson plans, the teachers reviewed their lesson plans just prior to coteaching each day. They made certain to offer choices to all students and allowed each student to pick his or her individual preference. They were careful not to require a consensus on the choice at hand, as this would not allow students the individual autonomy to make a personal choice, thus reducing the effectiveness of the strategy. When presented to students, the choices were written on the board and explained verbally. In some instances, either Miss Messenger or Mrs. Brayfield provided other visual demonstrations, such has holding up a box of crayons and a box of sparkly markers to make it clear that either one was an option. During this step, they answered any clarifying questions.

• **Step 4: Ask the student to make his or her choice.** Next, the teacher leading instruction for that particular activity prompted the students to make their choices. If additional questions were raised, those were also answered in a swift yet respectful manner.

• **Step 5: Provide wait time for the student to select his or her choice.** As part of step 5, teachers were careful to ensure students had sufficient time to make their choices. The wait time varied according to the task at hand. For example, if the choice was an option between writing with an ink pen, a mechanical pencil, or a wooden pencil, the window for choice might be 30 seconds. If the choice was picking a storybook to read from the class library, the wait time might be 3 minutes. In still other cases, it might be the students have two pictures in front of them and they are asked to pick one picture within 1 minute to write a short story about that would later be edited and shared with a friend. In either case, the window of time for making the choice (e.g., 30 seconds, 3 minutes, or 1 minute) was explained to all students, and a timer was used if necessary.

• **Step 6: Listen to (or observe) the student's response.** After being given sufficient time to make the decision, the teachers listened to or observed each student's response, noting his or her choice.

• **Step 7: Prompt the student to make a choice from one of the available options if the student has not made a choice within the time allotted.** If a particular student was struggling to make a choice within the allotted time, either Miss Messenger or Mrs. Brayfield quietly prompted the student to make a choice from the available options. Both teachers were cautious to remain positive yet firm to ensure the students had enough time to successfully complete the selected task. In some cases, they encouraged them to try new experiences when appropriate—always before the selection was made.

• **Step 8: Reinforce the student's choice, providing him or her with the option selected.** The teachers praised students' individual choices and allowed them access to whichever choice was made. Both teachers agreed ahead of time that students would each be allowed the full range of choices offered, as it is important to honor people's individual choices. They also decided it was important for students to stick with their initial choice each time choice was offered but students could make a new choice on another day/activity.

• **Step 9: Offer students an opportunity to give feedback on the choice they selected.** About once a week, either Miss Messenger or Mrs. Brayfield would offer students the opportunity to give feedback on the choices they selected during the previous week. They also asked for input on other choices they would like to be given in future days.

Looking at How Well Instructional Choice Worked

Miss Messenger and Mrs. Brayfield decided to collect specific data on academic engagement (referred to as academic engaged time; AET) and work completion (percentage of items completed) for Gus, Dan, and Steve to see how they responded to this low-intensity support. Together they created an operational definition of AET that included a label, a definition, and both examples and non-examples so that everyone would be certain they were observing the same behaviors.

- *Label.* AET.
- *Definition.* AET refers to a behavior related to the instruction task assigned by the teachers.
- *Examples.* These included reading the assigned book, working on the assigned worksheets, engaging in conversations related to the instructional task, and using materials according to their intended purposes.
- *Non-examples.* These included engaging in tasks other than those assigned by the teacher, talking about topics not related to the instructional task, and using materials for other than their intended purpose.

AET was collected using a momentary time-sampling procedure in which Miss Messenger wore an electronic device (a MotivAider®) preprogrammed to vibrate every 2 minutes over a 40-minute period during independent work time in language arts. Before collecting data, Miss Messenger and the paraprofessional, Mrs. McDonald, practiced using this recording system together to make sure they collected AET data reliably. Specifically, they practiced observing the three boys using a self-constructed data entry form over 3 consecutive days.

Figure 8.1 presents three graphs showing Gus's (Panel A), Dan's (Panel B), and Steve's (Panel C) percentage of AET. Notice that some of the data points in Gus's graph are marked with an asterisk (*) to indicate which sessions were observed by both Miss Messenger and Mrs. McDonald to make sure they were seeing the same behavior. On these sessions (2, 7, 10, 16, and 19), they collected reliability data on the AET data for each of the boys.

In addition to collecting information on AET, Mrs. Brayfield also collected data on work completion (not graphed in Figure 8.l). Work completion was evaluated using a daily report card on which Mrs. Brayfield or Miss Messenger evaluated the assigned instruction task, with scores ranging from 0 to 100% completion.

To make certain the intervention was happening as planned, either Mrs. Brayfield or Miss Messenger completed a daily treatment integrity form (see Figure 8.2 for treatment integrity data on the second introduction of the choice intervention). Each day they recorded whether the intervention component was *not in place* (0), *partially in place* (1), or *fully in place* (2). Figure 8.2 shows a percentage of implementation for each session (at the end of each column). These data were very important, as they helped with interpreting how students responded to instructional choice. For example, in looking at Panels A, B, and C in Figure 8.1, you can see that AET was much lower during baseline compared with the first introduction of instructional choice. Then the levels of AET and work completion again declined when choice was removed during the withdrawal phase (A2) and again increased when the intervention was reintroduced (B2)—with the exception of April 4 (session 19) in Figure 8.2. On this day, the level of integrity was quite low (33%) for all students, and (not surprisingly) their percentage of AET was also low and assignments were not completed. In general, when the intervention was in place as planned, all three students were more engaged and completed more work.

Prior to beginning and at the end of the intervention, Miss Messenger, Mrs. Brayfield, and Mrs. McDonald decided to see what the students thought about this little "test run" of instructional choice. They asked all students in the class to rate four short statements about their experience. In brief, all students—including Gus (whose ratings are shown in Figure 8.3), Dan, and Steve—enjoyed having choices and indicated they felt they got more work done in reading when they had choices. For Gus, the intervention actually exceeded his initial expectations (his scores increased from 75 to 100%), and he indicated having choices made reading time more enjoyable.

After running this "test," Miss Messenger, Mrs. Brayfield, and Mrs. McDonald put the intervention back in place and continued to monitor student performance. They continued this process until each student had 5 consecutive weeks of daily academic engagement at a level of 80% or better and work completion at 90% or better. After all three students met these criteria, the teachers decided to leave the intervention in place as part of regular instruction, as they saw benefits for other students as well and as it was such a simple strategy to add to their daily instruction.

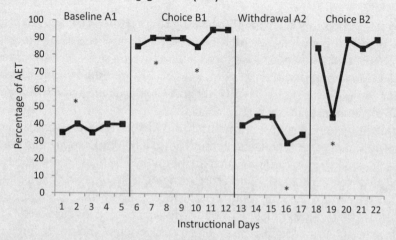

Panel A. Gus's Academic Engaged Time (AET)

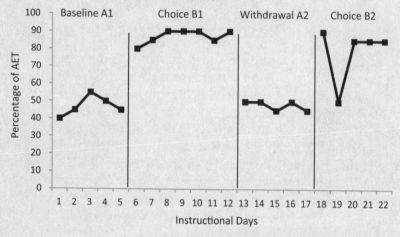

Panel B. Dan's Academic Engaged Time (AET)

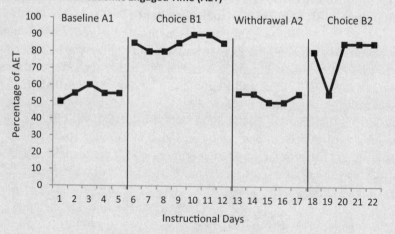

Panel C. Steve's Academic Engaged Time (AET)

FIGURE 8.1. Examining the effects: First-grade students' percentage of academic engaged time during reading instruction.

TREATMENT INTEGRITY CHECKLIST: INSTRUCTIONAL CHOICE

Teacher: Miss Messenger   Scale: _____

Lesson: Story Writing

☑ Self-report   ☐ Observer

0 = Not in place   1 = Partially in place   2 = Fully in place

Component	Session 18 Monday 4/4/2016			Session 19 Tuesday 4/4/2016			Session 20 Wednesday 4/6/2016			Session 21 Thursday 4/7/2016			Session 22 Friday 4/8/2016		
	Gus	Dan	Steve	Gus	Dan	Steve	Gus	Dan	Steve	Gus	Dan	Steve	Gus	Dan	Steve
I offered _____ the established choices.	2	2	2	2	2	2	2	2	2	2	2	2	2	2	2
I asked _____ to make his choice.	2	2	2	2	2	2	2	2	2	2	2	2	2	2	2
I provided _____ wait time to select his choice.	2	2	2	0	0	0	2	2	2	1	1	1	2	2	2
I listened or observed _____'s response.	2	2	2	0	0	0	2	2	2	2	2	2	2	2	2
I prompted _____ to make a choice from one of the available options if he had not made a choice within the time allotted.	2	2	2	0	0	0	0	0	0	2	2	2	2	2	2
I praised _____'s choice and provided him with the option selected.	2	2	0	0	0	0	2	2	2	0	0	2	2	2	2
Percentage session integrity: (Total points earned/# points possible) × 100	100%	100%	83%	33%	33%	33%	83%	83%	83%	75%	75%	92%	100%	100%	100%

FIGURE 8.2. Making certain the strategy is in place: Treatment integrity checklist used by Miss Messenger to monitor the extent to which each step of instructional choice strategy was implemented as planned for each boy when the intervention was reintroduced following the withdrawal phase.

SOCIAL VALIDITY FORM: INSTRUCTIONAL CHOICE

Before we get started . . . What do you think, Gus?	☹ 0 No, not really	1 Sometimes	☺ 2 Yes, definitely
I would like to have choices during reading time.			✓
Having choices would make reading time more enjoyable.		✓	
I could get more of my work done if I had choices.		✓	
Other students in my class would enjoy having choices.			✓
Percentage: (total number/total number possible) × 100 =		75%	

Now that you have tried it . . . What do you think, Gus?	0 No, not really	1 Sometimes	2 Yes, definitely
I liked having choices during reading time.			✓
Having choices made reading time more enjoyable.			✓
I got more of my work done because I had choices.			✓
Other students in my class enjoyed having choices.			✓
Percentage: (total number/total number possible) × 100 =		100%	

FIGURE 8.3. Examining stakeholders' views: Social validity form developed by Miss Messenger to examine the three students' views on instructional choice, with Gus's individually completed sheets shown.

Summary

Instructional choice is an effective, efficient, relatively easy-to-use strategy requiring minimal preparation. It can decrease challenging behaviors, increase academic engaged time, and increase work completion (Ramsey et al., 2010). Similar to increasing opportunities to respond (OTR), instructional choice can be used to support one or more students to become more engaged while continuing to meet the academic needs of an entire class. Oftentimes teachers report feeling ill prepared to manage student behavior, feeling less confident in behavioral programming relative to academic programming. By offering within- and across-task instructional choices, teachers provide a PBIS that involves simple yet important instructional shifts that yield important changes in student behavior—particularly for students with behavioral challenges. Another feature many teachers enjoy about instructional choice-making activities is they increase student autonomy by giving students more control over their educational experiences (Jolivette et al., 2001). Instructional choice is also a powerful strategy to use in inclusive placements for students with behavioral challenges (Rispoli et al., 2013).

CHAPTER 9

Tips for Success

A Few Closing Thoughts

As school-site administrators, teachers, and other professionals draw on research to improve students' educational outcomes, many have focused on implementing multi-tiered systems that are comprehensive, integrated, and systematic to meet students' multiple needs in academic (response to intervention; RTI), behavioral (positive behavior interventions and support; PBIS) and social (using validated curricula) domains. As we discussed in Chapter 1, effective Tier 1 programming addresses each of these components and has the capacity to provide the majority of students with a successful school journey by building schools that are inviting, nurturing, and joyful places that students want to be—places characterized by equity, opportunity, and quality (Horner, 2014). For students needing instruction and support beyond Tier 1, these models include Tier 2 (low-intensity supports for some) and Tier 3 (high-intensity supports for a few). However, without solid Tier 1 efforts implemented with a high level of integrity, subsequent levels of support are less likely to be as powerful.

In this book we complement multi-tiered prevention models, offering a closer look at low-intensity, teacher-delivered supports that can be easily integrated into routine instructional practice (Lane, Oakes, & Menzies, 2014). Specifically, in a comprehensive, integrated three-tiered (CI3T) model of prevention that address academic, behavioral, and social needs in an integrated fashion, low-intensity strategies are used to prevent challenging behaviors from occurring, increase instructional time, as well as establish a positive school climate and productive learning environments (Lane, Menzies, et al., 2013).

Yet, too often, calls for reform do not fully consider how demanding teachers' jobs are and how little time they have to try new techniques. The strategies introduced in this book are already familiar to many teachers and have an evidence base for their success. What is new here is how to use them systematically as a Tier 1 practice for a school or classwide by teachers whose student-level screening data suggest additional strategies are needed to assist an entire class in accessing instruction (e.g., when more than 20% of a class presents with moderate or high behavioral risk), as well as how to leverage the strategies as a Tier 2 intervention for students who need additional support (see Figure 9.1 for summary screening data).

Under optimal conditions, most of these strategies would be used as part of Tier 1 practices to support all students in fully accessing instruction. It may be that teachers also incorporate some of the strategies presented as part of their Tier 2 and 3 practices, with each increasing in intensity (see Figure 1.1 in Chapter 1). Applications of these strategies as possible Tier 2 supports are illustrated in the secondary (Tier 2) grids included in each of the boxes across Chapters 2–8. For example, it may be instructional choice (Chapter 8) and behavior-specific praise (BSP; Chapter 3) are implemented as Tier 1 practices. Yet students with moderate behavior challenges are offered targeted or individualized instructional choices and further supported with higher rates of BSP to assist them in fully engaging in the instructional choices they make (e.g., Lane, Royer, et al., 2015). As part of the successful implementation, teachers are careful in remembering to praise effort ("Great job completing all the assigned problems!", "Well-done! The third try was a charm. Your pinch-pot stood!"), not ability ("You are the smartest student I have had in years!"), given effort is a malleable factor (Harks, Rakoczy, Hattie, Besser, & Klieme, 2014), meaning this is something that students can control that supports an internal locus of control (compared with things that are beyond their control; see Chapter 5).

In this last chapter, we briefly discuss a few remaining ideas that will help teachers and school sites use the strategies optimally, within and beyond the context of CI3T models of prevention. In the pages that follow, we first explain how these strategies are grounded in applied behavior analysis, with an emphasis on understanding the principle of reinforcement. Next, we focus on the importance of establishing a positive school climate in which the culture of expectations is shifted to place as much emphasis on students' social and behavioral needs as we do their academic outcomes (Yudin, 2014). Then we focus on the strategies discussed in this book, with a look toward considerations for professional learning. This final piece is important as we seek to eliminate existing disparities in learning opportunities and how behavior is managed, keeping in mind that students themselves do not create disparities. Instead, disparities often occur from differences in teacher training experiences, professional learning, and discipline policies (Yudin, 2014). Here the focus is on leveling the playing field so all educators can access the resources and supports needed to develop their knowledge, confidence, and use of the strategies discussed in this book (Lane, Menzies, Bruhn, & Crnobori, 2011).

TEACHER NAME J. Roberts

Date: 12/2016

	Grade-Level Assessment					
	0 Above Target	0–3 Low	0–1 Low	0–1 Low		
	1 At Target	4–8 Moderate	2–3 Moderate	2–5 Moderate		
	2 Below Target	9–21 High	4–15 High	6+ High		

Student Name	Student ID	Reading	Math	SRSS Behavior (SRSS-E7)	SRSS-I5 Internalizing (Preliminary)	ODR	Days Absent
Angel, Julio	2310	1	1	1	1	0	0
Akins, J'Monte	2013	1	1	0	0	0	0
Backer, Brent	2031	2	2	4	0	3	0
Boxwell, Kylie	2001	1	1	0	2	1	3
Cartright, Ashley	2152	1	3	0	8	0	3
Cox, Lucille	2002	2	3	2	10	0	8
Hankins, Erin	2017	1	1	0	0	0	0
Illio, Helen	2132	3	2	6	2	9	7
Jackson, Ronald	2003	2	2	3	1	0	3
Kemp, Patrice	2009	1	2	0	3	0	5
Parker, Stephanie	2004	1	2	4	0	0	1
Reed, Kent	2010	1	2	3	0	0	1
Sterling, Michael	2022	3	0	7	2	9	3
Thomas, James	2018	1	2	0	0	0	1
Walsh, Carter	2215	2	3	14	4	18	0

FIGURE 9.1. Summary screening data. SRSS, Student Risk Screening Scale; SRSS-I5, internalizing subscale of the Student Risk Screening Scale Internalizing and Externalizing (currently available for use at the elementary level only). Light gray shading suggests moderate risk, dark gray shading suggests high risk. Missing more than 10 days of school per year places students at heightened risk (Walker, Block-Pedego, Tids, & Severson, 2014).

Grounded in Applied Behavior Analysis

We reiterate that the strategies presented in this book can be used across the PreK–12th-grade continuum independent of any multi-tiered system of supports. Each offers an effective, feasible approach to assist students in demonstrating behaviors that facilitate the instructional experiences of all learners. None of the strategies presented here are punishment-based; they are grounded in applied behavior analysis (ABA; Baer et al., 1968; Cooper et al., 2007), with an emphasis on PBIS. They are offered to support skill building for teachers and students alike.

For the interested reader, we want to explain the relation between these strategies and ABA. ABA is a science dedicated to "the understanding and improvement of human behavior" (Cooper et al., 2007, p. 3). More precisely, ABA is a scientific approach used to describe, predict, and shape behavior. It involves determining the specific environmental variables that impact socially important (or socially valid) behaviors and developing a technology of behavior change based on the information learned about the environmental variables discovered (Cooper et al., 2007). ABA is at the heart of PBIS.

A major principle of ABA is the use of reinforcement, which is simply the process of either increasing or eliminating the occurrence of a specific behavior. In education (and in parenting!), reinforcement is a powerful tool for helping students learn and use the behaviors that are instrumental for success in specific settings. These behaviors range from readiness skills, such as paying attention to a classroom task or an adult, to good organizational habits such as having a notebook neatly arranged for a particular class. They also include skills that are critical for interactions with peers and teachers, for example, demonstrating self-control when upset or angry and actively listening when others are sharing ideas, feelings, or information. Such behaviors are often taught across the PreK–12th-grade continuum, recognizing that academic enabling skills (Gresham, in press) and self-determined behaviors (e.g., goal setting, decision making) not only influence students' performance during their educational years but also foster success as students transition out of the structured PreK–12th-grade school settings. Moreover, these skills affect how people transition into postsecondary education and employment and how they negotiate a range of relationships after leaving school (e.g., with loved ones, employers, and community members; Shogren, Wehmeyer, & Lane, 2014). Reinforcement is an effective tool for teachers to use in guiding students in the development of these behavioral skills; however, the use of reinforcement is an often discussed and sometimes misunderstood practice.

Understanding Reinforcement

In the most basic sense, reinforcement occurs when "a stimulus change immediately follows a response and increases the future frequency of that type of behavior in similar conditions" (Cooper et al., 2007, p. 702). The basic concept of reinforcement describes a contingent relation between a behavior and the environmental variables that shape it (see Figure 9.2). A reinforcer is any action or object that affects the future probability of a behavior. Reinforcing involves three related concepts. First is the idea that the target behavior changes when a reinforcer is introduced. The reinforcer (the stimulus) can be either an action or an object of some type, also called a stimulus. The second component is that there is a presentation of the stimulus, because that is what causes the change. Finally is the concept of contingency, meaning the stimulus is contingent on evidence of the behavior. In other words, the stimulus is offered when the behavior occurs. A common scenario illustrating these ideas occurs when parents offer an allowance for completing chores. The behavior is completing chores, and the reinforcer is the allowance. The allowance is contingent on the chores being completed. Some children do not need allowance as a reinforcer and will do their chores whether or not they receive it, but others will be motivated by allowance as a reinforcer. This leads to another important premise in reinforcement: the action or object offered as a reinforcer must be motivating to the child to whom it is presented. Otherwise, it will not work to increase the occurrence of the behavior. See Figure 9.3 for examples of

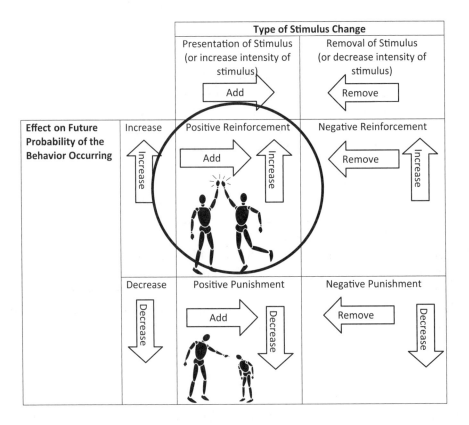

FIGURE 9.2. Principles of applied behavior analysis: Understanding reinforcement.

Function	**Seeking** *Positive Reinforcement*	**Avoiding** *Negative Reinforcement*
Attention	• Lunch with friend • Lunch with staff of choice • Preferential seating • Reading time with adult • Meeting with the principal • Tutor/mentor younger class • Award given in front of class/school • Featured in a PBIS video/skit • Praise postcard sent home • Tell jokes to the class • Be a guest announcer at a sporting event or on the school announcements	• Lunch in private area with peer and staff of choosing • Quiet time in the library pass • Get out of class • participation pass • Get out of P.E. or be the time keeper • Preferential seating during school event • Participate in class discussions through anonymous clickers or other media • Multiple roles for participation in group project that do not require presenting in class
Tangibles/ Activities	• Lunch with a friend • Leading the pledge of allegiance • Lunch with staff of choice • Movie (on-campus) • Preferential seating • Class helper • Extra reading time • PBIS assembly • Additional computer time • Additional recess time • Game of choice • Ticket to school event (e.g. sporting, dance, play) • Extra basketball time • Feature spot in PBIS video • Cleaning the white board • School supplies (e.g., pens, pencils) • Books • Stickers • Food coupon • School t-shirt or sweatshirt • Bike, radio, I-pod • Candy, soft drinks • Gift cards (e.g. movie, stores, restaurants) • Discounted yearbook, dance ticket, sporting event	• Extra computer time (avoid class time) • Homework pass • Front of the lunch line pass • Additional free time • Extra library time • Preferred parking (avoid the long walk to class!) • Doodling pad in class • Choice of activities to complete to demonstrate learning of concepts (so they may avoid a nonpreferred activity) • Early transition (between classes or after school) pass • Alternative assignment pass (e.g., complete a PowerPoint instead of an essay) • Teacher's helper (run errands to get a break from class)

(continued)

FIGURE 9.3. Types of reinforcers. Based on the function matrix developed by Umbreit, Ferro, Liaupsin, and Lane (2007).

Function	Seeking *Positive Reinforcement*	Avoiding *Negative Reinforcement*
Sensory	• Listen to music during independent work time • Hold a stuffed animal during listening activities • Use smelly markers or pencils for a writing or art activity • Use a light up pen for classwork • Sit on the yoga ball at your desk • Bring a snack to class • Listen to a book on tape • Cooking activity • Sitting on the bean bag • Playing board games • Fidget toy at desk • Pencil grip • Seat cushion • Special seat	• Eat lunch in the classroom, library, or other quiet space • Recess with a friend in the gymnasium • Choice of location pass for completing independent work • Wear your sunglasses in class pass • Use of head phones during noisy activities • Earplugs • Noise-cancelling headphones • Work in a quiet room or room with lights off/dimmed

FIGURE 9.3. *(continued)*

various types of reinforcers. Here it is important to remember that what is reinforcing to one student is not necessarily reinforcing to all.

In brief, all behavior is maintained by accessing (positive reinforcement) or avoiding (negative reinforcement) attention, activity/tangible, or sensory experiences (Umbreit et al., 2004). As such, reinforcement can be characterized as positive or negative. Positive reinforcement means a stimuli (i.e., attention, activities/ tangibles, or sensory experiences) is introduced contingent upon a behavior occurring that results in an increase in the future probability of the behavior occurring in similar conditions (e.g., completing chores to earn an allowance). Often, the term *positive reinforcement* is thought to be synonymous with "good," as in producing a good effect. However, positive reinforcement simply occurs when a behavior is followed quickly by the *presentation* of a stimulus that *increases* the future probability of the behavior occurring under similar conditions (see the arrows in Figure 9.2). It is possible to positively reinforce behaviors you do not want to continue. In fact, sometimes teachers do so unintentionally. For example, when teachers ask students to raise their hands to be called on but then acknowledge (positive reinforcement) students who call out answers, they are reinforcing the calling out (undesired behavior) and not the hand raising (desired behavior). The teacher's response of attending to the calling-out behavior is positive reinforcement and therefore increases the future probability of the calling-out behavior.

Negative reinforcement also results in an *increase* in the future probability of the behavior occurring under similar conditions; however, in this case it occurs when the stimulus is *removed* contingently. As with positive reinforcement, you can *increase* the occurrence of a behavior through negative reinforcement. In other words, a consequence strengthens the behavior that comes before it. For example, if a student sees a scarf in the foyer of a very loud cafeteria, he or she may pick up the scarf and use it to cover his or her ears to block the noise. In this way, the effect of the noise in the cafeteria is reduced. Or, similarly, removing a student from center time for cursing may be an illustration of negative reinforcement if the student's cursing continues or increases in the future (cursing increases to avoid center time). Rather than equating positive with good and negative with bad, they can be thought of as adding (positive) or taking away (negative).

Oftentimes people confuse the terms *negative reinforcement* and *punishment*. Punishment occurs when a stimulus change immediately follows a behavior (also referred to as a response) that *decreases* the future frequency of the behavior occurring under similar conditions (Cooper et al., 2007). Like reinforcement, there are two types of punishment: positive punishment and negative punishment. Positive punishment occurs when a behavior is followed immediately by the *presentation* of a stimulus (or an increase in the stimuli's intensity) that decreases the frequency of the response (or similar response) in similar conditions. An example is raising your voice (YELLING!—introducing an aversive stimuli) at a student who is being disruptive. Negative punishment occurs when a behavior is followed immediately by *removal* of a stimulus (or a decrease in the stimuli's intensity) that *decreases* the frequency of the response (or similar response) in similar conditions. An example is when two students are arguing over who gets to use the blocks during free play, and the teacher removes the blocks as a choice (resulting in the arguing ceasing; see Figure 9.2). As in the case of reinforcement, you cannot really determine whether something is a reinforcer or a punisher until you see the impact on *future* behavior. In essence, learning is shaped by consequences.

Although punishment is frequently used to control behavior, in the long term it is a much less effective strategy than reinforcement. Although it is often associated with a desired short-term change in behavior, it does not skill build for students. In addition, punishment is associated with increases in aggression and often the behavior reoccurs (spontaneous recovery; Cooper et al., 2007). Maladaptive behaviors are almost certain to occur again unless a student has learned to self-regulate his or her actions and/or acquired a new set of skills to take the place of the less desirable behavior. Tiered prevention models—PBIS, specifically, as the behavioral component of the CI3T model—take a problem-solving approach to behavioral issues and provide teachers with many more tools than simply responding with punishment when behavior problems occur. Therefore, punishment procedures should only be used in a few cases and only after all other techniques have been exhausted. We do not recommend the use of punishment procedures in most cases given these and other concerns (see Behavior Analyst Certification Board [BACB] website for ethical considerations; *www.bacb.com*).

Promoting Positive School Climate

Okay, if the last five paragraphs gave you a headache, just know the information is here if you need to explain to someone the difference between these ABA principles: positive reinforcement, negative reinforcement, positive punishment, and negative punishment (see Figure 9.2). Please keep this in mind when you need to respond to someone who says "Reinforcement is just bribery!" *Reinforcement is not bribery.* Reinforcement is used to support the use of socially appropriate behaviors. Bribery, on the other hand, is attempting to coerce someone into doing something that is not in his or her best interest (e.g., drink it, smoke it, jump off it). We focus on describing when and how behavior occurs because, if we can predict when it is likely to occur, we can make adjustments (often minor) and shape behavior, enabling students to have a positive experience in school, academically, behaviorally, and socially. Clearly, a complete discussion of reinforcement is beyond the scope of this chapter, but it can be found elsewhere (e.g., BACB website; *www.bacb.org*; Cooper et al., 2007). But we want you to remember the basics are here for your convenience.

We also want you to be clear that having a schoolwide approach to PBIS does not mean that you eliminate a reactive plan (also referred to as a disciplinary plan). Each school-site leadership team absolutely needs a clearly delineated plan as to how to respond when minor and major rule infractions occur. When used correctly, these plans can be effective, but emphasizing proactive and positive strategies first has many benefits. We believe, and evidence supports, that when schools use a prevention framework, they increase their capacity to create a climate of respect and trust among teachers, students, and staff. And, of course, a positive school climate is a critical element in promoting student success (e.g., Bradshaw, Waasdorp, & Leaf, 2012).

In fact, schools in the United States are tasked with the responsibility of preparing a competent and caring citizenry (Horner et al., 2009). Many schools struggle to provide such environments, as evidenced by higher rates of suspension, exclusion, and academic failure for students of certain minority groups, including those with disabilities (Office of Civil Rights, 2014). Reducing the achievement gap between subgroups of students, as well as promoting mental health, is a national priority (U.S. Department of Education, 2014). Therefore, it is paramount that educators create positive, safe learning environments for all children and youth to develop and learn. Schoolwide PBIS models are being implemented in schools across the country as a framework for installing practices to create such schools in which students are physically and intellectually safe—safe to make mistakes and be assured that positive adults will provide additional instruction and appropriate supports. There is mounting evidence that PBIS practices, such as the strategies presented in this book, lead to safer, more positive school environments. Schools must be places where students can be free to make mistakes and learn from them—places free of criticism and punitive responses to learning errors.

In 2014, the U.S. Department of Education released a resource guide for schools on improving school climate and discipline. Action steps for improved climate and student achievement include engaging in purposeful and deliberate efforts to create positive school environments and implementing evidence-based strategies (within a tiered structure) to promote positive behavior. Schoolwide PBIS (the behavioral component in the CI3T model of prevention) has been examined for impact on school climate and student school outcomes. For example, Horner et al. (2009) found that elementary schools reported increased perceptions of school safety in their first year of implementing PBIS. Further, schools implementing PBIS practices experienced lower rates of office discipline referrals (ODRs) and reductions in suspensions (Bradshaw, Mitchell, & Leaf, 2010) and improvements in academic outcomes (Bradshaw et al., 2010; Horner et al., 2009). As mounting evidence supports the use of PBIS practices for student outcomes, teachers also benefit from more positive working environments (Bradshaw et al., 2008). Teachers also report having more instructional time (Cheney, Blum, & Walker, 2004). The strategies we focus on in this book are intended to support teachers in using this instructional time in the most effective, efficient manner. Now, back to the low-intensity strategies at hand.

Exploring the Strategies at Hand:
Considerations for Professional Learning

Figure 9.4 presents a brief listing of the seven strategies presented, which rely heavily on the principle of positive reinforcement: opportunities to respond (OTR; Chapter 2), behavior-specific praise (Chapter 3), active supervision (Chapter 4), instructive feedback (Chapter 5), high-probability requests (Chapter 6), precorrection (Chapter 7), and instructional choice (Chapter 8). We provide a brief description of each strategy to help guide your decision-making process as you determine which strategies to explore and potentially incorporate into your instructional toolkit. For example, if you were to examine your academic and behavior screening data and determine that more than 20% of students in a class or period were struggling behaviorally (Figure 9.1), then you might first consider incorporating one or more of these strategies into your classwide routine of instructional practices. It might be you decide to look at your behavior screening data (e.g., comparing fall to winter time points to see how students are responding). Or you might collect more frequent, repeated assessments for a small group of students with moderate behavioral risk to see how they respond to the strategies implemented with the whole class or with students on a more individual basis. For example, teachers might use an individual student preference menu for instructional choice (Chapter 8) or high-probability requests (Chapter 6) or increase rates of reinforcement for specific students around targeted behaviors (Chapter 3). This is far more efficient than moving forward with student-level interventions such as self-monitoring and behavior contracts.

Strategy	Chapter	Definition	On-site or district-level coach	To explore	Explored
Opportunities to respond (OTR)	2	Providing students with frequent opportunities, within a set time period, to respond to teacher questions or prompts about targeted academic material.		☐	☐
Behavior-specific praise (BSP)	3	Using praise statements that include reference to the specific behavior for which the student is being recognized.		☐	☐
Active supervision	4	Using obvious behaviors such as proximity, scanning, and interacting with students to avert problem behavior.		☐	☐
Instructional feedback	5	Providing students with specific information about their performance to clarify misinformation, confirm or fine-tune understanding, or restructure current schemas.		☐	☐
High probability (high-p) requests	6	Requesting behaviors the student is likely to respond to, providing reinforcement for appropriate responding, and then delivering a low-probability request in close succession to the previous reinforcement.		☐	☐
Precorrection	7	Identifying predictable contexts that result in problem behavior and providing students with supports, prompts, and reinforcement for engaging in appropriate behavior.		☐	☐
Instructional choice	8	Providing students with two or more options and allowing them to select their preferred option.		☐	☐

FIGURE 9.4. *Strategies to explore.* All definitions are those stated in the respective chapters.

From *Supporting Behavior for School Success: A Step-by-Step Guide to Key Strategies* by Kathleen Lynne Lane, Holly Mariah Menzies, Robin Parks Ennis, and Wendy Peia Oakes. Copyright 2015 by The Guilford Press. Permission to photocopy this figure is granted to purchasers of this book for personal use only (see copyright page for details). Purchasers can download a larger version of this figure from *www.guilford.com/lane4-forms*.

If you are a school-site administrator, district-level administrator, instructional coach, behavioral specialist, or school psychologist, you might decide to support teachers in learning these strategies through a range of professional learning offerings, such as:

1. Developing a book study on each topic, with teachers sharing their successes in applying each strategy (e.g., Lane, Swogger, Royer, Oakes, & Common, 2015).

2. Offering a 10-minute "strategy of the month" as part of regularly scheduled faculty meetings or online professional learning videos or webinars.

3. Identifying "onsite experts" among educators who are knowledgeable and confident in the use of these strategies. These individuals can serve as peer models and coaches in a nonevaluative manner for teachers who identify themselves as learners of these strategies. There is a place to record the names of onsite or district-level coaches in Figure 9.4. We would recommend including their names, positions, and contact information (e.g., email addresses and phone numbers) for easy access (no one has the time to go looking for that information).

4. Creating teacher toolkits for these strategies. The toolkits may include the tools we offer in this book (e.g., social validity surveys, step checklists, treatment integrity measures). Additionally, school educators may create videos to model the strategy. Then, using professional learning release time, educators may observe strategies modeled in classrooms or ask for peer feedback on their use of the strategy, creating collaborative communities of practice.

5. Onsite professional learning using free access opportunities such as those available at *www.pbis.org* and *www.ci3t.org* (PowerPoints, pacing sheets, and suggested resources) or accessing other local and national professional learning opportunities through your state education department, technical assistance networks, and local and national conferences (e.g., Association of Positive Behavior Support [APBS]; Council for Children with Behavioral Disorders [CCBD]).

6. Subscribing to journals such as the *Journal of Positive Behavior Interventions* (JPBI), which was explicitly designed to offer "sound, research-based principles of positive behavior support for use in school, home and community settings with people with challenges in behavioral adaptation" (JPBI mission statement, *http://pbi.sagepub.com*). Faculty, staff, and parents gather together monthly in small groups to discuss topics of interest from the most current literature.

7. Review the related resources listed in Figure 9.5 to expand your own professional learning library. This figure contains books, journals, practice guides, and websites that align with strategies discussed in this book. In addition, we offer information on data collection tools that can support you in examining (1) the extent to which the interventions are put in place (treatment integrity), as well as (2) changes in student performance, by directly measuring a range of behaviors

Type of resource	To	
Reference	explore	Explored
Books		
Colvin, G., & Scott, T. M. (2015). *Managing the cycle of acting-out behavior in the classroom* (2nd ed.). Thousand Oaks, CA: Corwin.	☐	☐
Crone, D., Horner, R., & Hawken, L. (2004). *Responding to problem behavior in schools: The Behavior Education Program.* New York: Guilford Press.	☐	☐
Gast, D. L., & Ledford, J. R. (Eds.). (2014). *Single case research methodology: Applications in special education and behavioral sciences* (2nd ed). New York: Routledge.	☐	☐
Lane, K. L., Cook, B., & Tankersley, M. (Eds.). *Research-based strategies for improving outcomes in behavior.* Boston: Pearson.	☐	☐
Lane, K. L., Menzies, H., Bruhn, A., & Crnobori, M. (2010). *Managing challenging behaviors in schools: Research-based strategies that work.* New York: Guilford Press.	☐	☐
Lane, K. L., Menzies, H. M., Oakes, W. P., & Kalberg, J. R. (2012). *Systematic screenings of behavior to support instruction: From preschool to high school.* New York: Guilford Press.	☐	☐
McIntosh, K., & Goodman, S. (in press). *Multi-tiered systems of support: Integrating academic RTI and school-wide PBIS.* New York: Guilford Press.	☐	☐
Sailor, W., Dunlap, G., Sugai, G., & Horner, R. (2009). *Handbook of positive behavior support.* New York: Springer.	☐	☐
Simonson, B., & Myers, D. (in press). *Classwide positive behavior interventions and supports: A guide to proactive classroom management.* New York: Guilford Press.	☐	☐
Stormont, M., & Newman, C. (2014). *Simple strategies for teaching children at risk.* Thousand Oaks, CA: Corwin.	☐	☐
Journals		
Beyond Behavior www.ccbd.net/publications/beyondbehavior	☐	☐
Intervention in School and Clinic http://isc.sagepub.com	☐	☐
Journal of Positive Behavior Intervention http://pbi.sagepub.com	☐	☐

(continued)

FIGURE 9.5. Resources to explore.

From *Supporting Behavior for School Success: A Step-by-Step Guide to Key Strategies* by Kathleen Lynne Lane, Holly Mariah Menzies, Robin Parks Ennis, and Wendy Peia Oakes. Copyright 2015 by The Guilford Press. Permission to photocopy this figure is granted to purchasers of this book for personal use only (see copyright page for details). Purchasers can download a larger version of this figure from *www.guilford.com/lane4-forms*.

| Type of resource | To | |
Reference	explore	Explored
Preventing School Failure *www.tandfonline.com/toc/vpsf20/current#.VE0VI_nF-So*	☐	☐
Teaching Exceptional Children *http://journals.cec.sped.org/tec*	☐	☐
Practice guides		
Cabeza, B., Germer, K., Magill, L., Lane, K. L., Carter, E. W., & Oakes, W. P. (2013). *The CI3T model of prevention: Supporting academic, behavioral, and social development of students.* Nashville, TN: Vanderbilt University. Available at *http://vkc.mc.vanderbilt.edu/ci3t/wp-content/uploads/2014/06/Model-of-Prevention-Brief.pdf*	☐	☐
Epstein, M. H., Atkins, M., Cullinan, D., Kutash, K., & Weaver, R. (2008). *Reducing behavior problems in the elementary school classroom: A practice guide* (NCEE #2008-012). Washington, DC: National Center for Education Evaluation and Regional Assistance, Institute of Education Sciences, U.S. Department of Education. Retrieved from *http://ies.ed.gov/ncee/wwc/PracticeGuide.aspx?sid=4*	☐	☐
Hamilton, L., Halverson, R., Jackson, S. S., Mandinach, E., Supovitz, J. A., & Wayman, J. C. (2009). *Using student achievement data to support instructional decision making: A practice guide* (NCEE #2009-4067). Washington, DC: U.S. Department of Education, Institute of Education Sciences, National Center for Education Evaluation and Regional Assistance. Retrieved from *http://ies.ed.gov/ncee/wwc/PracticeGuide.aspx?sid=12*	☐	☐
U.S. Department of Education. (2014). *Guiding principles: A resource guide for improving school climate and discipline.* Washington, DC: Author. Retrieved from *www2.ed.gov/policy/gen/guid/school-discipline/guiding-principles.pdf*	☐	☐
Yoder, N. (2014) *Teaching the whole child: Instructional practices that support social and emotional learning in three teacher evaluation frameworks.* Washington, DC: American Institutes for Research Center on Great Teachers and Leaders. Retrieved from *www.gtlcenter.org/sites/default/files/TeachingtheWholeChild.pdf*	☐	☐
Websites		
Behavior Analyst Certification Board (BACB) *www.bacb.com*	☐	☐
Comprehensive Integrated Three-Tiered Model of Prevention *www.ci3t.org*	☐	☐
The IRIS Center *www.iris.peabody.vanderbilt.edu*	☐	☐
NorthEast School-wide Positive Behavior Support (NE-SWPBS) *www.neswpbs.org*	☐	☐

(continued)

FIGURE 9.5. *(continued)*

Type of resource	To	
Reference	explore	Explored
Positive Behavioral Interventions and Supports—OSEP National Technical Assistance Center *www.pbis.org*	☐	☐
What Works Clearinghouse *http://ies.ed.gov/ncee/wwc/default.aspx*	☐	☐
IRIS website: Modules and case studies addressing behavior		
Addressing Disruptive and Noncompliant Behaviors (Part 1): Understanding the Acting-Out Cycle • Module discussing the acting-out cycle stages and strategies for responding to student behavior. *www.iris.peabody.vanderbilt.edu/module/bi1*	☐	☐
Addressing Disruptive and Noncompliant Behaviors (Part 2): Behavioral Interventions • Module describing interventions for increasing compliance and decreasing disruptive and noncompliant behaviors. *www.iris.peabody.vanderbilt.edu/module/bi2*	☐	☐
Classroom Management (Part 1): Learning the Components of a Comprehensive Behavior Management Plan • Module highlighting the importance of establishing a comprehensive classroom behavior management system (rules, procedures, consequences). *www.iris.peabody.vanderbilt.edu/module/beh1*	☐	☐
Defining Behavior • Case study describing how to define behavior in a way that is observable and measurable. *www.iris.peabody.vanderbilt.edu/wp-content/uploads/2013/05/ICS-015.pdf*	☐	☐
Measuring Behavior • Case study providing information on how to collect data on student behavior (event, interval, duration, and latency recording). *www.iris.peabody.vanderbilt.edu/wp-content/uploads/2013/07/ICS-014.pdf*	☐	☐
Norms and Expectations • Case study providing strategies for establishing classroom norms and expectations. *www.iris.peabody.vanderbilt.edu/wp-content/uploads/2013/07/ICS-003.pdf*	☐	☐
Data collection tools		
Behavior Observation System for Students (BOSS; $29.99) Pearson Education. Inc. • Records and graphs momentary time-sampling data. Available for Apple and Android products. *www.pearsonclinical.com/education/products/100000780/behavioral-observation-of-students-in-schools-boss.html#tab-details*	☐	☐

(continued)

FIGURE 9.5. *(continued)*

Type of resource	To explore	Explored
Reference		
Behavior Tracker Pro ($29.99) Marz Consulting, Inc. • Records and graphs frequency, duration, interval, and ABC data. Available for Apple products. *www.behaviortrackerpro.com*	☐	☐
D.A.T.A (Free) Behavior Science.org, LLC • Records event and duration of up to four behaviors. Available for Apple products. *https://itunes.apple.com/us/app/d.a.t.a/id448028783?mt=8*	☐	☐
Interval Timer (Free) Deltaworks • Prompts data recording at any interval length. Requires pen and paper to record data. Available for Apple products. *https://itunes.apple.com/us/app/interval-timer-timing-for/id406473568?mt=8*	☐	☐
Professional organizations		
Association of Positive Behavior Support (APBS) • Journal: *Journal of Positive Behavioral Interventions* • *www.apbs.org*	☐	☐
Council of Administrators of Special Education (CASE) • Journal: *Journal of Special Education Leadership* • *www.casecec.org*	☐	☐
Council for Children with Behavioral Disorders (CCBD) • Journals: *Behavioral Disorders, Beyond Behavior* • *www.ccbd.net*	☐	☐
Council for Exceptional Children (CEC) • Journals: *Exceptional Children, Teaching Exceptional Children* • *www.cec.sped.org*	☐	☐
Council for Exceptional Children—Division of Research (CEC-DR) • Journal: *Journal of Special Education* • *www.cecdr.org*	☐	☐
CEC Pioneers Division (CEC-PD) • *www.community.cec.sped.org/pd/home*	☐	☐
Council for Educational Diagnostic Services (CEDS) Journal: *Assessment for Effective Intervention* • *www.community.cec.sped.org/CEDS/home*	☐	☐
Division on Autism and Developmental Disabilities (DADD) • Journals: *Education and Training in Autism and Developmental Disabilities, Focus on Autism and Other Developmental Disabilities* • *www.daddcec.org*	☐	☐

(continued)

FIGURE 9.5. *(continued)*

Type of resource	To explore	Explored
Reference		
Division for Communicative Disabilities and Deafness (DCDD) • Journal: *Communication Disorders Quarterly* • *www.community.cec.sped.org/DCDD/home*	☐	☐
Division on Career Development and Transition (DCDT) • Journal: *Career Development for Exceptional Individuals* • *www.community.cec.sped.org/dcdt/home*	☐	☐
Division for Culturally and Linguistically Diverse Exceptional Learners (DDEL) • Journals: *Multiple Voices for Ethnically Diverse Exceptional Learners* • *www.community.cec.sped.org/DDEL/homepage*	☐	☐
Division for Early Childhood (DEC) • Journals: *Journal of Early Intervention, Young Exceptional Children* • *www.dec-sped.org*	☐	☐
Division of International Special Education and Services (DISES) • Journal: *Journal of International Special Needs Education* • *www.dises-cec.org*	☐	☐
Division for Learning Disabilities (DLD) • Journal: *Learning Disabilities Research and Practice* • *www.teachingld.org*	☐	☐
Division for Physical, Health and Multiple Disabilities (DPHMD) • Journal: *Physical Disabilities: Education and Related Services* • *www.community.cec.sped.org/DPHMD/Home*	☐	☐
Division on Visual Impairments and Deafblindness (DVIDB) • Journal: *DVI Quarterly* • *www.community.cec.sped.org/DVI/home*	☐	☐
Association for the Gifted (TAG) • Journal: *Journal for the Education of the Gifted* • *www.cectag.com*	☐	☐
Technology and Media Division (TAM) • Journal: *Journal of Special Education Technology* • *www.tamcec.org*	☐	☐
Teacher Education Division (TED) • Journal: *Teacher Education and Special Education* • *www.tedcec.org*	☐	☐

FIGURE 9.5. *(continued)*

(e.g., engagement, compliance). Finally, we include a listing of professional organizations you might consider joining to assist with your individual professional learning plans. Although not all organizations are directly related to the content provided in this book, all are reputable organizations focused on meeting students' multiple needs within and beyond the school setting.

Summary

We offer this book for the busy educator—teacher, paraprofessional, behavior specialist, school psychologist, social worker, mental health provider, administrator, technical assistance provider, and/or teacher preparation professor—who may already have knowledge of specific behavioral strategies but needs a quick and easy guide for implementing them.

We also hope this will be a useful tool to those educators who are new to PBIS or who had limited preprofessional preparation in classroom management practices. Each strategy is grounded in ABA, with sufficient evidence to suggest that, if implemented as intended (with integrity), it will likely yield the desired changes in student performance, such as decreased levels of disruption and increased levels of engagement.

References

Achenbach, T. M. (1991). *Manual for the Child Behavior Checklist/2–3 and 1992 profile.* Burlington: University of Vermont Department of Psychiatry.

Adams, G., & Brown, S. (2007). *Six-minute solution: A reading fluency program.* Dallas, TX: Voyager Sopris Learning.

Alber, S. R., Heward, W. L., & Hippler, B. J. (1999). Teaching middle school students with learning disabilities to recruit positive teacher attention. *Exceptional Children, 65,* 253–270.

Algozzine, B., Browder, D., Karvonen, M., Test, D., & Wood, W. M. (2001). Effects of interventions to promote self-determination for individuals with disabilities. *Review of Educational Research, 71,* 219–277.

Allday, R. A., Hinkson-Lee, K., Hudson, T., Neilsen-Gatti, S., Kleinke, A., & Russel, C. S. (2012). Training general educators to increase behavior-specific praise: Effects on students with EBD. *Behavioral Disorders, 37,* 87–98.

Ardoin, S. P., Martens, B. K., & Wolfe, L. A. (1999). Using high-probability instruction sequences with fading to increase student compliance during transitions. *Journal of Applied Behavior Analysis, 32,* 339–351.

Austin, J. L., & Agar G. (2005). Helping young children follow their teachers' directions: The utility of high probability command sequences in pre-K and kindergarten classrooms. *Education and Treatment of Children, 28,* 222–236.

Baer, D. M., Wolf, M. M., & Risley, T. R. (1968). Some current dimensions of applied behavior analysis. *Journal of Applied Behavior Analysis, 1,* 91–97.

Bambara, L., Ager, C., & Koger, F. (1994). The effects of choice and preference on the work performance of adults with severe disabilities. *Journal of Applied Behavior Analysis, 27,* 555–556.

Banda, D. R., & Kubina, R. M. (2006). The effects of a high-probability request sequencing technique in enhancing transition behaviors. *Education and Treatment of Children, 29,* 507–516.

Barth, R. P., Lloyd, C. Green, R. L., James, S., Leslie, L. K., & Landsverk, J. (2007). Predictors of placement moves among children with and without emotional and behavioral disorders. *Journal of Emotional and Behavioral Disorders, 15,* 159–167.

Beland, K. (1992). *Second Step: A violence prevention curriculum for grades 1–5, Revised.* Seattle, WA: Committee for Children.

Belfiore, P. J., Lee, D. L., Vargas, A. U., & Skinner, C. H. (1997). Effects of high-preference single-digit mathematics problem completion on multiple-digit mathematics problem performance. *Journal of Applied Behavior Analysis, 30,* 327–330.

Blood, E., & Gulchak, D. (2013). Embedding "clickers" into classroom instruction: Benefits of strategies. *Intervention in School and Clinic, 48,* 246–253.

Bradshaw, C. P., Buckley, J., & Ialongo, N. (2008). School-based service utilization among urban children with early-onset educational and mental health problems: The squeaky wheel phenomenon. *School Psychology Quarterly, 23,* 169–186.

Bradshaw, C. P., Mitchell, M. M., & Leaf, P. J. (2010). Examining the effects of school-wide positive behavioral interventions and supports on student outcomes: Results from a randomized controlled effectiveness trial in elementary schools. *Journal of Positive Behavior Interventions, 12,* 133–148.

Bradshaw, C. P., Waasdorp, T. E., & Leaf, P. J. (2012). Effects of school-wide positive behavioral interventions and supports on child behavior problems. *Pediatrics, 130,* 1136–1145.

Brophy, J. (1981). Teacher praise: A functional analysis. *Review of Educational Research, 51,* 5–32.

Brophy, J. E. (1979). Teacher behavior and its effects. *Journal of Educational Psychology, 71,* 733–750.

Bruhn, A. L., Lane, K. L., & Hirsch, S. E. (2014). A review of tier 2 interventions conducted within multi-tiered models of prevention evidencing a primary behavioral plan. *Journal of Emotional and Behavioral Disorders, 22,* 171–189.

Brunsting, N. C., Sreckovic, M. A., & Lane, K. L. (2014). Special education teacher burnout: A synthesis of research from 1979 to 2013. *Education and Treatment of Children, 37,* 681–712.

Burns, M. K. (2007). Comparison of opportunities to respond within a drill model when rehearsing sight words with a child with mental retardation. *School Psychology Quarterly, 22*(2), 250–263.

Burns, M. K., Egan, A. M., Kunkel, A. K., McComas, J., Peterson, M. M., Rahn, N. L., et al. (2013). Training for generalization and maintenance of RtI implementation: Front-loading sustainability. *Learning Disabilities Research and Practice, 28,* 81–88.

Butler, D. L., & Winne, P. H. (1995). Feedback and self-regulated learning: A theoretical synthesis. *Review of Educational Research, 65,* 245–281.

Cabeza, B., Germer, K., Magill, L., Lane, K. L., Carter, E. W., & Oakes, W. P. (2013). *The CI3T model of prevention: Supporting academic, behavioral, and social development of students.* Nashville, TN: Vanderbilt University. Available at *http://vkc. mc.vanderbilt.edu/ci3t/wp-content/uploads/2014/06/Model-of-Prevention-Brief. pdf.*

Carnine, D. (1976). Effects of two teacher-presentation rates on off-task behavior, answering correctly, and participation. *Journal of Applied Behavior Analysis, 9*(2), 199–206.

Carter, E. W., Lane, K. L., Crnobori, M. E., Bruhn, A. L., & Oakes, W. P. (2011). Self-determination interventions for students with and at risk for emotional and behavioral disorders: Mapping the knowledge base. *Behavioral Disorders, 36*, 100–116.

Cavanaugh, B. N. (2013). Performance feedback and teachers' use of praise and opportunities to respond: A review of the literature. *Education and Treatment of Children, 36*(1), 111–136.

Cazden, C. B. (2001). *Classroom discourse: The language of teaching and learning* (2nd ed.). Portsmouth, MA: Heinemann.

Cheney, D., Blum, C., & Walker, B. (2004). An analysis of leadership teams' perceptions of positive behavior support and the outcomes of typically developing and at-risk students in their schools. *Assessment for Effective Intervention, 30*, 7–24.

Codding, R. S., & Lane, K. L. (2014, September 26). A spotlight on treatment intensity: An important and often overlooked component of intervention inquiry. *Journal of Behavioral Education.* Available at *http://link.springer.com/article/10.1007/s10864-014-9210-z.*

Codding, R. S., & Lane, K. L. (2015). Spotlight on treatment intensity: An important and often overlooked component of intervention inquiry. *Journal of Behavioral Education, 24*, 1–10.

Colvin, G. (2004). *Managing the cycle of acting-out behavior in the classroom.* Eugene, OR: Behavior Associates.

Colvin, G., & Scott, T. M. (2015). *Managing the cycle of acting-out behavior in the classroom* (2nd ed.). Thousand Oaks, CA: Corwin.

Colvin, G., Sugai, G., Good, R. H., III, & Lee, Y.-Y. (1997). Using active supervision and precorrection to improve transition behaviors in an elementary school. *School Psychology Quarterly, 12*(4), 344–363.

Colvin, G., Sugai, G., & Patching, B. (1993). Precorrection: An instructional approach for managing predictable problem behaviors. *Intervention in School and Clinic, 28*, 143–150.

Committee for Children. (2002). *Second Step: A violence prevention curriculum.* Seattle, WA: Author.

Common, E. A., Lane, K. L., Swogger, E. D., Brunsting, vN., & Oakes, W. P. (2015). *Teacher-driven strategies to increase students' opportunities to respond: A methodological review.* Manuscript in preparation.

Conroy, M. A., Sutherland, K. S., Snyder, A. L., & Marsh, S. (2008). Classwide interventions: Effective instruction makes a difference. *Teaching Exceptional Children, 40*(6), 24–30.

Coogan, B. A., Kehle, T. J., Bray, M. A., & Chafouleas, S. M. (2007). Group contingencies, randomization of reinforcers, and criteria for reinforcement, self-monitoring, and peer feedback on reducing inappropriate classroom behavior. *School Psychology Quarterly, 22*, 540–556.

Cook, B., & Tankersley, M. (Eds.). (2013). *Effective practices in special education.* Boston: Pearson.

Cooper, J. O., Heron, T. E., & Heward, W. L. (2007). *Applied behavior analysis.* Upper Saddle River, NJ: Pearson Education.

Crick, N., Grotpeter, J., & Bigbee, M. (2002). Relationally and physically aggressive children's intent attributions and feelings of distress for relational and instrumental peer provocations. *Child Development, 73,* 1134–1142.

Crone, D., Horner, R., & Hawken, L. (2004). *Responding to problem behavior in schools: The Behavior Education Program.* New York: Guilford Press.

Crone, D. A., Hawken, L. S., & Horner, R. H. (2010). *Responding to problem behavior in schools: The Behavior Education Program* (2nd ed.). New York: Guilford Press.

Crosby, S., Jolivette, K., & Patterson, D. (2006). Using precorrection to manage inappropriate academic and social behaviors. *Beyond Behavior, 16,* 14–17.

Darch, C. B., & Gersten, R. (1985). The effects of teacher presentation rate and praise on LD students' oral reading performance. *British Journal of Educational Psychology, 55,* 295–303.

Davis, C. A. (1995). Peers as behavior change agents for preschoolers with behavioral disorders. *Preventing School Failure, 39,* 4–9.

Davis, C. A., & Brady, M. P. (1993). Expanding the utility of behavioral momentum with young children: Where we've been, where we need to go. *Journal of Early Intervention, 17,* 211–223.

Davis, C. A., Brady, M. P., Hamilton, R., McEvoy, M., & Williams, R. (1994). Effects of high-probability requests on the social interactions of young children with severe disabilities. *Journal of Applied Behavior Analysis, 27,* 619–637.

Davis, C. A., Brady, M. P., Williams, R. E., & Hamilton, R. (1992). Effects of high-probability requests on the acquisition and generalization of responses to requests in young children with behavior disorders. *Journal of Applied Behavior Analysis, 25,* 905–916.

Davis, C. A., & Reichle, J. (1996). Variant and invariant high-probability requests: Increasing appropriate behaviors in children with emotional-behavioral disorders. *Journal of Applied Behavior Analysis, 29,* 471–482.

Dawson, J. E., Piazza, C. C., Sevin, B. M., Gulotta, C. S., Lerman, D., & Kelley, M. L. (2003). Use of the high-probability instructional sequence and escape extinction in a child with food refusal. *Journal of Applied Behavior Analysis, 36,* 105–108.

De Pry, R. L., & Sugai, G. (2002). The effect of active supervision and pre-correction on minor behavioral incidents in a sixth grade general education classroom. *Journal of Behavioral Education, 11*(4), 255–267.

Deci, R. M., & Ryan, E. L. (2000). Intrinsic and extrinsic motivations: Classic definitions and new directions. *Contemporary Educational Psychology, 25,* 54–67.

Delisle, J. (2012). Reaching those we teach: The five Cs of student engagement. *Gifted Child Today, 35*(1), 62–67.

Denton, C. A., Fletcher, J. M., Anthony, J. L., & Francis, D. J. (2006). An evaluation of intensive intervention for students with persistent reading difficulties. *Journal of Learning Disabilities, 39,* 447–466.

DePry, R. L., & Sugai, G. (2002). The effect of active supervision and precorrection on minor behavioral incidents in a sixth-grade general education classroom. *Journal of Behavioral Education, 11,* 255–267.

DiCarlo, C. F., Baumgartner, J., Stephens, A., & Pierce, S. H. (2013). Using structured choice to increase child engagement in low-preference centres. *Early Child Development and Care, 183,* 109–124.

DiPerna, J. C., & Elliott, S. N. (2002). Promoting academic enablers to improve student achievement: An introduction to the mini-series. *School Psychology Review, 31*, 293–297.

Drago-Severson, E., & Pinto, K. (2006). School leadership for reducing teacher isolation: Drawing from the well of human resources. *International Journal of Leadership in Education, 9*(2), 129155.

Drummond, T. (1994). *The Student Risk Screening Scale (SRSS)*. Grants Pass, OR: Josephine County Mental Health Program.

Duchaine, E. L., Jolivette, K., & Fredrick, L. D. (2011). The effect of teacher coaching with performance feedback on behavior-specific praise in inclusion classrooms. *Education and Treatment of Children, 34*, 209–227.

Dunlap, G., DePerczel, M., Clarke, S., Wilson, D., Wright, S., White, R., & Gomez, A. (1994). Choice making to promote adaptive behavior for students with emotional and behavioral challenges. *Journal of Applied Behavior Analysis, 27*, 505–518.

Eber, L., Hyde, K., Rose, J., Breen, K., McDonald, D., & Lewandowski, H., (2009). Completing the continuum of schoolwide positive behavior support: Wraparound as a tertiary-level intervention. In W. Sailor, G. Dunlop, & G. Sugai (Eds.), *Handbook on positive behavior support* (pp. 671–703). New York: Springer.

Elliott, S. N., & Gresham, F. M. (2007). *Social Skills Improvement System—Classwide Intervention Program Guide*. Bloomington, MN: Pearson Assessments.

Engelmann, S., Meyer, L., Carnine, L., Becker, W., Eisele, J., & Johnson, G. (1999). *Corrective reading program*. Columbus, OH: SRA/McGraw-Hill.

Ennis, R. P., Schwab, J. R., & Jolivette, K. (2012). Using precorrection as a secondary-tier intervention for reducing problem behaviors in instructional and non-instructional settings. *Beyond Behavior, 22*, 40–47.

Epstein, M. H., Atkins, M., Cullinan, D., Kutash, K., & Weaver, R. (2008). *Reducing behavior problems in the elementary school classroom: A practice guide* (NCEE #2008-012). Washington, DC: National Center for Education Evaluation and Regional Assistance, Institute of Education Sciences, U.S. Department of Education. Retrieved from *http://ies.ed.gov/ncee/wwc/PracticeGuide.aspx?sid=4*.

Esch, K., & Fryling, M. J. (2013). A comparison of two variations of the high-probability instructional sequence with a child with autism. *Education and Treatment of Children, 36*, 61–72.

Faul, A., Stepensky, K., & Simonsen, B. (2012). The effects of prompting appropriate behavior on the off-task behavior of two middle school students. *Journal of Positive Behavior Interventions, 14*(1), 47–55.

Felce, D., & Perry, J. (1995). Quality of life: Its definition and measurement. *Research in Developmental Disabilities, 16*, 51–74.

Fisher, D., & Frey, N. (2009). Feed up, back, and forward. *Educational Leadership, 69*(3), 20–25.

Flocabulary. (2007). *The Word Up Project, Level Blue*. New York: Author.

Forness, S. R., Freeman, S. F. N., Paparella, T., Kauffman, J. M., & Walker, H. M. (2012). Special education implications of point and cumulative prevalence for children with emotional or behavioral disorders. *Journal of Emotional and Behavioral Disorders, 20*, 4–18.

Fuchs, D., & Fuchs, L. (2006). Introduction to response to intervention: What, why, and how valid is it? *Reading Research Quarterly, 41*(1), 93–99.

Fullerton, E. K., Conroy, M. A., & Correa, V. I. (2009). Early childhood teachers' use of specific praise statements with young children at risk for behavioral disorders. *Behavioral Disorders, 34,* 118–135.

Frey, N., & Fisher, D. (2011). Feedback and feed forward. *Principal Leadership, 11*(9), 90–93.

Fyfe, E. R., DeCaro, M. S., & Rittle-Johnson, B. (2014). When feedback is cognitively demanding: The importance of working memory capacity. *Instructional Science,* 1–19. Available at *http://link.springer.com/article/10.1007%2Fs11251-014-9323-8#page-2.*

Gable, R. A., Hester, P. P., Rock, M., & Hughes, K. (2009). Back to basics—Rules, praise, ignoring, and reprimands revisited. *Intervention in School and Clinic, 44,* 195–205.

Gan, M. J. S., & Hattie, J. (2014). Prompting secondary students' use of criteria, feedback specificity and feedback levels during an investigative task. *Instructional Science, 42,* 861–878. Available at *http://link.springer.com/article/10.1007%2Fs11251-014-9319-4#page-1.*

Gast, D. L., & Ledford, J. R. (Eds.). (2014). *Single case research methodology: Applications in special education and behavioral sciences* (2nd ed.). New York: Routledge.

Gettinger, M., & Walter, M. J. (2012). *Classroom strategies to enhance academic engaged time.* In S. L. Christenson, A. L. Reschly, & C. Wylie (Eds.), *Handbook of research on student engagement* (pp. 653–673). New York: Springer Science & Business Media.

Godfrey, S. A., Grisham-Brown, J., Schuster, J. W., & Hemmeter, M. L. (2003). The effects of three techniques on student participation with preschool children with attending problems. *Education and Treatment of Children, 26*(3), 255–272.

Gresham, F. M. (1989). Assessment of treatment integrity in school consultation and pre-referral intervention. *School Psychology Review, 18,* 37–50.

Gresham, F. M. (in press). Evidence-based social skills interventions for students at-risk for EBD. *Remedial and Special Education.*

Gresham, F. M., & Elliott, S. N. (2008a). *Social Skills Improvement System: Performance Screening Guide.* Bloomington, MN: Pearson Assessments.

Gresham, F. M., & Elliott, S. N. (2008b). *Social Skills Improvement System: Rating Scales.* Bloomington, MN: Pearson Assessments.

Gresham, F. M., & Lopez, M. F. (1996). Social validation: A unifying construct for school-based consulting research and practice. *School Psychology Quarterly, 11,* 204–227.

Hall, R. V., Lund, D., & Jackson, D. (1968). Effects of teacher attention on study behavior. *Journal of Applied Behavior Analysis, 1,* 1–12.

Hamilton, L., Halverson, R., Jackson, S. S., Mandinach, E., Supovitz, J. A., & Wayman, J. C. (2009). *Using student achievement data to support instructional decision making: A practice guide* (NCEE #2009-4067). Washington, DC: U.S. Department of Education, Institute of Education Sciences, National Center for Education Evaluation and Regional Assistance. Retrieved from *http://ies.ed.gov/ncee/wwc/PracticeGuide. aspx?sid=12.*

Harks, B., Rakoczy, K., Hattie, J., Besser, M., & Klieme, S. (2014). The effects of feedback on achievement, interest and self-evaluation: The role of feedback's perceived usefulness. *Educational Psychology, 34,* 269–290.

Hattie, J. (2009). *Visible learning: A synthesis of over 800 meta-analyses relating to achievement.* New York: Routledge.

Hattie, J., & Timperley, H. (2007). The power of feedback. *Review of Educational Research, 77*, 81–112.

Hawkins, S. M., & Heflin, L. J. (2011). Increasing secondary teachers' behavior-specific praise using a video self-modeling and visual performance feedback intervention. *Journal of Positive Behavior Interventions, 13*, 97–108.

Haydon, T., Conroy, M. A., Scott, T. M., Sindelar, P. T., Barber, B. R., & Orlando, A. (2010). A comparison of three types of opportunities to respond on student academic and social behaviors. *Journal of Emotional and Behavioral Disorders, 18*(1), 27–40.

Haydon, T., DeGreg, J., Maheady, L., & Hunter, W. (2012). Using active supervision and precorrection to improve transition behaviors in a middle school classroom. *Journal of Evidence-Based Practices for Schools, 13*(1), 81–94.

Haydon, T., & Hunter, W. (2011). The effects of two types of teacher questioning on teacher behavior and student performance: A case study. *Education and Treatment of Children, 34*(2), 229–245.

Haydon, T., Mancil, G. R., & Van Loan, C. (2009). Using opportunities to respond in a general education classroom: A case study. *Education and Treatment of Children, 32*(2), 267–278.

Haydon, T., & Musti-Rao, S. (2011). Effective use of behavior-specific praise: A middle school case study. *Beyond Behavior, 20*, 31–39.

Haydon, T., & Scott, T. M. (2008). Using common sense in common settings: Active supervision and precorrection in the morning gym. *Intervention in School and Clinic, 43*, 283–290.

Heward, W. L. (1994). Three "low-tech" strategies for increasing the frequency of active student response during group instruction. In R. Gardner III, D. M. Sainato, J. O. Cooper, T. E. Heron, W. L. Heward, J. Eshleman, et al. (Eds.), *Behavior analysis in education: Focus on measurably superior instruction* (pp. 283–320). Monterey, CA: Brooks Cole.

Horner, R. H. (2000). Positive behavior supports. In M. L. Wehmeyer & J. R. Patton (Eds.), *Mental retardation in the 21st century* (pp. 181–196). Austin, TX: PRO-ED.

Horner, R. H. (2014, October). *Opening remarks.* Keynote address presented at the National Positive Behavioral Interventions and Supports Leadership Forum, PBIS Building Capacity and Partnerships to Enhance Educational Reform, Rosemont, IL.

Horner, R. H., Sugai, G., Smolkowski, K., Eber, L., Nakasato, J., Todd, A. W., et al. (2009). A randomized, wait-list controlled effectiveness trial assessing school-wide positive behavior support in elementary schools. *Journal of Positive Behavior Interventions, 11*, 133–144.

Hulac, D. M., & Benson, N. (2010). The use of group contingencies for preventing and managing disruptive behaviors. *Intervention in School and Clinic, 45*, 257–262.

Individuals with Disabilities Education Improvement Act of 2004, 20 U.S.C. 1400 *et esq.* (2004).

Ingersoll, R. M., & Smith, T. M. (2003). The wrong solution to the teacher shortage. *Educational Leadership, 60*, 30–33.

Institute for Global Ethics. (2008). *Building decision skills.* Retrieved from *www.globalethics.org/.*

Jackson, P. W. (1990). *Life in classrooms.* New York: Teachers College Press.

Janney, D. M., Umbreit, J., Ferro, J. B., Liaupsin, C. J., & Lane, K. L. (2013). The effect of the extinction procedure in function-based intervention. *Journal of Positive Behavior Interventions, 15*, 113–123.

Johnson-Gros, K. N., Lyons, E. A., & Griffin, R. R. (2008). Active supervision: An intervention to reduce high school tardiness. *Education and Treatment of Children, 31*(1), 39–53.

Jolivette, K., Alter, P., Scott, T. M., Josephs, N. L., & Swoszowski, N. C. (2013). Strategies to prevent problem behavior. In K. L. Lane, B. G. Cook, & M. Tankersley (Eds.), *Research-based strategies for improving outcomes in behavior* (pp. 22–33). Boston: Pearson.

Jolivette, K., Stichter, J. P., & McCormick, K. M. (2002). Making choices—improving behavior—engaging in learning. *Teaching Exceptional Children, 34*, 24–30.

Jolivette, K., Wehby, J. H., Canale, J., & Massey, N. G. (2001). Effects of choice-making opportunities on the behavior of students with emotional and behavioral disorders. *Behavioral Disorders, 26*, 131–145.

Kamins, M. L., & Dweck, C. S. (1999). Person versus process praise and criticism: Implications for contingent self-worth and coping. *Developmental Psychology, 35*, 833–847.

Kamphaus, R. W., & Reynolds, C. R. (2008). BASC-2. *Behavioral and Emotional Screening System*. Bloomington, MN: Pearson.

Kennedy, C., & Jolivette, K. (2008). The effects of positive verbal reinforcement on the time spent outside the classroom for students with emotional and behavioral disorders in a residential setting. *Behavioral Disorders, 33*, 211–221.

Kennedy, C., Jolivette, K., & Ramsey, M. (2014). The effects of written teacher and peer praise notes on the inappropriate behaviors of elementary students with emotional and behavioral disorders in a residential school. *Residential Treatment of Children and Youth, 31*, 17–40.

Kern, L., Bambara, L., & Fogt, J. (2002). Class-wide curricular modification to improve the behavior of students with emotional or behavioral disorders. *Behavioral Disorders, 27*, 317–326.

Kern, L., & Clemens, N. H. (2007). Antecedent strategies to promote appropriate classroom behavior. *Psychology in the Schools, 44*(1), 65–75.

Kern, L., Mantegna, M. E., Vorndran, C. M., Bailin, D., & Hilt, A. (2001). Choice of task sequence to reduce problem behaviors. *Journal of Positive Behavior Interventions, 3*, 3–10.

Kern, L., & Manz, P. (2004). A look at current validity issues of school-wide behavior support. *Behavioral Disorders, 30*, 47–59.

Kern, L., & State, T. M. (2009). Incorporating choice and preferred activities into class-wide instruction. *Beyond Behavior, 18*, 3–11.

Kern, L., Vorndran, C. M., Hilt, A., Ringdahl, J. E., Adelman, B. E., & Dunlap, G. (1998). Choice as an intervention to improve behavior: A review of the literature. *Journal of Behavioral Education, 8*, 151–169.

Kettler, R. J., Elliott, S. N., Davies, M., & Griffin, P. (2009). *Using academic enabler nominations and social behavior to predict students' performance level on Australia's national achievement test*. San Diego, CA: American Educational Research Association.

Konrad, M., Helf, S., & Joseph, L. M. (2011). Evidence-based instruction is not enough:

Strategies for increasing instructional efficiency. *Intervention in School and Clinic, 47*, 67–74.

Kounin, J. S. (1970). *Discipline and group management in classrooms.* New York: Holt, Rinehart & Winston.

Kulhavy, R. W. (1977). Feedback in written instruction. *Review of Educational Research, 47*, 211–232.

Kulhavy, R. W., & Wager, W. (1993). Feedback in programmed instruction: Historical context and implications for practice. In J. V. Dempsey & G. C. Sales (Eds.), *Interactive instruction and feedback* (pp. 3–20). Englewood Cliffs, NJ: Educational Technology.

Kulik, J. A., & Kulik, C. C. (1988). Timing of feedback and verbal learning. *Review of Educational Research, 58*, 79–97.

Lambert, R., & McCarthy, C. (Eds.). (2006). *Understanding teacher stress in an age of accountability.* Greenwich, CT: Information Age.

Lane, K. L., & Beebe-Frankenberger, M. E. (2003). *School-based interventions: The tools you need to succeed.* Boston: Allyn & Bacon.

Lane, K. L., Carter, E. W., Jenkins, A., Magill, L., & Germer, K. (in press). Supporting comprehensive, integrated, three-tiered models of prevention in schools: Administrators' perspective. *Journal of Positive Behavior Interventions.*

Lane, K. L., Cook, B., & Tankersley, M. (Eds.). (2012). *Research-based strategies for improving outcomes in behavior.* Boston: Pearson.

Lane, K. L., Eisner, S. L., Kretzer, J. M., Bruhn, A. L., Crnobori, M. E., Funke, L. M., et al. (2009). Outcomes of functional assessment-based interventions for students with and at risk for emotional and behavioral disorders in a job-share setting. *Education and Treatment of Children, 32*, 573–604.

Lane, K. L., Harris, K., Graham, S., Driscoll, S. A., Sandmel, K., Morphy, P., et al. (2011). Self-regulated strategy development at tier-2 for second-grade students with writing and behavioral difficulties: A randomized control trial. *Journal of Research on Educational Effectiveness, 4*, 322–353.

Lane, K. L., Kalberg, J. R., Bruhn, A. L., Driscoll, S. A., Wehby, J. H., & Elliott, S. (2009). Assessing social validity of school-wide positive behavior support plans: Evidence for the reliability and structure of the Primary Intervention Rating Scale. *School Psychology Review, 38*(1), 135–144.

Lane, K. L., Kalberg, J. R., & Menzies, H. M. (2009). *Developing schoolwide programs to prevent and manage problem behaviors: A step-by-step approach.* New York: Guilford Press.

Lane, K. L., Menzies, H. M., Bruhn, A. L., & Crnobori, M. (2011). *Managing challenging behaviors in schools: Research-based strategies that work.* New York: Guilford Press.

Lane, K. L., Menzies, H. M., Ennis, R. P., & Bezdek, J. (2013). School-wide systems to promote positive behaviors and facilitate instruction. *Journal of Curriculum and Instruction, 7*, 6–31.

Lane, K. L., Menzies, H. M., Oakes, W. P., & Kalberg, J. R. (2012). *Systematic screenings of behavior to support instruction: From preschool to high school.* New York: Guilford Press.

Lane, K. L., Oakes, W. P., & Cox, M. (2012). Functional assessment-based interventions:

A university-district partnership to promote learning and success. *Beyond Behavior, 20,* 3–18.

Lane, K. L., Oakes, W. P., Jenkins, A., Menzies, H. M., & Kalberg, J. R. (2014). A team-based process for designing comprehensive, integrated, three-tiered (CI3T) models of prevention: How does my school-site leadership team design a CI3T model? *Preventing School Failure, 58,* 129–142.

Lane, K. L., Oakes, W. P., & Magill, L. (2014). Primary prevention efforts: How do we implement and monitor the Tier 1 component of our comprehensive, integrated, three-tiered (CI3T) model? *Preventing School Failure, 58,* 143–158.

Lane, K. L., Oakes, W. P., & Menzies, H. M. (2014). Comprehensive, integrated, three-tiered (CI3T) models of prevention: Why does my school—and district—need an integrated approach to meet students' academic, behavioral, and social needs? *Preventing School Failure, 58,* 121–128.

Lane, K. L., Oakes, W. P., Menzies, H. M., & Harris, P. J. (2013). Developing comprehensive, integrated, three-tiered models to prevent and manage learning and behavior. In T. Cole, H. Daniels, & J. Visser (Eds.), *The Routledge international companion to emotional and behavioural difficulties* (pp. 177–183). New York: Routledge.

Lane, K. L., Robertson, E. J., & Graham-Bailey, M. A. L. (2006). An examination of school-wide interventions with primary level efforts conducted in secondary schools: Methodological considerations. In T. E. Scruggs & M. A. Mastropieri (Eds.), *Applications of research methodology: Advances in learning and behavioral disabilities* (Vol. 19, pp. 157–199). Oxford, UK: Elsevier.

Lane, K. L., Royer, D. J., Messenger, M., Common, E., Ennis, R. P., & Swogger, E. D. (2015). *Empowering teachers with low-intensity strategies to support academic engagement: The effects of instructional choice for elementary students in inclusive settings.* Manuscript in preparation.

Lane, K. L., Smither, R., Huseman, R., Guffey, J., & Fox, J. (2007). A function-based intervention to decrease disruptive behavior and increase academic engagement. *Journal of Early and Intensive Behavioral Intervention, 3.4–4.1,* 348–364.

Lane, K. L., Swogger, E. D., Royer, D., Oakes, W., & Common, E. (2015). *Shoring up classroom management within CI3T models of prevention: Practical strategies that work.* Manuscript in preparation.

Lane, K. L., & Walker, H. M. (in press). The connection between assessment and intervention: How does screening lead to better interventions? In B. Bateman, M. Tankersley, & J. Lloyd (Eds.), *Enduring issues in special education: Personal perspectives.* New York: Routledge.

Lee, D. L. (2006). Facilitating transitions between and within academic tasks: An application of behavioral momentum. *Remedial and Special Education, 27,* 312–317.

Lee, D. L., Belfiore, P., Scheeler, M. C., Hua, Y., & Smith, R. (2004). Behavioral momentum in academics: Using embedded high-*p* sequences to increase academic productivity. *Psychology in the Schools, 41*(7), 789–801.

Lee, D. L., & Laspe, A. K. (2003). Using high-probability request sequences to increase journal writing. *Journal of Behavioral Education, 12,* 261–273.

Leming, J. S. (2001). Integrating a structured ethical reflection curriculum into high school community service experiences: Impact on students' socio-moral development. *Adolescence, 36,* 33–45.

Lewis, T. J., Colvin, G., & Sugai, G. (2000). The effects of precorrection and active supervision on the recess behavior of elementary students. *Education and Treatment of Children, 23*(2), 109–121.

Liaupsin, C. J., Umbreit, J., Ferro, J., Urso, A., & Upreti, G. (2006). Improving academic engagement through systematic, function-based intervention. *Education and Treatment of Children, 29,* 573–591.

Lynass, L., Tsai, S., Richman, T., & Cheney, D. (2012). Social expectations and behavioral indicators in schoolwide positive behavior supports: A national study of behavior matrices. *Journal of Positive Behavior Interventions, 14,* 153–161.

Lysakowski, R. S., & Walberg, H. J. (1982). Instructional effects of cue, participation, and corrective feedback: A quantitative synthesis. *American Educational Research Journal, 19,* 559–578.

Mace, C. F., & Belfiore, P. (1990). Behavioral momentum in the treatment of escape-motivated stereotypy. *Journal of Applied Behavior Analysis, 23,* 507–514.

Mace, C. F., Hock, M. L., Lalli, J. S., West, B. J., Belfiore, P., Pinter, E., et al. (1988). Behavioral momentum in the treatment of noncompliance. *Journal of Applied Behavior Analysis, 21,* 123–141.

Madsen, C. H., Becker, W. C., & Thomas, D. R. (1968). Rules, praise, and ignoring: Elements of elementary classroom control. *Journal of Applied Behavior Analysis, 1,* 139–150.

Marchant, M., & Anderson, D. H. (2012). Improving social and academic outcomes for all learners through the use of teacher praise. *Beyond Behavior, 21,* 22–28.

Martens, B. K., Witt, J. C., Elliott, S. N., & Darveaux, D. X. (1985). Teacher judgments concerning the acceptability of school-based interventions. *Professional Psychology: Research and Practice, 16,* 191–198.

McIntosh, K., & Goodman, S. (in press). *Multi-tiered systems of support: Integrating academic RTI and school-wide PBIS.* New York: Guilford Press.

Meyer, A. L., Farrell, A. D., Northup, W. B., Kung, E. M., & Plybon, L. (2000). *Promoting non-violence in early adolescence: Responding in peaceful and positive ways.* New York: Kluwer/Plenum.

Miller, N. E., & Dollard, J. (1941). *Social learning and imitation.* New Haven, CT: Yale University Press.

Mooney, P., Ryan, J. B., Gunter, P. L., & Denny, R. (2012). Behavior modification/traditional techniques for students with emotional and behavioral disorders. *Advances in Special Education (MS)* (ERIC Document Reproduction Service No. ED540065). Available at *http://eric.ed.gov/?id=ED540065.*

Mooney, P., Ryan, J. B., Uhing, B. M., Reid, R., & Epstein, M. H. (2005). A review of self-management interventions targeting academic outcomes for students with emotional and behavioral disorders. *Journal of Behavioral Education, 14,* 203–221.

Morgan, P. L. (2006). Increasing task engagement using preference or choice-making: Some behavioral and methodological factors affecting their efficacy as classroom interventions. *Remedial and Special Education, 27,* 176–187. Available at *http://rse. sagepub.com/content/27/3/176.short.*

Myers, D. M., Simonsen, B., & Sugai, G., (2011). Increasing teachers' use of praise with a response-to-intervention approach. *Education and Treatment of Children, 34,* 35–59.

National Governors Association Center for Best Practices & the Council of Chief State School Officers. (2010). *Common Core State Standards Initiative.* Washington, DC: Author.

Nevin, J. A. (1996). The momentum of compliance. *Journal of Applied Behavior Analysis, 29,* 535–547.

Nevin, J. A., Mandell, C., & Atak, J. R. (1983). The analysis of behavioral momentum. *Journal of the Experimental Analysis of Behavior, 39,* 45–59.

Nicol, D. J., & MacFarlane-Dick, D. (2006). Formative assessment and self-regulated learning: A model and seven principles of good feedback practice. *Studies in Higher Education, 31,* 199–218.

No Child Left Behind Act of 2001, Pub. L. No. 107-110, § 115, Stat. 1425 (2002).

Office of Civil Rights. (2014). *The transformed civil rights data collection (CRDC).* Washington, DC: U.S. Department of Education.

Oswald, K., Safran, S., & Johanson, G. (2005). Preventing trouble: Making schools safer places using positive behavior supports. *Education and Treatment of Children, 28*(3), 265–278.

Partin, T. C., Robertson, R. E., Maggin, D., Oliver, R., & Wehby, J. (2010). Using teacher praise and opportunities to respond to promote appropriate student behavior. *Preventing School Failure, 54,* 172–178.

Pianta, R. C., Hamre, B. K., & Allen, J. P. (2012). Teacher-student relationships and engagement: Conceptualizing, measuring, and improving the capacity of classroom interactions. In S. L. Christenson, A. L. Reschley, & C. Wylie (Eds.), *Handbook of research on student engagement* (pp. 365–386). New York: Springer.

Positive Action. (2008). *Positive Action: Positive development for schools, families and communities.* Twin Falls, ID: Positive Action. Retrieved from *www.positiveaction. net.*

Powell, S., & Nelson, B. (1997). Effects of choosing academic assignments on a student with attention deficit hyperactivity disorder. *Journal of Applied Behavior Analysis, 30,* 181–183.

Pressey, S. L. (1927). A machine for automatic teaching of drill material. *School and Society, 25,* 549–552.

Ramsey, M. L., Jolivette, K., Patterson, D. P., & Kennedy, C. (2010). Using choice to increase time on-task, task completion, and accuracy for students with emotional/behavioral disorders in a residential facility. *Education and Treatment of Children, 33,* 1–21.

Rathel, J. M., Drasgow, E., & Christle, C. C. (2008). Effects of supervisor performance feedback on increasing preservice teachers' positive communication behaviors with students with emotional and behavioral disorders. *Journal of Emotional and Behavioral Disorders, 16,* 67–77.

Ravitch, D. (2010). *The death and life of the great American school system: How testing and choice are undermining education.* New York: Basic Books.

Reimers, T. M., & Wacker, D. P. (1988). Parents' ratings of acceptability of behavioral treatment recommendations made in an outpatient clinic: A preliminary analysis of the influence of treatment effectiveness. *Behavior Disorders, 14,* 7–15.

Reinke, W. M., Lewis-Palmer, T., & Martin, E. (2007). The effect of visual performance feedback on teacher use of behavior-specific praise. *Behavior Modification, 31,* 247–263.

Rhode, G., Jenson, W. R., & Reavis, H. K. (1992). *The tough kid book: Practical classroom management strategies.* Longmont, CO: Sopris West.

Richards, J. (2012). Teacher stress and coping strategies: A national snapshot. *Educational Forum, 76*(3), 299–316.

Rispoli, M., Lang, R., Neely, L., Camargo, S., Hutchins, N., Davenport, K., et al. (2013). A comparison of within- and across-activity choices for reducing challenging behavior in children with autism spectrum disorders. *Journal of Behavioral Education, 22,* 66–83.

Romaniuk, C., & Miltenberger, R. G. (2001). The influence of preference and choice of activity on problem behavior. *Journal of Positive Behavior Interventions, 3,* 152–159.

Roth, J. L., Brooks-Gunn, J., Livner, M. R., & Hofferth, S. L. (2003). What happens during the school day?: Time diaries from a national sample of elementary school teachers. *Teachers College Record, 105,* 317–343.

Royer, D. J., Lane, K. L., Swogger, E. D., & Messenger, M. (2014). Instructional choice interventions that promote on-task and other appropriate behaviors in students. *Manuscript in preparation.*

Sadler, R. (1989). Formative assessment and the design of instructional systems. *Instructional Science, 18,* 119–144.

Sailor, W., Dunlap, G., Sugai, G., & Horner, R. (2009). *Handbook of positive behavior support.* New York: Springer.

Scott Foresman Reading Street. (2004). Upper Saddle River, NJ: Pearson Education.

Shogren, K., Wehmeyer, M., & Lane, K. L. (2014). *Embedding interventions to promote self-determination within multi-tiered systems of supports.* Manuscript submitted for publication.

Shogren, K. A., Faggella-Luby, M. N., Bae, S. J., & Wehmeyer, M. L. (2004). The effect of choice-making as an intervention for problem behavior: A meta-analysis. *Journal of Positive Behavior Interventions, 6,* 228–237.

Sigafoos, J., Roberts, D., Couzens, D., & Kerr, M. (1993). Providing opportunities for choice-making and turn-taking to adults with multiple disabilities. *Journal of Developmental and Physical Disabilities, 5,* 297–310.

Simonsen, B., Britton, L., & Young, D. (2010). School-wide positive behavior support in an alternative school setting: A case study. *Journal of Positive Behavior Interventions, 12,* 180–191.

Simonsen, B., & Myers, D. (2015). *Classwide positive behavior interventions and supports: A guide to proactive classroom management.* New York: Guilford Press.

Skerbetz, M. D., & Kostewicz, D. E. (2013). Academic choice for included students with emotional and behavioral disorders. *Preventing School Failure, 57,* 212–222.

Spear, C. F., Strickland-Cohen, K., Romer, N., & Albin, R. W. (2013). An examination of social validity within single-case research with students with emotional and behavioral disorders. *Remedial and Special Education, 34,* 357–370.

Spriggs, A. D., Gast, D. L., & Ayres, K. M. (2007). Using picture activity schedule books to increase on-schedule and on-task behaviors. *Education and Training in Developmental Disabilities, 42,* 209–223.

Stichter, J. P., Lewis, T. J., Whittaker, T. A., Richter, M., Johnson, N. W., & Trussell, R. P. (2009). Assessing teacher use of opportunities to respond and effective classroom management strategies: Comparisons among high- and low-risk elementary schools. *Journal of Positive Behavior Interventions, 11,* 68–81.

Stipek, D. J. (1993). *Motivation to learn: From theory to practice* (2nd ed.). Boston: Allyn & Bacon.

Stokes, T. F., & Baer, D. M. (1977). An implicit technology of generalization. *Journal of Applied Behavior Analysis, 10,* 349–367.

Stormont, M., & Newman, C. (2014). *Simple strategies for teaching children at risk.* Thousand Oaks, CA: Corwin.

Stormont, M., & Reinke, W. (2009). The importance of precorrective statements and behavior-specific praise and strategies to increase their use. *Beyond Behavior, 18,* 26–32.

Stormont, M. A., Smith, S. C., & Lewis, T. J. (2007). Teacher implementation of precorrection and praise statements in Head Start classrooms as a component of a program-wide system of positive behavior support. *Journal of Behavioral Education, 16,* 280–290.

Sugai, G. (2013,). *Keynote address.* Unpublished talk presented at North East Positive Behavior Support Conference. Cromwell, CT.

Sugai, G., & Horner, R. H. (2002a). Introduction to the special series on positive behavior support in schools. *Journal of Emotional and Behavioral Disorders, 10*(3), 130–135.

Sugai, G., & Horner, R. H. (2002b). The evolution of discipline practices: School-wide positive behavior supports. *Child and Family Behavior Therapy, 24,* 25–50.

Sugai, G., & Horner, R. H. (2006). A promising approach for expanding and sustaining school-wide positive behavior support. *School Psychology Review, 35*(2), 245–260.

Sutherland, K. S., Alder, N., & Gunter, P. L. (2003). The effect of varying rates of opportunities to respond to academic requests on the classroom behavior of students with EBD. *Journal of Emotional and Behavioral Disorders, 11*(4), 239–248.

Sutherland, K. S., Copeland, S. R., & Wehby, J. H. (2001). Catch them while you can: Monitoring and increasing the use of effective praise. *Beyond Behavior, 11,* 46–49.

Sutherland, K. S., & Wehby, J. H. (2001). Exploring the relationship between increased opportunities to respond to academic requests and the academic behavioral outcomes of students with EBD: A review. *Remedial and Special Education, 22*(2), 113–121.

Sutherland, K. S., Wehby, J. H., & Copeland, S. R. (2000). Effect of varying rates of behavior-specific praise on the on-task behavior of students with EBD. *Journal of Emotional and Behavioral Disorders, 8,* 2–8.

Sutherland, K. S., Wehby, J. H., & Yoder, P. J. (2002). Examination of the relationship between teacher praise and opportunities for students with EBD to respond to academic requests. *Journal of Emotional and Behavioral Disorders, 10*(1), 5–13.

Sutherland, K. [S.], & Wright, S. A. (2013). Students with disabilities and academic engagement: Classroom-based interventions. In K. L. Lane, B. G. Cook, & M. Tankersley (Eds.), *Research-based strategies for improving outcomes in behavior* (pp. 34–45). Boston: Pearson.

Tapp, J., Wehby, J., & Ellis, D. (1995). A multiple option observation system for experimental studies: MOOSES. *Behavior Research Methods, Instruments, and Computers, 27,* 25–31.

Thompson, M. T., Marchant, M., Anderson, D., Prater, M. A., & Gibb, G. (2012). Effects of tiered training on general educators' use of specific praise. *Education and Treatment of Children, 35,* 521–546.

Tomlinson, C. (2005). *An educator's guide to differentiating instruction.* Boston: Houghton Mifflin.

Trussell, R. P. (2008). Classroom universals to prevent problem behaviors. *Intervention in School and Clinic, 43*(3), 179–185.

Ttofi, M. M., & Farrington, D. P. (2011). Effectiveness of school-based programs to reduce bullying: A systematic and meta-analytic review. *Journal of Experimental Criminology, 7*(1), 27–56.

Tyre, A., Feuerborn, L., & Pierce, J. (2011). Schoolwide intervention to reduce chronic tardiness at the middle and high school levels. *Preventing School Failure, 55*(3), 132–139.

Umbreit, J., Ferro, J., Liaupsin, C., & Lane, K. (2007). *Functional behavioral assessment and function-based intervention: An effective, practical approach.* Upper Saddle River, NJ: Prentice-Hall.

U.S. Department of Education. (2014). *Guiding principles: A resource guide for improving school climate and discipline.* Washington, DC: Author.

Van Acker, R., Grant, S. H., & Henry, D. (1996). Teacher and student behavior as a function of risk for aggression. *Education and Treatment of Children, 19,* 316–334.

Van Bramer, J. (2003). Conversation as a model of instructional interaction. *Literacy Teaching and Learning, 8*(1), 19–46.

Vaughn, B. J., & Horner, R. H. (1997). Identifying instructional tasks that occasion problem behavior and assessing the effects of student versus teacher choice during these tasks. *Journal of Applied Behavior Analysis, 30,* 299–312.

Walker, H. M., Block-Pedego, A. Todis, B., & Severson, H. H. (2014). *School Archival Records Search (SARS).* Eugene, OR: Pacific Northwest.

Walker, H. M., & Gresham, F. M. (2013). The school-related behavior disorders field: A source of innovation and best practices for school personnel who serve students with emotional and behavioral disorders. In W. M. Reynolds, G. E. Miller, & I. B. Weiner (Eds.), *Handbook of psychology: Vol. 7. Educational psychology* (2nd ed., pp. 411–440). Hoboken, NJ: Wiley.

Walker, H. M., Ramsey, E., & Gresham, F. M. (2004). *Antisocial behavior in school: Evidence-based practices* (2nd ed.). Belmont, CA: Wadsworth.

Walker, H. M., & Severson, H. (1992). *Systematic screening for behavior disorders: User's guide and technical manual.* Longmont, CO: Sopris West.

Walker, H. M., Todis, B., Holmes, D., & Horton, G. (1988). *ACCESS program: Adolescent curriculum for communication and effective social skills.* Austin, TX: PRO-ED.

Webster-Stratton, C., Reid, M. J., & Stoolmiller, M. (2008). Preventing conduct problems and improving school readiness: Evaluation of the Incredible Years Teacher and Child Training Programs in high-risk schools. *Journal of Child Psychology and Psychiatry and Allied Disciplines, 49,* 471–488.

Wechsler, D. (2003). *Wechsler Intelligence Scale for Children—4th edition* (WISC-IV). San Antonio, TX: Harcourt Assessment.

Wehby, J., & Hollahan, S. (2000). Effects of high-probability requests on the latency to initiate academic tasks. *Journal of Applied Behavior Analysis, 33,* 259–262.

Wehby, J. H., Symons, F. J., Canale, J. A., & Go, F. J. (1998). Teaching practices in classrooms for students with emotional and behavioral disorders: Discrepancies between recommendations and observations. *Behavioral Disorders, 24,* 51–56.

Witt, J. C., & Elliott, S. N. (1985). Acceptability of classroom intervention strategies. In T. R. Kratochwill (Ed.), *Advances in school psychology* (Vol. 4, pp. 251–288). Mahwah, NJ: Erlbaum.

Wolfe, P., & Nevills, P. (2004). *Building the reading brain, PreK–3.* Thousand Oaks, CA: Corwin Press.

Yoder, N. (2014). *Teaching the whole child: Instructional practices that support social and emotional learning in three teacher evaluation frameworks.* Washington, DC: American Institutes for Research Center on Great Teachers and Leaders. Retrieved from *www.gtlcenter.org/sites/default/files/TeachingtheWholeChild.pdf.*

Ysseldyke, J. E., Christenson, S. L., Thurlow, M. L., & Bakewell, D. (1989). Are different kinds of instructional tasks used by different categories of students in different settings? *School Psychology Review, 18,* 98–111.

Yudin, M. (2014, October). *PBIS: Providing opportunity.* Keynote address presented at the National Positive Behavioral Intervention and Supports Leadership Forum, PBIS Building Capacity and Partnerships to Enhance Educational Reform, Rosemont, IL.

Index